THE CELESTIAL CAFÉ

THE CELESTIAL CAFÉ

STUART MURDOCH

Edited by Sean Guthrie

Illustrations by Graham Samuels

POMONA

A Pomona Book

P - 0 2 3

Published by Pomona Books 2011
PO Box 50, Hebden Bridge, West Yorkshire HX7 8WA, England, UK
Telephone 01422 846900 · e-mail admin@pomonauk.co.uk

www.pomonauk.co.uk

1

A CIP catalogue record for this book
is available from the British Library

ISBN 978-1-904590-24-8

Set in Monotype Bembo Book
Typeset by Bracketpress

Printed and bound in England by
CPI Cox & Wyman, Reading, RG1 8EX

This book is dedicated to The Button,
if she wants it.

Thanks to John Williamson, Katrina House, Neil Robertson,
Mark Hodkinson, Christian Brett, Ciara MacLaverty
and the members of Belle And Sebastian

THE YEAR BEFORE

When I was a child I couldn't wait to grow up, get a car and perhaps have a job as a jet pilot. Now I'm old, I'd give that stuff up in a flash. Now I'm old, with a political conscience.

Jet pilot — that's a laugh. My fear of flying plus all the fun that comes with terrorism and trouble at work conspire to make gloom slip along lightly into panic.

I need to go on a long flight soon, and I'm worried. The cosy surrounds of this café certainly help though. What I'd pay to exchange the fuselage of a jumbo jet for this railway carriage of a café. While the rest of the group travelled by plane I'd spend the 12 hours in here instead, giving free recitals, loving pensioners and sorting out minor tax problems. Outside it would rain, become sunny, then rain again. I'd watch the changing shifts of the girls. I'd eke out details of their private thoughts from their gestures and whispers. I'd find out their secrets by simply asking about them, as boredom turned to boldness.

They would know of my secret, and serve my meals on a

small tray for the sake of neatness. I'd insist on spreading myself wide to help me forget all aspects of the flight.

"But I'd love to be in a plane," the waitress would say.

"Well, you go then, instead of me."

"Brazil will be fabulous!"

"I know it will, it's just the air space in between."

I'd try not to take my café flight on a school holiday though. There's a boy at the next table going a bit mad. Hush, child — this is my library! Your youth is haunting the ambience, chasing it out through the windows.

God, what I could achieve in this place while the rest of the group were flying over the Atlantic. The way I feel about this place, love is too small a word, as Woody Allen once said. I need this place to physically survive, and yet it's going to be sold. I mentally add this to the list of things which conspire to doom me.

I have a mental picture of terrorists raiding the café like they might a plane. The bearded spoilsports suddenly stand up at their tables, but when they fire their guns, instead of bullets they are dismayed to find they are firing flowers, and flee in disgrace. I barely bother to look up as the waitress rushes to the door to bid them farewell, clutching the flowers.

"That's so nice, nobody ever gives us flowers!"

Nothing bad can happen in this place. I love it. After it's gone I will construct a pocket religion of the place and see if it catches on. It will consist of good advice and small matters of coffee etiquette, and I will spring it unawares on customers. But they will be in just the right mood to listen to me, and my carefully chosen words will be as effective as the waitress topping up their cups.

To summarise, I'm encased in the booth of a celestial café. I've exchanged time in here for time on a plane plus a forfeit.

When the plane lands, I will be ushered through the kitchen entrance to the arrival lounge, where my travelling companions will magically await me.

In the meantime, I'm not going to feel short on company as long as I have you to talk to.

Stuart Murdoch
October 17, 2001

THE AUTUMN BOWLING SEASON

Glasgow, Scotland

I've just rushed up the road to write the first instalment of a diary before I lose momentum. It never occurred to me to write a regular diary before, mostly because I couldn't imagine who would want to read it, but with a modicum of encouragement from the people in our office, here I am. I've bought a gorgeous laptop that has become my new best friend, and by God I'm going to use it.

The staff and I had a meeting in the office, and among other things we decided we'd let the website go a bit. I think when Belle and Sebastian started out we seemed to be on the cutting edge of things, web-wise, but you, the fans, have taken over the momentum and we've been lagging, what with all your chat rooms and mailing lists. So we'll have a new website early next year, and in the meantime we'll try to keep you abreast of what we're doing.

One of my slight qualms about writing a diary before was that I was never quite sure who I was writing it for. It was easy to write for the *Glasgow University Guardian*, a student newspa-

3

per, because I had a precise idea of who might be reading. I've met many more of you in the past year than I have done previously, so that helps, but don't be shy of dropping us a line. It'll help set the tone for this diary.

SEPTEMBER 16, 2002

Keip Goudi, Athens, Greece and
Enzimi Festival, Rome, Italy

Those were the last gigs of the year, I think, though the thought torments me slightly. You can never take international travel for granted. The bottom might drop out of our market, and then where would we be? Not in the likes of Japan or Italy.

I had been looking forward to Athens and Rome for ages, playing outside in an amphitheatre in Greece then a park in Rome, but it pissed down in Athens and the venue in Rome turned out to be a bus station car park. Never mind — I couldn't imagine the Athens gig going any better. In the weeks before we came the city had experienced some of the worst weather in years, so the gig was moved to what seemed to be an equestrian centre in the middle of an army base. Then the cops turned up at the soundcheck and told us the gig wasn't going to happen anyway, the organisers apparently having failed to secure a licence for the show. So all 20 of us kicked back and sat in a circle, discussing contingencies and expressing doubts, and it felt quite good — as if we were in a fly-on-the-wall documentary and there was something to film for a change.

We hung about for a couple of hours, wishing we had a frisbee, and then somebody called the Greek minister for culture, who was on his holidays somewhere. Apparently he gave it the green light because they started letting the kids in. They were a good bunch, it was Friday and we were all in a good mood.

I'd given my whistle to a fan in Germany so I was struggling during *Roy Walker*, but we got this kid with a whistle like a jet engine to come on stage and oblige us. She was very good. I like the way that can happen. Somebody usually marches on stage without a semblance of nerves, as if they know what's expected of them before I've even asked. Like we've planted them or something, which we haven't. I, for one, would shit myself if anybody put me on a stage all of a sudden in front of all those people. So well done, whoever the girl with the burst buttons is. I ought to start making medals again — I used to give them out like sweeties, but I've got quite stingy recently.

Then it was on to Rome. We were staying on a little campus for visitors to the Vatican, so there wasn't much action to be had when we arrived. Me, Rosie, Derv and Emma went sightseeing on the Sunday morning, the first time I've managed to have a look around. I still had a map in my head of what I thought the Forum ought to be like from Roman history at school, so it was quite dreamy to be walking about. I thought the Colosseum was breathtaking. It's funny how, perhaps until fairly recently, the inhabitants of the city must have simply tolerated their ruins. Some of them will have survived because it was easier to let them lie after they'd been plundered for all the best stone. Then there must have been a time when they became venerated and somebody started putting fences up. It's all speculation, though — just what I was thinking. We could have done with a decent tour guide, to tell the truth.

There was certainly a lot of pish talked on this trip, with Beans one of the main culprits, but it was amusing pish, and it does get you by. He was in an extraordinarily good mood for the trip, spending the whole time laughing at everything. What's good about Beans is that he's quite brainy so you can actually learn something from him, and that's important because otherwise your brain would rot, wouldn't it? We might employ a tour tutor in future, like child actors get, because we're missing out, aren't we?

Brian suggested that if Britain declared war on Iraq he would leave the country, since it would be the only thing he could do to prove he didn't support what was happening. I can see his point. It would be a complete sickener. Who the hell do we think we are? The five permanent members of the UN Security Council have already split the Iraqi oil share between them, pending a new, US-friendly Iraqi government. It makes you want to sell your car as well. They can keep their stinking oil. Well, they can wait until I've sold my car Max, then they can keep it. I'd feel like getting out of here as well if we went to war. The trouble is, I'd probably fancy going to New York or somewhere. And there's the hypocrisy. America: a great place, but run by a load of tossers. Come on, spread the wealth! And Europe is just as bad, or it would be if the world paid as much attention to it as it does the United States. I'm sure if you met them you'd find not all politicians are tossers, but, really, they're all so mean. None of them is prepared to give an inch. Sometimes if you take a decent person and put them in a car, they act towards others in a way they would never do if they were walking down the street. Put someone in charge of a country and it's the same thing.

SEPTEMBER 24, 2002
Glasgow, Scotland – Newark, New Jersey, US

I woke up this morning to realise I'd left my car in a street that was halfway through being resurfaced. I looked out the window and it was still there, surrounded by diggers and tanks and stuff, so I put on my trainers and ran downstairs to move it. By the time I got down the car was gone. I was resigned to the fact it would be on its way to the pound, but I asked one of the workers anyway. I was expecting a hostile reaction but he was sympathetic, albeit in a gruff way. Then a couple of his colleagues shouted that the car was round the corner, so I ran there to find it had already been unloaded. I apologised but the first guy smiled as though he was happy to oblige, as if he was doing it for good karma.

I went back inside to check my plane tickets on the internet only to discover I'd booked the wrong week. I wanted to go tomorrow and had tickets for the following Tuesday. I phoned the airline and they couldn't have been nicer. They cancelled the tickets immediately even though they weren't changeable, then found me a better ticket for the next day, straight from Glasgow to New York. Well, to Newark, which is equally good. Result! And I skipped to the bathroom, acknowledging my good fortune for the second time.

And that brings me here, halfway over the Atlantic in a Boeing 767 with Stevie Jackson on what is ostensibly a song-writing exercise. In reality we're going to watch baseball and hang out for a week. Hang out — the perfect American expression. There's no phrase quite like it in Britain. We're too uptight to admit we're going to do nothing for a while: everybody has to be doing something.

The first time I went to the States was in 1993. It was a pretty random choice. A friend and I wanted to go somewhere warm for the winter. We got out our Weetabix atlas, looked at all the climates marked 'Mediterranean' on the map then went to southern California, where we were liberated by the warmth and the people we met. When I got back, I was lying under a tree in a park in Glasgow when an old lady passed by and said to me:

"Is that you having a sleep?"

"I'm just thinking," I said, a bit dazed.

"And that's work, is it?" she said.

Welcome home, I thought.

We're both in a restless mood after the touring. The funny thing is, just yesterday Glasgow started to work its magic on me and pull me back into the fold. It was a still, sunny day and Byres Road was feeling busy again, settling into its autumn purpose, so I know that's going to be waiting for me when I return. But a week in New York will do just fine for now, thank you very much. It'll be a rare privilege. I always liked it when Bertie Wooster packed his trunk and headed for New York. So we'll follow in that slacker's wake.

OCTOBER 4, 2002

Hillhead Library, Glasgow, Scotland

I'm back from my holidays. There is a row going on downstairs. Some poor guy is reacting really badly to the concept of library fines. I mean, the fight started out of nothing. He looked like the kind of guy who would get into a fight buying a newspaper or crossing the road. I feel sorry for him.

"I'm no' the gallus one, right? Av goat a card for that door. Whit dae ye mean av goat to leave? She thinks she IS someone, fuckin' speccy auld bastard!"

Then he was thrown out. I heard one of the men saying to the staff good-naturedly:

"You keep your boyfriends out of here!"

My ex-neighbour Agnes is collecting signatures outside the library. Glasgow University is building 200ft-tall chimneys at the back of her house and she's not very happy about it. She and the other neighbours are on the pavement with a table and pictures of the new development. Good on her! She's not young, but I think this sort of action keeps her occupied. She's the kind of woman whom the action seems to follow, if you know what I mean. Eugene told me she was in Boots the other day and there was a bit of a commotion. Then he saw me talking to her later and thought she must be my gran. She wears big blue glasses that look like lab specs. Pure Joan Collins.

"Could they not build it out at the science park?" I ask her.

"They could, but it's all about money, Stuart," she says, grimacing and rubbing her thumb and middle finger together. Too true, Agnes. That's what it's always about.

To most people, at any rate, but not seemingly to one man. THE man. He was born in Galloway, got into pop music, burned a million quid then turned to writing books. Bill Drummond! I went to see him the other day—what a treat! Sarah gave me 45 to read recently. He's such a nice writer that his book is a pleasure to read from the off. He writes about his life and all the silly things that infect him. Infectious is the word. He is driven by the beauty he sees and feels, and chases after it because his life depends on it. And that's how he lives every day, getting into one scam after another and writing about it.

It was fun to hear him talk. He was telling us about a particular strand of thought and circumstance and how it had led him to create art and think differently about things. The results of his creativity were displayed in the room we were sitting in: photos, text, paintings, pamphlets, pots of paint marked 'Drummond's International Grey' and his proposed new British flag, which looked like a roadside chevron but in yellow, blue, black and green.

Drummond must be almost 50 years old, but he looks very boyish. Sarah and I agreed his outlook must keep him looking young. His story involved him and his sister taking off for

9

Iceland in a fishing boat when he was 17. They vowed to walk across the country starting from the north, but they didn't quite make it, and the experience had stayed with him. Eleven years later, in 1981, he came across an artist, Richard Long, whom he came to admire very much. One day in 1996, after he had retired from pop, he decided he would buy a Richard Long painting. He went to a gallery and looked through the pictures. There was one taken while the artist had been on a trek across Iceland, only he had completed the journey. Bill recognised the spot, the hills and the stone circle pictured, and bought the painting for $20,000. The rest of the talk was about how he planned to get rid of the picture.

One crazed night he divided it into 20,000 little rectangles. He cut the first one out with his Stanley knife and ate it. But he decided to travel round the country selling the rest of the pieces for a dollar each. When he gets the $20,000 he's going to go to Iceland and finish his walk. He's going to bury the cash, take a picture of the location and hang it in his room. It will be called *The Smell of Money Underground*.

I still had dollars left from my trip to New York, so Sarah and I bought a few pieces.

It crossed my mind to ask Bill to manage us while Neil is away for a year. We'd still need Katrina to 'manage the manager' though.

OCTOBER 9, 2002
Glasgow, Scotland

I feel as if I've been out the house for days so I'd better write this up because I'll fall asleep if I go home. I don't know what you expect from a so-called rocker's diary. When I stop to think about this stuff, nothing seems to happen. I'm sorry about that, but you're reading this, so I'll carry on in the same vein because you must have a perverse interest in the mundane. I'm trying, though: I do try. Thing is, I don't feel like telling you a lot of stuff because that's for me to know and you to find out, but I will tell you a bit about the group today and what we get up to when we're at home.

This morning I was on the bus on the way to meet the band when it passed a bowling green. It got me wondering about bowling greens and what happens to them in the winter. All year round they are beautiful little pools of green scattered across Glasgow. The Japanese have their driving ranges, but we have our grass bowling greens, hedged off, with the inevitable little social club attached. I thought it would be an idea to take a series of pictures called *The Autumn Bowling Season* or something like that, visiting some of the nicer bowling greens in Glasgow and depicting some of the things that go on after the playing season is over. It would be a funny mixture of nature and hedonism, with strange women dressed in fur and the colours of the season, drinking tea.

After band practice I went to see a film at the CCA. When I worked there and had a chip on my shoulder I used to call it the the Centre for Contemporary Arseholes (it should be Arts), but now it's been done up it's great. They've had some good stuff on. I was going to say it has shed its elitist image but then I realise only three people turned up to the film, two of whom left after an hour, leaving me and the girl who works there. Have I changed or has art? Have I grown up and grown to like olives? Or was it just a quiet night?

They showed three episodes of Janet Street-Porter's *London Weekend Show*, mostly about punk, from 1976, 1977 and 1979 or so. The Sex Pistols, The Clash, fashion in the King's Road, X-Ray Spex, Ian Dury, John Cooper Clarke. The Pistols were so sweet when they started, and Ian Dury was priceless. He was talking about punk but looking forward to a time when the whole family could go to a punk gig. "You know, the retarded son, banging his head off the wall. And Gran complaining about the noise. And dogs too." He was serious too. Janet Street-Porter was laughing her big toothy laugh and so was I.

We had a laugh with our lawyer today. Our Legal Man, Robert White. When he came in and handed us all 40-page contracts Bob's face just dropped. It was like double maths. I thought it was going to be quick. We did our best to steer the conversation on to general topics and get Robert talking about the old days and Spandau Ballet and people like that. When we did eventually get back to the contract Beans decided he wanted the next record to be issued in minah bird — far and away the most inspirational format yet thought up. We sent Robert away after a couple of hours and got back to our songs.

OCTOBER 17, 2002
Glasgow, Scotland

A newspaper asked me to write a diary of what I've been up to this week, but I want to start by recommending a film. I've just watched *All The President's Men*. It's a great film! I'm sure you know what it's about — the Watergate break-in, the investigation by the *Washington Post* and the eventual resignation of Richard Nixon. Robert Redford and Dustin Hoffman play the reporters, Bob Woodward and Carl Bernstein.

"Woodward, Bernstein, you're on the case. Don't fuck it up!"

I'm really into Redford and Hoffman. The shirts; the coffee; the cigarettes; the way the office lighting shows up their hair; the way they're driven by the investigation. They've no time for girls or eating or sleeping. They are constantly moving.

They mumble to each other, caught up in their own world. You have to strain to catch some of the dialogue. I always liked the film, even before I could work out what it was about.

I'd like to be like them and have a job like theirs. Maybe in a tiny way I do have a job like theirs. It's the constant movement, things happening, the buzz of collaboration. If the reporters stopped looking, the story would die. If a group stops moving, a group like ours for instance, it will die. I never thought about this until recently but I'm prepared to go along with it because, as I said, that's the kind of job I want. So how do you keep things moving?

When our group started out there was the natural movement that comes from seven or so people trying to get to the same place at the same time. It wasn't easy! There were constant rendezvous in cafés, before the internet made things sensible. A meeting would turn into an afternoon as the stories got dafter, as the latecomers arrived and the early birds disappeared, as contingencies got wilder and the chance of actually practising became smaller. But nobody really cared because it was a happening!

These days we've got an office and sensible people running it. We've got goals and schedules. We've got contracts, we've got worldwide distribution. We've got to the stage where everything works. We're very lucky. I'm very lucky. But it's now, when everything is ticking along so well, that I want to feel like a straggler in a school cross-country race. I want to drop off the back of the field. I'm going to stand in a doorway. I'm going to take a left instead of a right to see what happens. I'm not going back to school! I want to go up the town and smoke a cigarette. I want to check out what's happening down the docks. I want to be Woodward and Bernstein. I want to get the buzz.

After that the reality of my weekly schedule might seem

13

mundane. Sorry about that. We did have Trevor Horn come to see us a week ago while we were practising because we're looking for a producer for our next record.

Our group is very much entrenched in the old ways when it comes to recording. We've never had much to do with the proper pop industry, so we've always had to follow our noses, and our noses always led us to the records we loved, most of which come from the 1960s and 1970s. I ought not to go into some of the things we've done to get the sound we're after — it might take a while — but in the past it has involved parking a massive mobile recording studio outside my house for two weeks.

During the conversation, Trevor admitted he doesn't use tape at all when he records — it all goes straight to computer. We were all a little shocked. We've been sticklers for expensive analogue tape to the point of lunacy before.

"Think of it like this," he said. "We had an outside toilet when I was a boy. I used to like going outside to use the toilet. You get used to it. But I wouldn't have an outside toilet now."

After he said that there was a moment of thoughtfulness, and then you could see some of the worries lifting from various members' faces, myself included. And I think that's when we all threw our lot in with him.

On Monday I put my car Max up for auction on our website. It's still got a week to run. It would be convenient to say I'm selling it as a small protest against the threat of the West's war for oil, but it wouldn't be true. The real reason is I'm too lazy to work on my car, so it's going. It's a nice 1970s Ford. I'll be sad to see it go, but then I'm looking forward to flexing the power of my new 10-week ZoneCard. Actually, I started already. It was my girlfriend's day off yesterday and she wasn't feeling too great.

14

"Let's go to the pictures," she said.

"No. I've got a better idea."

And then I took her round the Cathcart Circle! I'm a bad boyfriend, I admit. But what a show, what a free ride! The south side looks so pretty in the sun. Those south-side train routes should be listed with Historic Scotland or something. Can you list a train route? I'd do it.

On a similar theme, I wrote to the council's parks department to ask for an update on the Kelvingrove Park bowling greens. I'd heard there was a plan to build a car park there, which is beyond comprehension. It's all very well rushing to create areas of natural beauty in the countryside, but what about the towns? I care for that area around the park and the university more than I care for any mountain or glen in Scotland, and, like many others, use the place a lot. Where are we going to bowl? The man who replied to my letter was nice but not terribly reassuring.

"We are very sensitive to the high-quality views of the Kelvingrove Museum and Art Gallery. A multi-disciplinary working group has been created involving consultants and council officers to resolve the car parking provision challenge. The options we are looking at include creating an underground car park specifically for the reasons you mention in your email."

Does that mean the bowling greens and tennis courts are going on top?

NOVEMBER 7, 2002
Glasgow, Scotland

I should have written this last night when I was in the mood, but satisfied myself with the thought that I'd have a clearer head for the job this morning. I'm in escape mode again — we're in the

15

studio in about 45 minutes and I really don't feel like rushing this. I just feel like sitting here talking to you.

I was going to go to see a porn flick last night. I'm glad I didn't. I had a headache. That sounds pretty lame. I can't even watch somebody having a shag when I've got a headache.

I've never seen a hardcore porn film. This night was dressed up in the guise of an art happening at the local arts centre designed to keep dirty old men out. I wonder if any of the distinctly non-art fraternity got in? I'll never know. I know the girl who sells tickets and she put one aside for me. The show was a sequence of films introduced by Annie Sprinkle, a famous porn star. She was in the films, and was taking us through her own sexual history. It was respectable hardcore for middle-class kids like me.

I'm really bored of sex though. I don't mean the act, but I mean everything else. It's on the telly, in newspapers, in adverts, on billboards, and especially in pop music. It's OK to talk about sex and I'm no prude, but all these magazine guys, all those image makers and programme makers are guilty of a greater crime than being lurid. They are guilty of being boring.

Anyway, I'm being a hypocrite. Sorry, I flip from one mood to the next. I'm bored with it but you might be feeling really horny—and fair play to you. I'll get off the subject. The reason I had and still have a headache is that I was at the dentist yesterday. I feel kind of grotty anyway—oncoming winter and all that. Well, I was lying back and the dentist was jabbing away, and the assistant had her whole hand in there as well. My saliva glands were working overtime. The girl was meant to be sucking that stuff up, but there was too much and it overflowed, running down my neck into my hair. It felt like a flood, like a tributary of the Nile or something, so I was trying to draw the assistant's attention to what was happening, but of course it's hard when you've got two people pinning you down like that. When I motioned with my hands, they just took me for a coward and pressed on me harder. So the spit kept running to the back of my head until there was quite a damp patch.

After they finally let me get up, I tried to dry my hair with paper hankies. When I went to pay the bill, who was in the reception but a couple of good-looking girls. And I was standing there like I'd just come from a punk gig and I'd gobbed all over my own hair!

Enough of that. I've been pretty restless since I came back from Sussex. It was such a peaceful fortnight, with a nice family atmosphere.

"Little naps in the afternoon," said Sarah.

"Great food!" said Bob.

"Ah, the country air," said Mick.

Richard never set foot out of the house for the first week. Sarah insisted on taking him for a drive to the village. He didn't know where the front door was.

OK, I better make a move, but first I have a little assignment for you. I want you to write in and tell me something you found sexy but which doesn't include any sex. I was going to give you an example, but I'm so jaded you're going to have to use your imagination.

NOVEMBER 11, 2002
Sleeper train, Glasgow, Scotland – London, England

Today's been a bit of a disaster, but all is being set to rights. I'm in my pyjamas in my sleeping berth by the window on the 23.40 to London. Rutherglen is whizzing by and I'm already glued to the window. (I'm right over the brakes. I could hear them catch-

17

ing as we slowed down, and now it smells like someone's smoking a cigarette right beside me.)

This trip never goes by too slowly. I never anticipate a good night's sleep. I look at it more like a painless way to get to London. I just love the aspect of being put in a tube and passively fired through the night.

At this very moment in the dining car there will be some real characters prepared to spend the night drinking, smoking and talking themselves up to the other passengers. Quite often I'll pop along and see what's happening, but I can't be bothered tonight. They are the kind of characters dreamed up by Graham Greene, or maybe Somerset Maugham. Tonight I'm in the mood for a WH Auden poem about night travel and the romance of the fleeting British countryside.

It's good at any time of year, but the overnight train from Glasgow to London is best in summer. I always keep my blind open and hardly ever sleep. I get comfortable with a book, but am content to watch what I would otherwise never see: the countryside through a summer night with only a hint of darkness. There are endless half-green greys as the hills settle down and become the Midlands.

I had a foolish day. I eventually got out the house, picking up the wrong set of keys on the way and realising my error just as the door snapped shut. That pretty much set the pattern for the day. Eventually I gave up and came home, had the locksmith out then lazed around until it was time to catch the train. I read some of the assignments I asked you for. They're really good! (Wow, the guy in the next berth is snoring for Scotland. I'm glad he isn't in with me.) Here are some of the best.

It's sexy when my boyfriend calls me his pumpkin pie. It makes me feel loved, and love is sexy.

    Elizabeth

I find it sexy when a guy takes me to a museum on a date, rather than a movie or dinner, but I find it super-sexy when a guy knows how to flamenco!

    Lorraine

My girlfriend only recently gained the confidence to play the piano for me. When she sat down and began to play, I became entranced by her fingers. They danced across the keys like waves. It wasn't as if she was even working to make a sound, but more like she was the one being played. Her body moved gently and corresponded perfectly to the emotion of the music. It was perfect.

    Ken

I was at my best friend's house with a boy who would later become my boyfriend when he picked up a guitar and started to play it. At first he was shy, singing and playing softly like he didn't really want anyone around, but then a switch must have flipped inside of him, because he started to get drawn into the music. He was staring into nothingness and lost that mask most people wear every day of their lives. For some it is a smile, for others a slight frown, while others still bite their lip. When he was playing the guitar he didn't need a mask any more. His face became serious as he concentrated on playing. His eyes became clearer and brighter too. It's always nice when a person tells you about something they really care about — it makes you feel special — but to see someone lose themselves so completely is something else.

    Rachel

I came across an interesting advert in a magazine recently. It had a picture of a man and a woman, and mocked those black-and-white shots you get for Ralph Lauren perfumes or whatever. Instead, this was an advert about domestic abuse, turning the photograph of a young couple into something far more disturbing but somehow sexy.

    Kristin

This past weekend my husband and I were fighting a lot, like ready to rip each other's head off with no remorse or reason. Not sexy. However, on Saturday, after I had stormed off to the bedroom yet again, I peered out the door to see if he was coming after me. He wasn't. He was standing by the kitchen counter, solemnly chopping vegetables for his pizza. And what was so sexy was his feet. He has small, kind of potato feet, and one of them was tipped up on its toe, facing into his other foot. A funny way to stand, but I found it kind of sexy, especially since he was oblivious to me and concentrating on his pizza. Pretty cute.

    Erin

Clear and malleable unpierced ears. I find them sexy.

    Raquel

It's sexy when people call me Robert, which is my name, rather than Bob, Rob or some other short form. It's a shame it doesn't happen more often.

    Robert

Sexy is waking up next to someone you truly fancy.

    Chelsea

I find it sexy when I am walking down a city street and for one moment all the buildings in the street conspire to form this perfect image of acute angles together, and I have to stop walking because all the angles together tear at my guts for a second.

  Jen

Whenever I had a fever, my ex-boyfriend used to hold my head against his chest to feel how hot I was. That was sexy.

  Corey

It's sexy when guys concentrate on something, for example reading or studying, and do not care about what's going on around them. I also find it sexy when they do little tricks with their pens or whatever they can get hold of.

  Wai Chan

My wife's pregnancy. Nothing sexier in the world.

  Robert

The way my boyfriend concentrates when he's driving, the way his nose crumples when he's thinking. Or when, after the second time we met, he told me he was afraid he had fallen in love with me. How he pretends not to be upset, but needs someone to talk to or hug. That's sexy to me — him showing real human emotions, and trusting me enough to share them with me and for letting me share mine with him.

  Jessica

Girls in retro-looking sweaters, that's sexy.

  Dan

Hands are sexy. When you look at someone's hands, you're seeing a part of their soul. Hands are the most creative and most sensual things. When you touch someone's hands, you're touching an intimate part of them, and I think we forget that sometimes, because they're so exposed. Hands are an important part of communication and expression — think of the artist or the musician, whom I feel does nothing more than follow the instincts in his fingers.

    Miranda

Spending my life with my wife is sexy — growing old together and living in a cottage with 20 dogs.

    Mark

I'm a sucker for a boy with protruding veins in his forearms. I'm pretty sure this stems from my first love who played a lot of tennis and had great forearms. This might sound as if I like men with tons of muscles, but that's not the case, just toned arms with active veins.

    Kristine

I always wake up before my boyfriend. Even though I am by no means a morning person, I find it hard to go back to sleep if there's someone next to me, so I attempt to wake him up. To elude me he sometimes goes foetal under the covers or grabs my teddy bear and curls up around it. He will even grab me and curl up all over me to try to force me to go back to sleep. Even with his messy morning hair, stinky morning breath and his general unwillingness to do what I want, it is too sexy for words. Of course, it's even sexier when he finally gets up and makes me breakfast tacos.

    Mandy

The boy I love has a mirror on the floor of his room, parallel to his bed, on which we often sit and listen to music. While doing that I love to look into the mirror to watch his expressions. He always looks so thoughtful, as if he is taking some complex problem and simplifying it into something bite-sized and easy to swallow. During these times, I often think of how sexy his thoughtfulness is. To see his mind working, even if he is thinking of something trivial, is sexy to me.

Lauren

Guys with really odd colouring, like really dark skin with light-blue or green eyes, or really pale with dark brown eyes, or someone who is really dark with freckles, or really light with exotic features.

Sophie

Panty lines. This thong trend has just got to go!

Joseph

I work at a university and yesterday there was a girl from the track-and-field team sitting and studying in the coffee shop. She was obviously a sprinter, and the torso of a young sprinter of Scandinavian descent is about as sexy as it gets.

Ray

Any bloke who works in an art-supply store is instantly, undeniably, mysteriously rendered sexy. This is because art-supply stores are the epitome of displaced sexual revelling in a controlled environment.

Libby

Intelligence (ie knowing lots of random facts and useless information) is very sexy. My boyfriend also does an almost flawless Scottish accent. Could anything be sexier than a Scottish accent?

Julie

It's sexy when a man cries.
  Mona

There's nothing sexier than a girl in her dressing gown, her hair still wet from the shower, curled up on the sofa trying to sip from a mug of tea, both hands clasping it to get all the warmth she can.
  Bruce

I like to see people dancing, singing and having an ace time while not under the influence of drugs or alcohol. Now that's sexy.
  Eddie

Long hair on a man. To keep long hair nice, clean and shiny takes dedication, and if a man can take the time to be that dedicated to his hair, you must wonder what else he could be dedicated to.
  Eve

Libraries are sexy. The books are so vibrant yet usually appeal exclusively to the mind, thus creating an imbalance that just longs to be tipped back over.
  Andrew Wheeler

Slapping paint on raw canvas. It doesn't get sexier, trust me!
  Si

Stockings are sexy. Putting them on always makes me feel like a French prostitute from one of Anaïs Nin's books. It's not about the sex but the act of wearing thick black stockings.
  Bridget

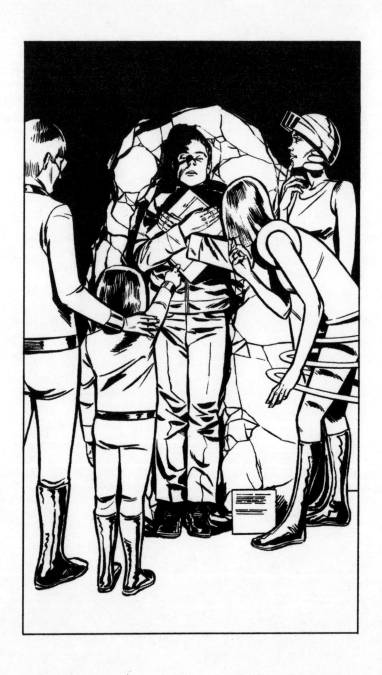

WHEN I DIE, ARCHAEOLOGISTS WILL KNOW MY RAGE

Glasgow, Scotland

I think Tony Blair is getting it way, way wrong. He's upping the stakes, getting everyone hysterical then using the panic to fuel his own crusade. Everyone should calm down!

I just don't get it. If Saddam's the problem then go after him with one of your shit-hot secret services, Tony. Why involve a whole country? The Iraqis are not a bad lot. Otherwise wait for Saddam to die — it won't be that long — or challenge him to man-to-man combat. I bet you could take him. I'm only half joking. I bet George Bush would do it, if only for the relief of getting out of all the trouble he's got himself into.

We know it's about oil now, and power and control and money. It's no longer just a gut instinct — it's a whopping big truth there for all to see — and it's going to bring the might of Allah and Buddah and Jesus Christ down on all of us in time, unfortunately, because this time we are in the wrong. And I'm not just talking about this scenario that's brewing. I'm talking about the fact we run our economy on the basis that we get richer while the poor countries of the world do our dirty work

29

for us, and still get poorer. If the world is a global village these days, how long can we act like village dictators and expect to get away with it?

The oil's going to run out soon anyway. In 50 years we will all be scratching our heads about this one, and hopefully getting on much better with our Middle Eastern neighbours. That's what I'm praying for anyway.

JANUARY 23, 2003
Glasgow, Scotland

When I've been back in Glasgow for a while, and this time I've been back for four or five months, I fall back into certain patterns of behaviour. Sometimes it starts to annoy me, but if you hang on long enough you reap benefits. Really good times of the week roll around to be enjoyed, while the bad times hang around like bad smells and you make the same promises to avoid them the following week. I will avail you of a few examples.

Good time
Sunday night, bath night. Sunday's a fairly busy day. I usually go to church twice, and I've got choir practice before the first service. I also help out with the youth club every second week. So after I've got the youth out of the door — about half past nine — it's free time. And it's nice because I look forward to Monday thanks to having such a cushy job. With my mind full of ideas and contingencies I quite often pick up my Walkman and walk the dark streets. I'll probably be listening to the title track of *Marquee Moon* by Television because it's at fast walking pace, it's brilliant and by the time it's over I can be round at my best pal Ciara's house. Or I might be listening to *There's Gonna Be a Storm* by The Left Banke, or *Jailbreak* by Thin Lizzy. All

30

firm and established favourites, I recommend them with hearty abandon.

Bad time
Saturday night. The loneliest night of the week. I wish I could get drunk and fall over and find myself in a club and shout in someone's ear for hours on end and go to someone's house for more drink. But I increasingly don't. I like to dance at Glasgow School of Art, but I'm often caught in a conundrum whether to go or not, and I hardly ever do. At about 11.30pm it reaches that point when you know you're not crossing the threshold, and the Sunday-night walk to Ciara's doesn't hold the same appeal. The malaise of themed TV beckons. I succumb like quicksand.

Good time
Thursday-night football. It's not even the actual football, which at the worst of times is still magic, it's the jog home. Even in freezing winter you're warm as toast and limber. I leave the changing rooms and slip up the road, trotting along in shorts. Great Western Road is still busy with people looking for pubs and pizza. I jog up and over Great George Street while I decide how I'm going to spend the rest of the night.

Bad time
Just getting to bed every night. It's such a palaver. The will is simply not there. I don't like going to bed. Unless my girl-friend's dragging me, I tarry by the fire playing endless games of Scrabble against the computer. You're drowsy but necessity implores you to put your pyjamas on, clean your teeth, fill your hot-water bottle, take your vitamins and do loads of annoying little things you've left until now.

31

Good time

Half past five on a week night. My girlfriend comes straight from work and jumps on me because I haven't seen her for a day or so. I make her a nice tea then she falls asleep on my shoulder watching the news.

JANUARY 31, 2003
Glasgow, Scotland

I've received the following email from Adam:

I've always been curious about that fact you allude to the Bible and some-times Christianity from time to time in songs, on record sleeves etc. I know you've mentioned you are not a Christian. I hesitate to call myself one, simply because of the strange meanings that word has taken on, but I was wondering, in particular, what you think about Christ. Do you think he is the son of God? Do you think he can be trusted? I ask because I think God is completely a part of music, art; everything for that matter. In anything excellent, regardless of an artist's philosophy, God makes himself known. He does this with any art that is real and that is getting at truth. That's why, when I listen to a song such as If You're Feeling Sinister, I feel closer to God for having listened to it. Despite the fact the song gives no positive message about God, it is a song about people try-ing to make sense of things and trying to get at the truth.

Well, this is exactly how I feel exactly, Adam, and I don't care who knows it! You're spot-on when you say *Sinister* is about people trying to make sense of things. The song is a rather neg-ative view of what I imagined some young people's experience with religion might be like, since you're not given much of a hand when it comes to that stuff.

You are left to your own devices in this day and age, and it takes a strong will to step over the threshold of a place of worship. And then it's extremely likely that, at that point, your views will be different to most of the people there, and that's daunting. But my advice is take the risk, stick with it. It will probably be worthwhile. Indoctrination is extremely unlikely! My experience is that I had so much in common with the people in the church after time, and they were so nice, that differences in belief exist and go along with the church as much as the choir and the pews.

Which brings me to Jesus. With each day I learn a little more about him, and for a non-believer I think about him rather a lot. There are so many amazing things about the whole situation. I'm not in a position to go into it just now, because I'm going to play football soon. I think I approach the son of God thing with an empirical vigour. I keep examining the facts. I think about Paul and his journeys; I am electrified by the Gospels; I have a slim grasp of how much sense the Crucifixion made. I think I understand the reason why it had to happen, and I think I can see to an extent how history changed from that point.

No amount of grappling will make you believe though. You either do or you don't. You either believe he rose from the dead or you don't. I don't know if that faith will ever come to me, but I will never stop thinking about it, or looking or listening out for it.

To change the subject a little, I'm back from football and the house is dark and cold, and I deserve it. As I was about to leave, all the fuses blew, with the bridge club still in the hall downstairs. Instead of helping them I snuck out in the general darkness and confusion. I didn't want to miss football, but I guess I knew I would pay for it later. I had a terrible game and then had to play *Blair Witch* in my house when I got in, and my house is

33

spooky at the best of times. So God was probably looking in on that as well. Or at least he might have had one of his many under-secretaries look into it. It's funny how we sometimes know we're making the wrong decision but we absolutely do it anyway.

FEBRUARY 9, 2003
Glasgow, Scotland

I had the most beautiful run yesterday. I got into a zone while I was drifting easily along Keppochhill Road up towards Springburn, and I thought of a lot of stuff I wanted to tell you. It was flicking through my mind in picture form, and it was Saturday so I was feeling good about the possibility of something happening, like when I used to run a club on a Saturday and I'd spend all day imagining the playlist, who would be there and stuff like that. It must have been the increased oxygen; I haven't felt that good in ages.

Anyway, my Saturday night turned out to be a big zero, involving *Harold and Maude* and some Japanese food, but you can't have everything, and I had that magical afternoon where I made it to friggin' Lenzie. That's a long way! I've hurt my foot but it was worth it.

My foot's an ongoing thing. It's been bugging me for years. I can't kick the football with my right foot, and I'm right-footed. I just run around the park these days like an impotent little chicken, but I can't not go because I'd be missing out. I broke a bone about three years ago but didn't realise it, and it healed funny. I went to a foot specialist recently and she said:

"You've broken a bone; it's healed funny."

"What can you do?"

"Not much."

34

She strapped me up though and that's the reason my foot is hurting, because the strapping gave me cramp.

When I'm about to die I'm going to head to a swamp so I topple in when the time comes. In 50,000 years when they dig me up, pretty well preserved, the scientists will have to work out what sort of life I led from my bone structure, teeth and whatnot. Maybe I'll be clutching a Felt record or something to give them a clue. They'll look at my foot and say: "This man broke a bone and it's healed funny." And they'll look at the Felt record, analysing the grooves with a Groove Analyser and they'll say: "He was obviously in an indie band and one day the pressure got too much, and he booted a wall." And they wouldn't be far from the truth, those crazy scientists.

Anyway, what I was going to tell you hasn't got much to do with my foot. It was the fact I forgot my foot for a while that allowed me to have such rich and abstract thoughts. I also think I've been skirting the subject slightly because it's always going to be hard to put such rich and abstract thoughts into words. I suppose that's what I'm aiming for when I write a song, a good one at least. It starts with an odd feeling that springs up from nowhere, and I clumsily try to turn the feeling into a song because I want to pass the feeling on.

I don't claim these thoughts are exclusive to me. I'm sure everyone gets them. They manifest themselves in different ways, and what people choose to do with them is unique and personal. Maybe you store them up, maybe you think about them when you're trying to get to sleep, maybe they're in your top 10 daydreams when you're in a boring meeting and your eye is drawn to the window and the sky beyond.

So I had my little Saturday afternoon/Saturday night feeling to myself as I drifted through Springburn Park and the grounds of Stobhill hospital. And I thought about writing this because

I wanted to describe a similar feeling I used to get, that maybe you could relate to a little. It has to do with a band called Orange Juice, a mid-1980s summer in Glasgow, fanzines from 1979, their love of The Byrds and The Velvet Underground, and a school film club I was too young to attend but which I perceived to be very cool.

In about 1986 I left my Led Zeppelin records, my Hendrix, my Van Halen, my Deep Purple and my Yes and became indie. I dropped out of university and followed my heart, and my heart led me to some funny places. I eventually became a real indie snob but didn't realise it. I had this longing for something and it was making all these minute decisions for me, but at the same time leading me down this inexorable path. But you can't see that at the time. There was nothing profound about the result, but it's revealing to stop and acknowledge what made you a dentist or a slacker, a computer games designer or a cinema usher, or what led to you to marry a certain person, or break up with another. And it all just starts as a little tickle, this feeling that comes over you on a dull Saturday in February, or on the bus on the way to your humdrum job. At least, that's what I'm wildly proposing.

You know the adage about six degrees of separation between you and any other person on the planet? That in six steps you can be connected with any other person? I'd like to propose a similar degree of separation between you and another person which makes you unique. (I don't know how many degrees because I haven't counted them yet.)

Take my mid-1980s 'mood' for example. I was into indie music, for want of a better word. I lived in that 'alternative' world. That's one. I was into Orange Juice and had a passion for them that went beyond simply liking the music. Something about the idea of them — that's two. Still thinking there was nothing unusual about my actions, I wandered up and down West Princes Street because that's where they used to live and where Postcard Records was, where they kept the records under their beds in 1980. That's three. I read fanzines from 1979–81, poring over them, looking for all the records that were in their chart at the time, wishing I had been around to witness gigs at the Bungalow and Edwyn dating Claire Grogan's younger sister. That's four. While I was wishing I lived in 1980, I also wanted a 1980 attitude to the music of the 1960s, where the greats were still rising to the top, where the post-punkers acknowledged The Velvets and The Byrds over all the crap of the 1970s.

Five degrees of informed choice, each getting a little deeper inside an idea, leading me to a place where nobody else in the world was at that time. And I know there was nobody else because I wouldn't have been able to find all the records I was looking for, and I would have spotted another bowl-cut waster across West Princes Street looking at me with sickening recognition.

Try it for yourself. Start with something quite general, something quite central to yourself. 'I like jazz', 'I've got four kids', 'I'm a former Miss Arkansas', 'I'm into trains'— something like that. Then work inwards, at each stage moving towards what it is that you get the greatest feeling for and I bet you will end up after four or five moves with a feeling or description of a person which could only be you. Then try examining the little feeling you've arrived at, which is at the centre of the description of yourself, and maybe you'll find that feeling is like the one I was talking about earlier, the one that had me jogging through Robroyston in a daze.

Apologies if I've been talking rubbish for a while though. I was just trying to see a train of thought through for once. Hard work for a bear of little brain.

I'm going to try it again to see if it works. I'm into films. One. I'm into Woody Allen, in fact *Annie Hall* is my favourite film. Two. One of the reasons that makes it easy for me to proclaim it's my favourite movie is that it was one of the films showing in Belmont Academy's Film Club season for 1980–81. I root for this sacred list inordinately. Three. Nobody else in the world has as clear a memory for what was on this list as me. *The Graduate* was there. *The Exorcist. The Deerhunter*, I think. *Freebie and the Bean*. (Check that one out! It's great. While overshadowed by the others in any critical league, I'd much rather see it than *The Exorcist*. I hate horror films, and have only a fleeting regard for *The Exorcist* because it was on the list.) *Annie Hall*, of course. It has always fascinated me the most because nothing is given away in the title, and it was given an AA certificate, which was just short of an X. I used to think, what could happen to this chick Annie Hall that would merit an AA? Did she kill people with a chainsaw? She must have been a stripper at least, but a stripper with intellect. Four.

Does that get to my initial thought? Pretty close, as I stood in the English department corridor when I was 12, missing out and dreaming, because I was too young to get in. I was standing on the outside while every cool person in the school went inside.

I was going to say that some of the movies were X-rated, but then how could anyone in the school see the films? But *The Exorcist* was there and that's an X, right? The English teachers must have had pretty cavalier attitudes in the 1980s. Fair enough. *All the President's Men* was there, maybe even *Slap Shot*. I could be fantasising here a bit. I'll tell you what, it was

Rollerball not *Slapshot*, with James Caan as the archetypal face of this list, of the time, and of this little idea I have.

I suppose I'd better creep out of the womb of this café booth and into the street. I've been dodging my homework for Trevor with various tasty distractions over the weekend. I couldn't even be bothered with the youth club last night. I had to kick them out. They like to hang about at the end of the night, which is nice I suppose, but last night they wouldn't budge, and I had to announce I had a hot date and I was going to strangle them with my driver's gloves if they didn't shift. That got them going.

MARCH 29, 2003
London, England

We're two weeks into the new record, and so far so good. It's early days, so I won't say too much, but we're all comfortable in our English country house with the horses, dogs, frogs, badgers and deep, dark woods. In the morning I go running on the bridle ways and paths of deepest Oxfordshire and it is a glorious way to start the day, a meditation of sorts, a peace away from the house and the record, miles away from Glasgow and our usual lives.

I'm in the smoke to do a voiceover for a short film by a guy called Bob who got in touch through the website. We spent a few hours this afternoon chatting about trains and songs and Dexy's and growing up, and that was it. I don't know how you'll get to see it, but when he's finished I'll ask him to send some details in case you're interested.

I'm tired. I've been running again, exploring the beautiful parks of west and north central London, so I'm going to retire to the bath with my Yes biography. (I'm sorry, I can't let that group go. If you can see beyond the vocal silliness — and I can — there is some terrific music to be found. Start by watching *Buffalo 66*, then maybe go for *The Yes Album*, but don't come hassling me for a refund!)

APRIL 21, 2003
Glasgow, Scotland

Crazy Lady Student's Secret Grump
The place is like a ghost town this morning, so thank goodness the café is open. It felt strange coming down the street this morning. I suppose what I like about ordinary weekdays is that I can blend in and pretend I'm busy. I'm sort of vogueing, though my dirty mac wouldn't pass me off for a business person. (I'm getting put off by a song playing in the café that is an instrumental version of a song we recorded and never released. It sounds just like it. I wish Stevie were here. He'd find it funny. "*Verity the Superagent*," he'd say. "Never liked that tune.")

It's a bank holiday today, and I felt people were looking at me going down the street. "Hey, you don't have to go to work," they would shout from their windows, but I'd grit my teeth and head on down here. The only other person on Byres Road is a mad female student whom I know for a fact has been trying to get a degree for about 20 years. She always carries a small reference section about on her humpy back, which can't be good for her posture. I wonder where she is going and why she can't work out a system whereby she leaves some of the books at her place of study and some of them at home so she doesn't have to carry all of them all the time. Maybe she's got a similar secret grump about me. I'm not going to think about the mad female student's secret grump. Oh no, now I am.

Whatever it is, I bet if there were a poll of a broad section of the population to see whose secret grump were more valid, she would win. Just because popular opinion will always swing against the person who's more indie, and I'm more indie than her. "Ha ha!" she would say. "I see that guy, I see him with the scarf on in June," or "I used to see him running backwards through Kelvingrove Park ... I used to see him sneak into the library without a card, with the trousers like tinfoil." Touché, lady, but you're still the crazy one.

So anyway, I'm in the café and still can't get comfortable, which is a pity, because I need to be comfortable to do anything remotely cerebral. I need to be warm for a start. I'm like an orchid. If it doesn't feel like a greenhouse in here then I can't put out any shoots. Last night I was really comfortable. I was running again, which seems to be a prerequisite to me writing any sort of diary entry these days. It was a magical time of the night. I was enshrouded in the dusk, which made me feel like the pressure of having to make something of the day was off. And then I started again with the flow of thoughts I wanted to write down, but I'm not in the mood for it now, dammit!

What's a bank holiday? I had to explain to my American friend that it's simply a day the banks decide to shut, and everybody else follows like sheep. For a non-working person it's bad, because it's just an extension to the boredom of the weekend. I try to give myself something broadly recreational to do, but it rarely staves off the threat of existential boredom. Then I feel like calling my dad.

"Dad, I'm bored!"

"You're bored, are you? I'll give you something to be bored about," he would say in a threatening tone. And suddenly the threat of existential boredom doesn't seem so bad.

Little Booze Bridges

I think part of the trouble is that I don't drink any more. I had a couple of years there when the odd drink was a very good thing. It could take you some interesting places when you were most in need of it. I had to give it up for health reasons. My liver wasn't knackered or anything like that — for a Scot I was a pretty moderate drinker — but I had skin trouble, and eventually, after a long string of doctors, a Chinese guy said:

"You need to give up coffee, alcohol, spicy foods and citrus fruits."

"Citrus fruits! Alcohol!"

I was already off dairy products as well at this point.

"Stopping drinking, that's going to be a hard one."

"You want to get better? You must have no alcohol."

Then he gave me ugly herbs and left me to think on, and think on I have continued to do. You know the rough edges booze smoothes out at the end of the week? And the little bridges booze builds between awkward and remote sections of the weekend, like Saturday night and Sunday morning? And you know how booze gives you a little padded suit in a tight social spot, and how it even gives you a little film to watch when the company gets a bit tiresome? Well, all those advantages are gone, and I'm left with the rough edges of the week. But it has certainly led me to think a bit more, and I'm a madman for the old creativity these days. Anyway, how did I get on to this?

The Chinese guy was right, though. If I have a drink these days my skin is like Braille the next day. Where did that come from? It started happened three years ago. Actually, it was trying to finish *Fold Your Hands* that did it. We were doing 16-hour days in the studio, ripping the songs up and starting again, and I was running out to the bandstand with my manuscript to try to get peace. There was a core of us in the group that had to get that record done. Us and Tony, God bless him. We had to work so hard. That record was our real apprenticeship. That's when we fucked up, but then I decided I couldn't put up with the fuck-ups of the past any more, couldn't stand any more wasted songs. And I'm glad the group went the distance with that record. I know it's got its weak spots, and there's still a sense within the group that it wasn't very good, but if I were to go back to listen to tracks off any of our LPs they would be from that one. It's got its moments. It points the way.

Today isn't so bad actually. It feels like it could be a good few years ago, with me wandering about looking for somewhere to keep warm. Earlier I went into the glasshouses in the Botanic Gardens and sat in the equatorial Africa section for a while, but even that isn't warm enough today. I think the council is cheating some of those equatorial African plants. I feel like the heat I need today only exists in memory — the memory of long, hot summers. It's fun to keep wandering though. Damned if I'm going back to the house.

The Hand in Front of My Face
OK, here's a little philosophical aside. I was talking to a boy the night before a friend's wedding, and somehow we got on to the topic of religion. It wasn't me who started it, it was him. It was maybe that he was faced with the prospect of going to church for the first time in ages, and it was making him edgy. He asked me if I believed in God and I said yes, but I think he was looking for some justification, and I wasn't giving it. Eventually I got a bit frustrated and lifted my hand a little to my face and told him that I believed there was a God more than I believed there was my hand in front of my face. That kind of stalled the conversation a little, but I wasn't kidding him.

I mention it now is because I'm reading *Sophie's World* by

43

Jostein Gaarder. Most of the book concerns itself with giving a layman's guide to philosophy. I've just reached the chapter about George Berkeley, who was an Irish bishop in the 18th century. He was an empiricist, which meant he believed we can't know any more about the world than what we can perceive through our senses, but he had great faith in God as the creator and preserver of all nature. That's a bit of a contradiction, I was thinking, but the author goes on to explain how Berkeley went further than the other empiricists, such as David Hume and John Locke, and how he came to some colourful conclusions.

Now I'm not saying Berkeley was right or anything. I'd have to read his book. He said the only things that exist are those we perceive. But he wouldn't take for granted that objects around about him had an underlying 'substance', because we have no 'experience' of that 'substance'. We do not perceive 'material' or 'matter'. He said we do not perceive things as tangible objects at all!

"Look!" Sophie thumped her fist hard on the table.

"Ouch!" she said. "Doesn't that prove that this table is really a table, both of material and matter?"

"How did you feel it?"

"I felt something hard."

"You had a sensation of something hard, but you didn't feel the actual 'matter' in the table. In the same way, you can dream you are hitting something hard, but there isn't anything hard in a dream, is there?"

The conclusion Berkeley was coming to was that everything we see and feel is 'an effect of God's power'. For God, according to him, is "intimately present in our consciousness, causing to exist for us the profusion of ideas and perceptions that we are constantly subject to". He said that "we can moreover claim that the existence of God is far more clearly perceived than the existence of man".

Well, I'm no philosopher, but it was fun to read something in black and white that I had felt distinctly from time to time. I'm jumping up and down on the chair thinking, "Hey, I think that too. I agree with you there, George!" If someone had told me when I was 18 that that's what they believed, I would have thought they were a crackpot. But that's how I think now.

Do you know something else I've been feeling lately? Imagine you are going away for a month. You carefully pack your stuff, anticipating all eventualities. You don't want to take too much, but you want to be prepared. A week into the trip you can tell you've packed too much stuff and you end up wearing the same comfortable clothes, leaving all your fancy shirts in the case. You wonder why you ever brought a dictionary with you, or shoe polish. You never even use that stuff at home.

Well, I've started feeling the same way. I fear I'll never be able to use all the stuff I brought. I'll be dead before I can use it all! My life is the equivalent of the month-long trip, and the baggage I was talking about is all the ideas and plans and tunes and things I've got to do. I think I'm going to run out of time! I know I'm only 34 but that's quite old, isn't it? It's almost halfway through. Not that it depresses me — I'm not in a panic about it. I'm grateful there's all this stuff I want to do, and that I can do it, but I get the feeling I'll be able to carry on with it in another place. I have a notion that this life is like the month away from home. I like it. It's trippy.

On a lighter note, last word from Hello Dolly. This guy is a poet! This correspondence was pointed out to me on a Morrissey online forum:

"*This is fucking great news. I didn't fucking know this was a fucking Belle and Sebastian fucking board, they're fucking over-hyped, plain and simple. I bought their fucking first fucking album on vinyl, it's fucking almost fucking unplayed, I fucking don't like them, and I fucking don't fucking see the fucking connection between fucking Belle and Sebastian and Morrissey. I mean, does he fucking like these fucking guys? They're not a fucking bad band, they're quite fucking good actually, but why the fucking why did you fucking mention them on this fucking message board? To fucking help them fucking sell some more fucking albums? Are You Fucking Feeling Fucking Sinister? is a fucking tasty LP. Anyway, I was fucking just wondering what the fucking connection is between these fucking two rather fucking good fucking artistes?*"

APRIL 24, 2003

Glasgow, Scotland

I'm looking through old pictures, old folders, old artwork. I'm trying to get a picture for the cover of the DVD. I came across a list of merchandising suggestions somebody sent me a long while ago. There are little drawings to accompany them. I remember these kids used to send drawings quite a lot, inspired by the songs. It was always nice to get, though I was lax in replying to them. So hi to Jon and Caroline from Cornwall — I've had your letter on my wall with the drawings for six years. There's a dog on wheels drawing, and beside that it says 'wuff trade', which is quite presentimental!

Your merchandising list is as follows:

1. 'Mayfly' special edition Stylophone
2. Belle and Sebastian sunstrip (for the car windscreen)
3. Liverpool and Widnes personalised discus (we wouldn't sell too many discuses, so how about a frisbee?)

4. Ubiquitous B&S bookmark
5. *If You're Feeling Sinister* nativity scene (I don't understand that one)
6. Seymour Stein executive jet, 1:24 scale, in die-cast metal
7. *Lazy Line Painter Jane* 20g tube of fungicidal cream (promotional use only)
8. *String Bean Jean* bubblebath
9. *I Could Be Dreaming* cloud formation (I think I read it right, though that's a strange one)

Some of these are really good — take note, Katrina!

APRIL 27, 2003

Glasgow, Scotland

I've been trying to sustain my slightly wistful mood by raiding the archives. I've been helping Blair finish the DVD and we've been bunging old footage and stills in and having fun. Well, I'm having fun because I like mucking around with that sort of stuff. While I was looking through old pictures I found a letter Isobel sent me just after we met. I remember because we met at a New Year party in 1996, and this letter is dated January 14.

We must have just played our first gig. It was at a party at Stuart David's house. I think I invited her to turn up with her cello, but she was so late she almost missed the whole show. At least she sent me a nice letter. I'm sure she won't mind if I let you see a bit of it because it's quite funny.

"The best thing about Stuart's party was Stevie Jackson, who really was as astounding as you had said. He's also a fan of Nancy and Lee, which makes me extra happy. Stevie spoke about trying out some three-part harmonies, which I've never tried before, but it would be good to practise. I reckon you know an ace flirt when you see one."

There would have been the four of us at least: me, Stu, Richard (who also lived in that house) and Stevie. I can't remember if Beans was playing, but he would have certainly been there.

She finished the note:

"Anyway, I had a good time playing with your band, meeting your dog, and am very sorry if my horrible lateness might have lessened the elegance of your performance. I hope I can hear the 'Stuart and Stevie baby songs' very soon."

The what songs?

MAY 22, 2003

Spain

I'm here doing nothing, having thought I earned it. I thought it would be relaxing but in fact it's making me uneasy. It's funny how doing nothing doesn't work out the way you think it should.

I was watching Juliette Binoche doing nothing in *Three Colours: Blue*. It was my favourite part of the film. But watching people do nothing on film is different from doing nothing. For Binoche's character, doing nothing was dunking sugar lumps and lighting up cigarettes in chic, ill-lit Parisian apartments, which is very appealing. Your mind wanders to hanging out with her, and doing nothing together, which isn't the same.

There was a gang of us who used to make an artform out of doing nothing. Me, Michael, Ciara, sometimes Lawrence. The Nothing Gang. Did you ever read *The Plague* by Albert Camus? There's an old man who lives in the town who moves peas from one pot to the other throughout the day. Then he moves them back again, one by one. We didn't quite get to the point of shifting peas, but we weren't a kick in the arse off it sometimes.

The good thing about quality nothing is that the daydreams flood in when conditions are ripe. I've mentioned my favoured conditions before — heat, stillness, having your back against a wall and being simultaneously on the periphery and in the centre, following your own course. You're not going to find these circumstances on a beach or in a theme park.

Ciara and I are doing nothing in a small Spanish seaside resort. We've just had breakfast. She looked great as she sat down, having come straight from bed. I told her the hairstyle she has is the one she's been after all these years. It had naturally emerged after eight hours in bed. All it took was a little pillow work and some night grease. She agreed.

"I need to steal a spoon so I can eat cereal in my room," she said.

She looked around like Frank Spencer and slipped a teaspoon under her top. The waitress came over to check our room number. Ciara fumbled for her key and almost pulled out the spoon. The threat over, she changed the subject.

"I can see your pants."

"I know. Some people pay a fortune for this look. These trousers cost me a dollar."

My trousers are way too big for me. Trucker chic.

"Jude and Claire always bought second-hand trousers but I never could," she said. "I was always afraid of crotch-to-crotch memory."

(Jude and Claire are her sisters, by the way.)

I laughed, pondering the memory left by the crotch of a trucker. She had a point. The danger lies in buying second-hand slacks with yellowing pockets. You're surely OK with jeans, right?

"When I was young I remember me and Claire fighting over the last bun," continued Ciara. "My mum got in between us

49

and decided we had to share it. And I was in a sulk, and my mum asked why I wouldn't eat it, and I said, 'Because I will feel Claire's feel!'"

I suggested *Crotch-to-Crotch Memory/I Feel Your Feel* would have made a great disco double A-side. We finished our breakfast and I cleaved to her side to avoid too much poolside attention from the ever-staring German boy-boy couples.

MAY 24, 2003
Primavera Festival, Barcelona, Spain

It's 11am and there's a party still going on in a room just above me. I am emphatically not at the party, though. I had a decent sleep. I slipped away from the festival while Mogwai were finishing and was planning to go back, but I must've fallen asleep watching *Amélie*, which is a little disturbing because I dreamed about Amélie, or at least an Amélie hybrid.

She was testing out for the group. She was staying with us while we recorded — never a good idea — so I suggested she try some backing vocals. She was a little insulted that someone of her intellect should be reduced to singing backing in a pop group, but she agreed in the end. The group were a little noncommital though.

There were a lot of Scots in Barcelona this weekend. I was out for a run and bumped into a guy called Mark who I went to primary school with. It was funny seeing him in Barcelona. He was here for the festival. Very nice guy, but unfortunately his niceness worked to his disadvantage the other night. He got a bit lost coming back from the festival, wandering around the little streets near Las Ramblas to try to find his hostel. He stumbled across a group of four or five guys and was about to ask directions when he realised they were all getting blow jobs.

When they saw him, one of them asked him:

"Do you have a mobile phone? I need to make a call."

Being a decent bloke Mark said 'yeah' and they subsequently made off with his phone and, I think, his wallet too. I hope it didn't spoil your weekend too much, Mark.

MAY 25, 2003
Glasgow, Scotland

After Spain, Glasgow is seducing me with its spring perfumes. It's nice to have a couple of days in the old hometown.

Once everybody went home from Barcelona, me and Ciara stayed to do the tourist thing in the city. We went to Ocean World along with about 1500 school kids. I was wearing my little blazer and my hat and a shirt, dressed smart for the plane in the evening. I must have stood out like a sore thumb though in Shark Themeland. I'm surprised Ciara doesn't get tired of my impeccable indie credentials. She suggested the newspapers might have to run a story headlined 'Glasgow man dies from lack of credibility' if we hung about there any longer, so we left.

On the plane a huge passenger decided to run a sweep to raise money for his local drug rehabilitation charity. Everyone had to pick a football team from his sheet (and I mean everyone. He was even trying to get into the cockpit to sell a ticket to the pilot! I suggested they better not let the big man anywhere near the cockpit or it was all over for us). Eventually he sold all his tickets. Everyone was clutching them feverishly because of the boredom of the journey. We were all reluctant to hand our money over, but now we had done it the €50 prize had gained mythical status.

Nobody saw the draw, but suddenly the big guy reached for

the steward's microphone and announced the winner was Everton. For quite a while nobody owned up — the winner was probably mortified — so the stewardess suggested they press his or her overhead service button and she would come and find them. But of course, in a rare moment of inter-passenger bonding/humour, most folk reached up and poked their button. The cabin crew couldn't get a word in as the whole ceiling lit up and the punters started pissing themselves with laughter. It was quite funny though. Eventually this wee camp ginger steward announced: "It's like Blackpool illuminations in here!"

But nobody seemed to pay any attention to him.

DEAR CATASTROPHE WAITRESS

London, England

Another working week draws to a close and I slide out the door and straight into a cinema. In this town there are many ways to relax; you just have to find the right one. Right now the LP feels like a baby and I haven't been the best father lately. That might sound like a strange analogy but I'm a strange person. Or at least I like to think I'm strange sometimes.

There's been a lot of talking this week and it came to a head today, but by midday I was feeling amused by it all. You can rely on Stevie thankfully to talk less and put the mix where his mouth is. Sometimes when he talks it comes out jumbled anyway. He bought a Rickenbacker today from a Rickenbacker dealer who came from Birmingham to see him. The guitar had 12 strings and as far as I know he's still holding on to all 12 of them.

We have to finish the record by next Friday. It's going to be one of the best weeks of my life or one of the worst. On Monday we travel across the city to N1 to lay down the orchestration on some of the tracks. Mick, who scores our records, has planned it like he might plan the building of a cantilever bridge across the River Tay. Monday's the day we get to lay the girders, so to speak.

I hope it's going to be a week like the one we made *Tigermilk*. It sort of feels like that, and I hope the rest of the group read this because that's how me and Stevie think it should be.

JUNE 14, 2003
London, England

We're meant to finish the LP tomorrow. Ha ha! Teacher's pet Stevie has mixed his songs already, while Rough Trade were in the room. He's always trying to make me look bad. I'm still singing and fretting, but hey, that's my job. I was out getting sound samples around Notting Hill yesterday afternoon. I was looking for a derelict area so I could smash a bottle and tape it, but I couldn't find a place. If you noticed me hanging around, looking totally shady under the Westway near the skate park, I was trying to get a chance to throw my glass, but people kept coming by! In the end we did it on the patio outside Bob's room, and he had to clean up the mess with his dustpan and brush. He claims to quite like housework anyway.

Another sound was of dropping coins on to a plate, which sounded like someone's alcoholic mother breaking into the kid's piggy bank. It was for *Roy Walker* by the way.

Right, I'm drowsy and ready to sleep, even though it's 11.26am and I've got to start in half an hour. We were all running about in our Y-fronts until about half past three last night, which explains my fatigue. Richard and Beans were slapping each other with mops! It was like Alan Bates and Oliver Reed in *Women in Love*.

London, England

All right, we're not going to get the record finished tonight. It's neither been the worst nor the best week of my life. We will live to mix another day. It's funny this business of not doing it all yourself. There are advantages and disadvantages, but if we get to the end and we're happy and it's quicker, I'll be happy enough. Actually, ignore that. I'm in it up to my ears. There's a long way to go.

Pretty much if each track doesn't bring me to tears with relief and pleasure combined at some point, it doesn't get on the record. I've got a pretty low tear threshold, it must be said, but at least you know it's costing us something. It would infuriate certain people I've known if they knew I shed tears so easily over dumb music, and not at more pertinent times, but that's just the way I am. I cry at the Olympics, for God's sake.

(Trevor just swore. "Piss off, you fucker," he mumbled at the computer. He only swears at technology. He said to Sarah, "This shouldn't hurt, but you're about to be stretched," referring to something he was doing on the computer. "That's OK," she replied. "I used to try to stretch myself when I was little. I used to spend hours hanging from the climbing frame, trying to get my arms long enough to reach the end of the flute!")

I've been watching *The Unbearable Lightness of Being* in the top lounge in the studio. A late-1980s fiesta (Binoche again) of rambling storylines, impeccable city scenes and magical Leos Janacek piano music. The gang's breaking up. We've got to keep working, but Richard, Bob and Beans are heading north. I was going to write some stuff about the tracks so far, but I feel a bit pooped, so I'll leave it.

I heard someone was selling the original dog on wheels on eBay. His name is Patch, by the way. It's funny considering me and Joanne found him up a lane, all soggy and bereft of a wheel. When she moved to London she took him with her but I guess he couldn't get settled. Maybe he was tearing up the furniture or fouling his basket or something. Whoever gets him, look after him, eh?

JUNE 20, 2003
London, England

I was booked to play records at a club in Nottingham on Saturday but I won't be able to make it. This weekend is the absolute deadline for the record and I can't get away. The week was unscheduled, so I haven't been home to get any records. I even sent my clothes home in the truck, so I've been wearing pyjamas in the studio.

I'll make it up to the guys in the club somehow. I would have been on pish form anyway. I tried to get some records at a record fair two weeks ago but all I got was a Kirsty MacColl single and *Down in the Tube Station at Midnight*. It's a pity — I keep getting ideas of what I would have played. Bob was going on about the *Return of the Los Palmas* 7-inch by Madness. He said he would like it played at his funeral (which I hope is a very long way off), and Stevie was talking about *Any Time at All* from *A Hard Day's Night*, which would have sounded great in the club. And I saw the 7-inch of *Maneater* by Hall and Oates in a shop round the corner. I would've played something by Haircut 100, *Down But Not Yet Out* by Felt and maybe *Roy Walker*! (Don't tell Stevie.)

I would've played *Black Coffee* by All Saints too. It's 4am and Dan's just gone home. He's the mix engineer on the record. He told me he once had to hold a bucket at puke level for one of the girls from All Saints while they recorded that song in this studio. You forget this place is steeped in proper pop history.

Here are some titles that emerged for the album during tea breaks today:

Schrödinger's Cat
Nazi Sinatra
If You're Going to Get Caught for Stealing a Horse, You Might as Well Shag It
If Your Gran Had Baws She'd Be Your Grandad (both Richard's, funnily enough)
I'm All Right, Jack
I'm All Right, Jane
Ken Dodd's Dad's Dog's Dead
Wanker's Forest

It's getting light, a time when instead of going to bed you'd rather hitch to Oxford, or the Midlands, following your nose, ending up in a strange person's spare bedroom. I once spent the night at Amelia Fletcher's house. Neil, Richard and I just turned up. We were driving around England because we got a few free days' van hire. It was nice of her to put us up.

You know which Amelia I'm talking about, right? Amelia from Talulah Gosh, Heavenly and Marine Research. Am I alone in thinking she personifies hardcore indie through the ages? How do you hold on to that position without actually being around or selling many records? Either you have it or you don't, I suppose. She should advertise Baby Belling cookers, or swirly brown acrylic-backed carpets, but she wouldn't because she's a brainy economist and a good conversationalist to boot.

I'm tarrying here because I think there is mouse action in my flat. Last night there was a cheeky mouse mincing around under my bed. The last thing I wanted to do when I got in from the studio was chase a mouse around for an hour, but chase I did because I didn't fancy him and his mates keeping me awake all night with their mouse barbecue. Or was it a fondue?

JUNE 25, 2003
Glasgow, Scotland

People go to bed pretty early where I live. I know this because in May I do house-to-house collections. I like having a wee nosey in their hallways and closes [stairways] while they rummage for change. There are so many women in their dressing gowns at eight in the evening! On a summer night, the kid in me will not suffer the thought of pyjamas at that time of day. I guess that was what I was thinking about when we wrote *Step Into My Office*. All the working couples and single women primed and bathed by half past eight, muscling their way into the heart of the Exchequer by their zealous duty to our balance of payments.

Tonight I forgot all about them because I was still on the bowling green at 9pm. We weren't bowling much though. I was with two friends, Isabelle and Melanie, who were endeavouring to teach me *Lord Anthony* in French. They were arguing over the pronunciation of Toblerone.

Michael from the band V-Twin was playing with three pals on the same green. They were pretty cool because they had brought a little record player with them and were playing Love and The Only Ones. It was a nice little scene. We were trying to finish Melanie's bottle of pastis before she returns to France tomorrow. They are sad to go. They love this town already and can't understand why some Glaswegians call it a shithole.

The park was surreally beautiful today. I walked through it very, very slowly, looking at the people from behind my shades. I hardly ever wear them, especially in Glasgow, and I feel a bit clumsy wearing them, especially because I have a fairly big head and therefore need huge goggles to match.

I was peeking at people, and wondering about a certain person, who of course I haven't seen for weeks because I haven't been here for weeks. Sure enough I saw this person in among a big gang of the hip and tanned, the rich and the emancipated. And there's me with my plastic bags and goggles. I just kept slinking, my heart in my mouth, mostly with the fatality of it all. Watch what you wish for! Don't wish for bad things for people because they could happen, and then you would feel terrible. Not that I was wishing for bad things. I was just trying to illustrate how powerful the whole wish system is.

JUNE 27, 2003
Glasgow, Scotland

I'm trying to sequence the record with all the new information available to me. By that I mean hearing the completed tracks instead of just imagining them. It's completely different, obviously. Your hopes for some tracks are inevitably dashed. I'll explain.

I was telling Stevie about my hopes for *I'm a Cuckoo*. At one point I told Trevor I didn't care about the other songs on the record as long as we 'got' this one. I guess I wanted it to be *Don't Fear the Reaper*, *Make Me Smile*, *Virginia Plain* and *There Is A Light That Never Goes Out* rolled into one. And I'm realising it isn't going to happen.

I should learn my lesson, but then I never do, and neither does Stevie. If we ever learned our lesson we would lay down our tools and go boating instead. We've still got work to do. I can see the sadness in Stevie's eyes and he can see the madness in mine.

In 1996 the band left me for a couple of evenings to mix *If You're Feeling Sinister*, but I quickly realised I couldn't get it going the same way as *Tigermilk*. I mean I didn't mix all of *Tigermilk*, just as I didn't mix all of *Sinister*, but I could feel like it was a different beast, and it disappointed me. My expectations were higher and my disappointment correspondingly greater. It's ironic that *Expectations* was on the most fully realised record.

I say all this with no hint of regret — I'm simply admiring the process the way you look back on old holiday snaps. The process is a friend, a magic that leaves you and stays with you according to its own will. For *Sinister* I ended up mixing up the vocals so you could hear them clearly. I couldn't have done anything else. I chose communication over chords, and I'm glad I did. And I suppose that at this very moment Trevor is doing exactly the same thing in London. And I'm rooting for him. I would take the message over the music if I absolutely had to. If you don't have that consistency of communication, what do you have? That's why I'm sitting here writing out the tracks again.

Of course I love it more than anything when the message and the music come together. It's an Olympic gold medal for a boy who will never be Sebastian Coe. It's Archie Gemmell's goal for a team that will never make it to the stadium. It's happened a few times, I think, but then we all want more.

You Don't Send Me
Roy Walker
Dear Catastrophe Waitress
If She Wants Me

64

That's as far as I got when Stevie came into the café a bit flustered and a little late. We settled down to a long and meandering conversation which maybe propped him up a little. He was a little deflated. We got talking about the record, the trouble with being back, the trouble with being away, relationships. He said:

"I'd rather give someone a foot massage and sit up talking. As long as it was the right foot."

"Or the left!" I replied.

Hurrah for the café, though. It's so much more valuable to society than the pub. OK, that's a sweeping statement I will come to retract, but I am fed up with yelling into someone's ear and sipping Coke until my teeth rot. If I can't hear and be heard all the way round the table I tend to switch off and run home.

JULY 1, 2003
Glasgow, Scotland

Have you noticed that I never tell you about anything very 'rock'? That's because scant little rockness ever happens to me. I did take a bit of a step towards it today though, and I can't believe I did it. I employed a cleaner! The janitor employs a cleaner. The bad janitor. The very bad janitor. Still, did you ever hear the one about the mechanic's car?

I was nervous before she came round. I spent all last night worrying about how I was going to get my flat sufficiently tidy so I could even let her in to assess it. I've never so much as let anybody from the church in to see the flat. It's probably a big dark secret among the ladies. If you show somebody your home they're going to know a lot about you straight away, and that's what worries me. Just a glance around the general squalor makes me shudder a little. Am I really this irresponsible? The average

65

thirtysomething couple around here would probably think I was destitute. I mean, I don't care, but it does make me nervous when people come round, especially 'adults'. It makes you want to act in one of two ways. Either you try to explain yourself in a blustering fashion — 'They were trying to knock this place down, you know. I never saw much point in trying to do the place up much' — or you act a little more eccentrically than is your wont, almost like a crazy person so they might think, 'Well, he is an artist after all.'

The point I was most acutely aware of on the eve of the visit by The Mopz Cleaning Co. was that I have a large, black declamatory phrase graffitied above my bookshelf. It says: "This beautiful house is condemned." I wrote it one New Year's Eve when I was in on my own, not drunk or anything, but just feeling a bit of empathy with the building I loved.

The irony is that I only started feeling comfortable here after five years, and that's when the church board told me it was to be flattened. So I wrote my graffiti to soothe the brickwork. I was glad of it, but I've been slowly trying to cover it up. I would die if the minister ever came up and saw it.

So last week I went out to my favourite bookshop, thinking I'd buy an old poster or two, an old map maybe, to cover up the sloganeering. You see, I don't think I could stand rejection by a cleaning company. Once you've made the phone call, you're vulnerable. I didn't want them to think I was nuts or anything.

I bought a poster depicting all the clans of Scotland, with a map showing how the country was split up about 400 years ago. The crests of all the families were shown, the coats of arms with the mottos too. I also bought a touring map of Ayrshire from the 1940s or so, which I love because it shows all the old railway routes that have now been lifted. So together with the clans, and a B&S tea towel for luck, I managed to get the thing covered. There was already a framed print of an Alasdair Gray picture covering one corner.

I was pleased with the result. I couldn't take my eyes off the clans poster. I loved the designs of all the crests and plumes. And not just the designs, but the way they had been reproduced. Whoever had done it had a real flair. I scoured the poster for a name but couldn't find one. I get off on good design and illustration, especially, it must be said, if it's from the 1960s or 1970s. This was from 1980, before computers had a chance to cast their dull shadow.

I thought about the illustrator working away, not even getting a credit. If you had laid out all those crests on a wall it would have got a first in any Scottish art school. At least, if I was marking! I looked closer. One coat of arms depicted a fierce-looking man, bare-chested, on top of the shield of his family. The face looked familiar, or at least the look. I glanced up at the Alasdair Gray picture, then back, and discerned a similarity in the styles. Maybe the guy had copied Scotland's greatest living writer and illustrator.

I looked at the wee fierce man down in the corner. Next to him was a crest where a bare-chested lady was depicted, holding a sword. Only then did I notice the man was checking her out, giving her a cheeky wee side glance. It was funny because it was, after all, a straight-laced academic chart. Then it dawned on me it was illustrated by Alasdair after all. He was just having a joke to himself after drawing about 300 po-faced family crests. It delighted me to make this discovery.

I need to leave the café now but I can't be arsed going home. I know I'm going to have to walk over the hill. I walk over it every day of my life in Glasgow, and I never tire of it. It's far away from my house, but I can get a bus back. I'll probably think some more about football today. Sorry to be a bore, but 24 people turned up for what was meant to be a seven-a-side match. Luckily there was nobody else there, so we played the full pitch. It was excellent, a desert of space. We stretched out our legs like butterflies emerging from the pupa.

Now I'm up at Park Circus casting a ghostly shadow across the park with my laptop. I hope it doesn't attract midges. You know about midges, right? They're our indigenous mosquito wannabe. Boy can they kill the mood! As Ciara's boyfriend Frank says,

"The midges, the midges, am no' gonna kid yis!"

It's beautiful up here, warm enough to hang out without clenching something. Glasgow's at its best in the summer. Only then, once the students have gone, does it settle down to its best rhythm. You should come over some time.

JULY 16, 2003
Glasgow, Scotland

The Way of the Egg
Today is a fine day in Glasgow. It feels like it's all kicking off. I don't think I've ever been so busy with band stuff, though I might be kidding myself. What's keeping me busy is stuff I make up and then feel compelled to do.

My current project is like Chicken Licken in the nursery story. Do you remember Chicken Licken? He got a fright or had a small accident or something, and he decided the sky was going to fall on his head, so he went off to find the king. He was a major panic merchant, alerting the whole countryside to his lunatic raving, but everyone he met was as daft as him. And, crucially, they all had nutty rhyming couplet names like Licken's—Henny Penny, Cocky Locky, Turkey Lurkey,

68

Goosey Loosey etc. They went for his story in a big way, and dropped everything to join the lunatic band.

OK, my analogy has gone a little far. Now that I got into the story of Chicken Licken I realise that. But there's a couple of things about the Chicken I like. I like the fact he's trying to keep the momentum up. He wants to keep the party going. You don't see his friends complaining much, do you? Fact is, it's probably the most excitement they've seen around the farmyard for quite some time. They're totally into it. They're getting a day-trip out of it and it's costing them nothing.

I've been taking pictures and knocking about on my bike, bumping into one person after the next, drinking tea and trying to get things going, feeling a little like Chicken Licken. But you have to be careful. In the end Chicken Licken gets eaten by a fox. I wonder if I'll reach a foxy end?

Actually I couldn't care less because I've been having a lot of fun. Glaswegians are nuts to want to leave this town at this time of year, when the city is reaching its most sublime point, where the sandstone and vegetation combine to create one big indie playground. That's how I found myself describing it to a friend the other night. She admitted to being 'geeky' about the town as well. I don't know why I used 'indie' as an adjective here, but then there are moves to keep altering the meaning of the word until it either doesn't mean anything or means all things to all people.

And that reminds me, one of the lunatic band I bumped into during photographic adventures last week was Jason from V-Twin. I bumped into him a couple of times in fact: once in the caff with Donald and Michael from V-Twin, and again when he was walking Fawcett, the cutest little indie raver of the lot. (Fawcett is a west highland terrier.) We got talking about our favourite words. I can't remember the context, but Jason's was 'obsequious' or 'meticulous' or one of those 'ouses'. (Sorry Jason, I can't remember which one.) Whatever, you can bet the conversation did nothing to contribute to the GNP of the Glasgow area — there was nothing about that hour and a half which would bolster the economy. We were just shooting the breeze over expensive coffees like we've been doing since 1993 when I first met Jason. I don't see him around so much now that he has switched cafés.

You kids think that guys don't talk about stuff. What I mean is there's a boring stereotype that says guys don't talk about stuff. If you get the right combination of people, though, you can have a good old chat. It just takes a couple in a group to get it going. And I like Jason because he likes to pull the barriers down any time, anywhere. It can be 9.15am at a bus stop in the rain and he'll be grinning from under his parka hood, talking about girl trouble or band trouble or dog trouble!

Justin Currie from Del Amitri was knocking about the caff. He's from a different era to us. It's funny that we still sit chattering about people like kids. I should grow up a little. I can't imagine having a coffee with Justin Currie. Not in the current situation. Well, I could, of course, but I'd have to behave myself and not talk rubbish. I put him in with the Lloyd Cole brigade — with Edwyn Collins, Alan Horne, Bobby Bluebell, James Kirk. It's a different generation! It'd take us both being drunk at a wedding to break the ice properly.

Anyway, Jason said a funny thing.

"Del Amitri are really underrated. They had their moments —*Always the Last to Know* is a great song."

Then he proceeded to quote the lyric, like John Gielgud on Radio 4 or something. What was equally disturbing is that Donald was quietly but steadfastly backing him up. I don't know where I stand! I owned a copy of *Sense Sickness*, which was released in 1983 and sounded like early Orange Juice. That's about it. What was funny was that Jason said:

"I mean, you've got to hand it to him, he's a big fucking handsome dude. If I was a girl, I'd bang him!" Ha ha!

My favourite word ... actually, I have two, but one of them would give away a current unhealthy obsession of mine. My favourite word has a Gielgud connection. He used to read the Bible on Radio 4. I mean, right from the start. They had him on for 10 minutes every day, reading from Genesis onwards. I like the word 'creepeth'. It's one that you would have trouble fitting into everyday conversation. But Gielgud used to roll the R, and it was good. Back in Genesis, everyone was always creepething around when everything was dark and lush and overhanging. The snakes talked and you strucketh your brother for the smallest of reasons, and the smallest of smotes would almost always kill!

So, as I was saying, my major thing in the last few days was taking pictures. I had the shoot for the front cover of *Dear Catastrophe Waitress* on Friday, and the shoot for the *Step Into My Office, Baby* single the Tuesday before. The whole week I was toying with the idea of buying a new camera. This was a fairly big deal to me. I knew the advantages of having the new camera but I didn't know how to work the frigging thing. Simply going into the shop to buy the thing was proving an ordeal. I mean, the first time I went in the guy did everything in his power not to sell me the camera. He didn't even get it out of the box. All the time I was standing there, sweating like a paedophile in a crèche, as though I would be found out as the nonphotographer I so clearly am. What the hell would I want with a Hasselblad?

I think I visited the shop four times before I got the thing, taking a different person to chum me on each occasion. It must be said, the underground artsy camera set in Glasgow rallied to the cause. Stand up Martin, Roxanne, Triss and Ian at the lab. And Marisa, of course, though she's in Boston.

Marisa's pretty much the perfect subject. She hands you the camera, primed and ready to shoot, then she strips off and poses meticulously. It was Marisa who opened my eyes to the possibility of the medium format. I imagine professionals are usually sniffy about lending equipment or handing over their tools, but Marisa must simply be comfortable in the knowledge that she can do it either side of the lens. And she can; she's a talented girl.

On the day I bought the Hasselblad I was meant to meet an acquaintance of an acquaintance, the aforementioned Triss, so he could give the camera the once over and talk knowledgeable bollocks to take the heat off me. But he stood me up! Later, his friend Roxanne told me his aquarium had broken, which is a hot one. I'm going to use that excuse the next time I can't make it to something. It was true, though — his aquarium had broken, threatening both flat and guppy. He came along to the shoot on Friday to make up for it, and to provide moral and technical support. As it turns out, everyone I had spoken to the previous week turned up, so there was an embarrassing surfeit of the knowledgeable and the artsy. Thank God we got some beers in. I felt a little self-conscious as I ponced about on top of a table, ordering the group around. They were very, very good.

The trouble with Glasgow at this time of year is that you never know how many layers to put on when you leave the house. I've had to become a layer expert over the years on account of my eskimo blood. And in Glasgow the sun can retreat and the wind advance in minutes. You can go from one to four layers accordingly. At least I can. Why is it that I can anticipate my own kids taking the piss out of me? Imagine I raised a real bruiser who has no sympathy whatsoever. I would have nowhere to hide.

Well, this particular sensitivity has even strained that most tolerable of friendships, that between a boy and his best friend. Even Ciara feigned to lose patience with me over this particular incident. I had gone into town while it was overcast, but the sun came out and showed no sign of going back in, leaving me feeling ripped off that I should have to lug my jacket around all day while I did my indie errands. So I went to the post office, bought a sheet of brown paper and posted my jacket home. That was a few years ago now, though, and I was less robust than you thankfully find me today.

It was a beautiful three-buttoned jacket of my dad's that I posted. I subsequently lost the jacket, and of all the things I have lost it is the one I have come to miss most. It was such a perfect item. I've never seen its like since, though I have searched. It was all the more annoying because it was my dad's. I left it in a changing room after playing football and it disappeared instantly.

I just came back to the house to have lunch and there's a package, a Felt DVD called *A Declaration*. This to me is very interesting. It's almost too much to take. Lawrence looks so good. It's too much, like a dream. I can't believe the band ever existed. They're perfect. Fuck the Smiths, fuck Orange Juice, Felt, FELT, FELT!! I have to stop watching it. I feel like I'm going to have a heart attack. They take me to a different place. "I wasn't fooling when I said/All the people I like are those that are dead." The quality of the DVD is shit, by the way, so don't go there unless you can join the dots for yourself.

Larkin, Cohen, Lawrence and Moz. The rest of you boys can leave your quills in your tunics.

Oh no. I'm in the park and I'm being checked out by a bald-headed guy. I must be in the pick-up zone. Serves me right for saying how beautiful Lawrence is. C'mon, you know what I meant. I'm a bit nervous, actually. What if he tries to wrench the laptop from me? Why do I never get propositioned by women? I suppose it's a law of nature. It would make life too easy. Like, what is the point of feedback? Why can't we make everything louder without the squeals? Like, what is the point of depth of field? Why can't the lens just capture everything flat, no matter how dark it is? But then we wouldn't strive. Digital has made a lot of things easy, but without the need to strive, the art has become worse. The exception is art that is digital to the core—video games and suchlike. Am I wrong?

So I ramble on to the steps to Park Circus, and on the way I bump into Allen, our drum tech, and his two mates, Chris and Edgy. They are in exactly the same spot I saw them in the last time I was in the park, a few days ago. They realise this and are a bit bashful as I approach.

"You are the *Three Coins in the Fountain*," I say.

They laugh. They are perched on the edge of the fountain. They had been to the transport museum but were disappointed the man wouldn't let them get in the cars and blow the horns. The subject eventually settles on *The Two Towers*.

"I mean, what were the Two Towers anyway?" asks Allen. "In the film it makes out they were Saruman's bit and Sauron's bit. I always thought it was meant to be Minas Tirith and Minas Morgul."

I kind of agree with him. That would make the most poetic sense. There are four towers to choose from, though: Orthanc, Morgul, Tirith and Barad-Dur.

"I'm surprised Tolkien didn't give the Hobbits a tower as well," I say, though they had a sort of mound.

Allen is one of the gang I was talking about earlier. He was helping me with both the photo shoots. We were in the same spot last Tuesday, the bandstand, where the baldy guy was trying to pick me up. Me, Allen, Katrina, Roxanne, Hannah and Bob, who were all modelling. Bob was wandering about in a straw hat smoking a roll-up. Allen motioned towards him, and said to me:

"Look at Bob, man. He just walks this land!"

And it's true. He just walks this land. Which reminds me, I was going to try to talk a bit about the other dudes in the group for a while, but I'm going to go and make dinner for a friend, so it will have to wait.

I may be a lousy cook, but at least I've learned the way of the egg.

AUGUST 26, 2003
Los Angeles, California, US

We've just finished a short tour of the States. The LP is finished and again I'm dangling at the end of a trip and heading off in a different direction, singing along with the radio too loudly in Los Angeles International Airport.

I'm watching the ground staff disembark an aircraft. I'm letting a flood of fatigue, relief, loneliness and unease wash through me, but it's all good. I'm heading up to San Francisco. There's magic in the streets and for once I've booked a hotel room. It's great when you drift away from a tour or a festival, from the job and the façade the life affords you. Now I can go at the pace of the street, I can take time to be polite, I can unclench my stomach, I can digest a meal, I can dish out the precise amount of sentiment appropriate to each situation I find myself in, because time is not a factor. In fact I can be generous with sentiment. Now I think of my shortcomings of the last couple of weeks and wish the relevant people were here to enjoy my generosity of spirit, but that's not how it works.

Farmer Dave with his drawings, Beans of the keyboard, Melora of the books, Jackson of the lingering doubt, I visit each in my thoughts and hope they are good and happy, and then I hope just as fervently that we'll be back to do it all again soon.

I can overhear a businessman at the next table on his mobile, eating Mexican food and yelping:

"Five hundred thousand? Five hundred thousand? You're kidding me. I wouldn't give that to an established act! They can make a record for 150. Good quality, good songs, y'know?"

I do know. Don't give them any more than 60, I say. He's got quite a good shirt on for a businessman.

What am I going to do when I get to San Fran? That's what people have been asking me a little, and I don't know. That's the thing. If I knew, I wouldn't want to go. All I know is that I want my fill of the town. I'm going to run from Ocean Beach to North Beach, from the marina to the top of the Twin Peaks. I'm going to put on my rose-tinted specs and imagine it's the 1970s again and I'm looking at the place through a Viewmaster. I'm going to go busking. I'm going to write songs for the next EP, one of them a boogie number, and we'll all get denim suits made specially for the cover.

On this trip I met Chris Squire from Yes. In April I met Steve Howe, so if you extrapolate I will have met the classic line-up in its entirety by November next year. I wonder who'll be next? Maybe I'll meet Jon Anderson in San Francisco. I don't know what we'd do if we met up. Maybe go out for dinner or something, though I'd rather go for dinner with my brother. I haven't seen him for ages.

San Francisco, California, US

Some holiday, this. I've spent most of it emailing, talking, walking and reading. Actually, this is what I do all the time and I wouldn't have it any other way. It's just trippy to walk outside and find it's still San Francisco, though it's doing its best to act like Scotland in October. The wind is whipping up and the clouds are touching the street. It's dark! I like it though. I've had to step into the Mission where it's a few degrees warmer. It's like Byres Road in Glasgow, or sunny Govan, a place where the local geography conspires to keep the air from moving around so much, or the cloud from obscuring the sun.

Mailing, mailing, talking my big fat head off. What are we building? What are we trying to achieve? Who's going to care in 50 years' time when I'm dead? In 50 years' time someone vaguely angelic — I hope — will show me a list of things, deeds and words I was responsible for, and high on the list will be the trivial and absurd, while low on the list will be the self-important and broadly general. High up there will be a chance word to a busker or directions to a woman and her kid (they asked the right tourist), and low down will be the dissection of *Stay Loose* for the listeners of public radio, and an email about which publicity shots to pick.

I wonder sometimes how important the strands of our lives really are in the bigger picture. I suppose we believe we are roughly trying to build a better life for ourselves. A lot of the time, thankfully, we are doing what we must because circumstances and our genetic make-up won't let us do anything else. But, from time to time, just by chance, we contribute a little brick, a little grain of sand toward something God would consider more worthwhile. I feel I've been caught up on the

77

worldly side of things, but at least by stopping to think about it I'm readjusting my sights.

I'm in a tiny park, what they call a commons, between Valencia and Guerrero streets in the Mission District. When I stayed here in 1993 I used to sit here waiting for my washing cycle to finish. It's nice to be here again.

I'm like a dog you throw a stick to. He'll keep fetching the stick until he wears his paws right through to the shins because it's in his genetic make-up. It's in my genetic make-up to walk over hills in pretty green cities. There are hundreds of hills in San Fran, so it's no fluke that I'm over here wearing out shoe leather and eating the odd burrito.

Speaking of which, I went looking for a burrito place I like in Noe Valley, a nice place in which to lean against the window and read a pocket novel. Unfortunately the place is now a card shop, so I wandered across the street to this rather well-to-do sandwich shop, which is where you find me now. A couple of hipsters of the best sort work here. The conversation between them seems to run at a tangent to what you might expect the clientele in this sort of place would talk about.

"You know, there's three crates of music here. How come every day I come in to Enya? I think Brad's got this little Enya thing going."

One of the waitresses is sitting at the next table, and she's yelling to waitress number two her musical opinions. And she's right. The Enya question has resonance for us all. For 99% of earth's population the line between the Cocteau Twins and Enya is an indiscernible little smudge, but for the 1% who are bothered about that kind of thing, it is a Red Sea parting of a kind, and we're leaving Enya to fight it out with the pharaoh, right? I'm going to the Promised Land with Liz Cocteau, oh yeah!

So she's rapping away with waitress number two, and she mentions The Gentle Waves! Was I not in them? Small world. Then she mentions that 'they' (whoever 'they' are) have all the Belle and Sebastian records as well, and a bunch of other stuff. I must admit, I start sweating a little bit. I would've sunk further into my pocket novel except I've forgotten my pocket novel so I have to sink further into the sports pages as if I'm finding the batting averages oh so interesting. When I get up to leave, waitress number one hopes I have a lovely day.

You too honey. Why didn't I just have a conversation with her? Oh well, never mind. Out on the sidewalk someone has written: "Fuck golf. Fuck Garth." And I'm inclined to agree.

SEPTEMBER 3, 2003
Glasgow, Scotland

While San Francisco would be a great place to live, Glasgow is working its inimitable charm tonight. I'm jet-lagged out my tree — out my face, man! I'm wandering about like Roy Walker. I'm working the same shift as all the late-summer foxes, thinking about a lot of stuff and listening to the new Camera Obscura record, which is gorgeous.

I've just had my breakfast, and it's 3.15am. The quietness causes you to mull things over. I thought this was going to be a happening summer, but it's raced by so fast. I can't remember doing much or getting much sleep. I can't remember loving much, but sometimes you have to shut down part of your brain, right?

It's been the summer of break-ups, of people moving on and moving house, and people trying to move so quickly the melancholy can't catch up with them. I wish it had been the summer when music came in and made up for all the shortcomings.

Music as the cleaning lady of the soul!

Glasgow, Scotland

I was going to get my computer out on the bus but I was fearful I might get it wrapped around my face. The 62 to Faifley is maybe not the bus to try it on. Now I forget what I was going to say. Probably something about girls.

There are some great-looking girls around Glasgow. I know that's always been the case, and I don't mean it in a drooling sense. What I mean is that people aren't scared of dressing up a bit. I like the fact some of the girls round here look a bit rough! San Francisco is maybe better for guys. I saw a lot of girls who looked like librarians with black-rimmed glasses and white faces while I was there. I saw a lot of other beautiful girls there too, but I'm just saying it's nice to be back. Things are looking up. There's nothing wrong with saying that, is there? My babbling is informed by civic pride. When I see a good-looking black girl coming along Argyle Street wearing a black tennis vest and a ruffled can-can type skirt, it gives me a good feeling. We can be hip and cosmopolitan too, you know.

Anyway, forgive me — I'm still moving with the motion of the plane. My inbox had a hundred new messages, and they were just from the time I spent on the plane. The last six meals I've eaten have been breakfast. I like breakfast, but this is a disturbing statistic. The only reason I'm telling you this is I'm convinced my mother will never read it, otherwise she would have something to say to me.

There was breakfast on the plane into London; breakfast at Heathrow because United's vegan breakfast wasn't exactly filling; breakfast on the plane to Glasgow; a veggie bacon breakfast butty when I got to Glasgow because I was dazed and still hungry. Then I fell asleep at 6pm and had breakfast at 3am. Then, when I got up this morning, I had cereal.

SEPTEMBER 8, 2003
Glasgow, Scotland

This weekend I said I would help with a gig taking place in the church hall. With that and the choir and the youth club all starting up again, I felt a bit like Bertie Wooster trying to escape old Aunt Agatha. And when the band turned up at the hall expecting to find a sound system that wasn't there, I began to fear the worst. Thankfully this was to turn into a weekend of three bands.

One of the things that happens when you're making a record is you invariably stop listening to new music. You don't have room in your brain. I tend to rely on old favourites when I want to hear something, being reluctant to take chances with my allotted half-hour of listening freedom. Now I'm a free man to an extent I'm back in the listening loop, which doesn't mean I'm listening to much, but I'm amenable to watching bands again and listening to new tunes. The first thing that happened this weekend was that I checked out the recording which popped through my door in a timely fashion. I say timely because I was actually looking forward to it. It was the new Camera Obscura album.

I was struck by a thought the other day while I was reading a review of the record in *The List* magazine. The review was a disinterested dawdle, lazily comparing the record to one of ours. It was so lukewarm it was almost tepid. I was annoyed at first, but then I realised the writer simply had no appetite for the record, nor for the kind of music in fact. The reviewer viewed this kind of music as a very narrow and specialised area, one in which our band and the Obscuras are side by side like two slim volumes in a dovecot.

You see, I've always imagined 'our kind' of music as a broad expanse of ocean, rolling woods and forests that goes on for ever. I thought our musical landscape was the one that would be populated by most right thinking people at one time or another, but I'm realising how unlikely this is in this day and age.

When it comes down to it, we're all carrying on where The Beatles left off, right? Sadly, I must admit that if they are Tolkien, the rest of us are the fantasy writers who try to tell stories of what happens next in the world Tolkien created. I haven't read any fantasy books apart from Tolkien, but I can imagine from the book covers what the deal is. I don't want to go there. Why should anyone therefore who has a Beatles record want to hear a Camera Obscura record or a Belle and Sebastian record?

I feel a bit older after thinking that. There will be kids coming through who will rightfully condemn us and our ilk to the musical grave. I did exactly the same in my listening days. For my part I think the Camera Obscura record is terrific, the only real record I've heard in the past year or so that I've loved. There are about six songs that are just so right. I love seeing certain bands live, but this is the only band that let me wander about with the headphones on, fully immersed in the sound, arrangements, singing and songs. The clincher is the fact Camera Obscura can't get a record deal in Britain. The Spanish seem to know a good thing when they see it, and they distribute their records all over the place. The group play headline theatre tours in Spain where they are perceived as proper pop stars.

So back to Saturday, the church hall and my house. I heard the posters said 'Belle and Sebastian present', which I thought was a bit cheeky. I knew what the presenting bit would mean: running about looking for equipment and mopping up afterwards, which was about right. But I was amply rewarded.

There were three acts on the bill. Jeremy Barnes, previously of Neutral Milk Hotel, who played a one-man-Jewish-wedding-band-vibe set. He was well received, reminding me of The Wedding Present's Ukrainian experiments. Then there was George from Manchester, who had an original, delicate, 1940s-tinged sound based around a female vocal. They had a couple of real moments.

By this point I thought the evening was going OK. Katrina and I even managed to polish off a complex Japanese meal while Jeremy was playing. Stevie said it looked like we were judging a talent contest as we sat at our trough indulging our various appetites. Next on stage were the organisers Scatter, a Glasgow seven-piece jazz-influenced beatnik group.

They were all buzzing about before they went on, obviously delighted the place was busy and the night had gone well so far. They were all slightly a-glow with booze, which I didn't think bode well for their performance. It was almost as if playing were an afterthought to pulling off the organisational side of things.

But I must report a spectacular success! They seemed to suddenly grow tall and fill their musical boots. I enjoyed them before, but maybe on account of the environment or their lack of experience I thought they were a bit skittery, and there were limits to the pleasure the mostly instrumental sound provided. Tonight, though, they were a revelation. Loose and confident, they chanted in unison, broke the jazz down to unexpected melodic passages then charged as one, becoming a tangled mesh of sound, the instruments being sax, flute, trumpet, organ, bass, kit and some form of amplified eastern lute-ish guitar.

It was a great performance, the limitations of the speaker

system meaning each instrument held equal importance in the sound and the blend wasn't taken over by the drum or bass tracks. I think Stevie was as inspired as me. We were catching them at a good time, when musicians derive real joy from playing with each other and the collaboration becomes a real force.

The third band that shaped the weekend had one member in common with Scatter: Nick McCarthy. They are Franz Ferdinand, whom I have also seen a few times. They seem to have got their set together too. Very tight and pretty funky, their angular sound and doubled vocals got The Sub Club moving on Sunday night. I was into it up to a point but couldn't quite lose myself. Halfway through I started feeling like a member of the wrong sex to be watching so close, so I retired to the sidelines and thought about my love life, or lack of it, and that got me safely to the end. I picked up my umbrella and escaped into a waiting cab.

I wasn't ready to go home so I gave the cabbie a made-up address. When we got there I realised I wanted to go home after all, so I told him we were at my girlfriend's house and that she would be asleep so she wouldn't miss me. The cabbie never twigged, and I wondered what other tall tales I could feed him before the end of the journey.

When I got in the Mets were on the telly, so I got on with some late-night eating and emailing, and kept an eye on the baseball. I must have been drifting off on the sofa, but when I came round I thought I heard someone calling my name. Right enough, the presenter of the baseball was talking about the group. Someone had written in to tell them we had a track called *Piazza, New York Catcher* on the new record. They said they wanted to hear it. When they hear it they will wish they never bothered.

I wrote into them none the less with some vague baseball-related adventure from the States and they mentioned it later in the show. I went to bed really, really late, but not before sticking my head out of the window. The Sub Club had made my ears ring and it was disconcerting to sit in bed with it echoing round the old noggin. So I stuck my head out for some background noise, saying my prayers out loud to the whispering poplars, the path and the faraway milkmen.

OCTOBER 2, 2003
Glasgow, Scotland

Today was going to be a beautiful day off. We've been practising, doing interviews and rushing about, and today was going to be the day where I finally caught up a bit and even managed to open my mail before rushing out. And true enough, the first five minutes or so were unrivalled. I had slept OK, and the promise of the new day was painted grey and circumspect just the other side of my green candlewick curtains.

But I quickly became swamped with second-degree thoughts of how I ought to go about achieving the first-degree goals. And then there was an hour tramping about in my pyjamas on a third-rate search for some French lyrics for *Lord Anthony*, the box for a cassette tape, the treatment for a video and my National Health number.

So eventually I stumbled down the road, seeing as we weren't practising today on account of Bob moving house.

(Stephen Pastel just came in for a second, looking a little forlorn. He'd just been practising and I think they were finding it hard going. He was trying to get *Baby Honey* going, and I said rather breezily,

"Ah well. It's just practice. You know what you want it to sound like, you'll get there."

He was nodding, not quite convinced. But then I had a good day's practice yesterday. He'd just begun.

"It always hard to get started," I added.

"Yeah, I know. I feel like we're conceptual musicians. It's not great."

He went off to get his pizza. Now I'm a little worried that we're leaving the practice room for a couple of days.)

Like I said, Bob was moving house. His last words were:

"Does anyone need a screen for a Super 8 projector? You've got until tomorrow morning."

This was at 1am.

"My shit's well and truly packed," he added.

Now I feel like a conceptual musician. I gave myself two things to do today — both of which were fairly conceptual — and I didn't do either of them. That's what I'm talking about. When I got into the caff my inbox was groaning under the weight of messages of varying importance, but I gave them all equal attention. And suddenly the morning was ebbing away. Sarah had picked up my signal and trawled into the caff at about midday with an idea. I was glad of the distraction. Or was it all the emails that had distracted me from her in the first place? That's what I'm talking about!

Miss Sarah Martin. The last cheep I heard out of her was a massive burp which she just managed to get to the microphone before it went unamplified. As a consequence the whole rehearsal room vibrated to the disturbance, and I declared weakly afterwards:

"Just the touch of glamour that we come to expect from you."

And she chuckled, her cheeks shining with the success.

Her idea though, was a good one. I'm not going into it just now, but you will reap the benefits eventually, don't you worry.

I went into the office to go over a few things with Iain and Katrina about our upcoming tours, party, website and record, then I felt a downer coming on so I went to get my hair cut. After that I went to see Ciara and we got the hell out of the city for a couple of hours, but I admit I was still painting fantasy scenarios in my mind about being in this lovely spot for a little longer with a certain person. I didn't feel engaged until I got home and curled up with Bogey and *In a Lonely Place* for an hour or so. I always think he's too wise to be playing the part he was given, but maybe that's his trick — to always seem like the wise person. And it's nice to be around wise people, isn't it? Because as you get older you're meant to wise up, when maybe all you want to do is let your tongue get you into trouble.

So that's that, the diary equivalent of a garbled prayer. All I know is I'm really looking forward to the tours. To be out with the family again, doing what we're best at, living within the rhythm and limitations of the touring life. The endless baths; fantasising about being back home, about a perfect Byres Road and a perfect black coffee; the tour book that couches your thoughts; the possibility of a true musical moment; the moment of unreality as you approach the microphone for the first time; your voice slipping into the first song like a foot into a sock; being home; being comfortable; daring to raise your eyes when you know you're settled; catching some kid's eye in the front row and feeling the way I feel about my nieces and nephews. Avuncular — that's the word. Be nice to your old uncle, eh?

Glasgow, Scotland

While I was wandering round I had some good thoughts about the possibility of music and writing and films — the usual. *Dear Catastrophe Waitress* isn't even out but I want to leave it behind. I've read a few reviews and most are fair enough. What the heck. It's up to you now, but I like to put myself in your shoes a bit.

I know what it's like waiting for a record to come out. It's different from coming to a group fresh and simply being delighted — some of the innocence has gone. Some of you will come to this record fresh, others will have guarded expectations and others still will be able to take it or leave it. Some of you will probably never hear the frigging thing.

Being on the vanguard with a band is a risk. It's like supporting a football club — you've got to take the rough with the smooth. I'm touched by the fact many of you are bigots for the group. You know where we're coming from, you'll excuse the weaker records, you might come in and out with us, but you will be there at the end. I know this because I remember eavesdropping on some of your remarks when *Fold Your Hands* came out. In retrospect, you remind me of the kid in *About a Boy* who is gracious in accepting the jumper his mother knitted for him for Christmas — uncomplaining and tactful.

Everyone has different album experiences. There's nothing like it. The record defines a moment, a season, more than any other artform (emphasis on the *season*). A good LP will accompany your summer, commiserate your autumn, usher in your winter and consummate your spring. Part of the trouble with an LP that becomes your daily bread is that the follow-up never meets your expectations.

I was lucky in that I was contemporary with *The Queen Is Dead* coming out. Although I knew The Smiths before its release, *The Queen Is Dead* was the one that struck me, the one that changed me and lived with me. The singles warmed me up and the LP was perfect. *Strangeways* was therefore on a hiding to nothing. The wait for it was greater than the consumption. It must be said, though, that I still hold *Strangeways* in high, high regard. It's my least favourite Smiths studio LP but it's still way up there, and I'm thankful to them for making it, just as I'm thankful they existed in the first place.

Another curious thing that occurs when an LP becomes your daily bread is that you often have to track down everything else the artist has recorded. This is usually rewarding, but again it is less likely that what you find will surpass the one you love. I'm sure you can think of many such occasions, and many exceptions to the rule.

Being contemporary with a group has both advantages and disadvantages. Most of the time you have to wait until the dust settles around a release before you figure out what you think about it. You can forget about what you're meant to think of it — what it comes down to is how inclined you are to listen to the record. That's like me and films. I've see many films that are critical dynamite but fairly unwatchable. Records are even more like that. It's the flash of a sleeve, a chance remark in a library, or putting the name to the sounds of a group in a second-hand clothes shop that are more likely to be my way in to an album.

So I'm leaving our record behind to start thinking about the next one, and before I throw myself into it I'm allowing myself to consider our next move before we make it, something you don't always have the luxury of doing (and something you perhaps ought not do too often, as it can readily lead to concepts and botched double albums).

I want to do another record for you really soon. I want to do an EP that turns into an LP, rather than the other way around. I want to do a 10-tracker that has plenty of space for the songs to breathe, that is less cluttered but keeps on pushing the sound. Once I start I'm going to get lost in it. This is the anticipation before the leap. I'm at the top of the luge and can't see any further than the first corner.

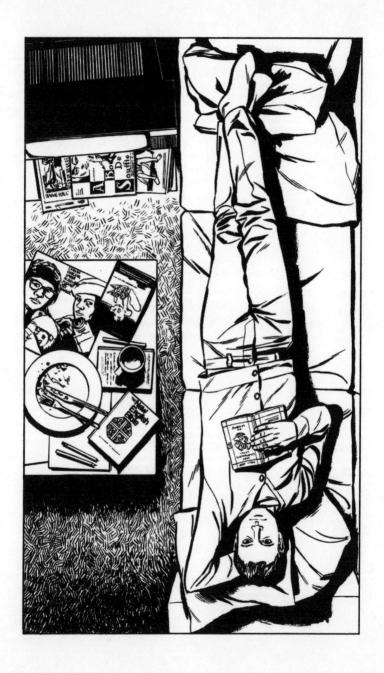

CELIBATE CITY CENTRAL

Glasgow, Scotland

I've been lying low on account of having a cold. When I get a cold my body grinds to a halt, as though all the Numskulls use it as an excuse to down tools and go on strike, so I resort to breezing along in a low gear, which would be OK were it not for the fact we have a tour coming up.

I worked with the youth club last night. Carol was leading the way and I was following. She was talking mostly about John the Baptist. We read certain passages from the Bible then the kids had to decide how John would have felt in certain circumstances. Our passage was the bit where he baptises Jesus. The kids had to give a list of words to describe how he felt. The reason I mention it is because I saw the list on the way out the door this morning, and I picked it up to have a look at. Among the suggestions were proud, humble, chatty, a bit guilty, tremendous, anxious and cheesed off.

It looks like John was running the gamut of human emotions. *Chatty*! That's funny. I bet John felt chatty. He'd been waiting

95

for the moment long enough. He must've wanted to have a good chat about it.

When I came into the café this morning there was a tape waiting for me by The Mars Hotel. I'm excited about hearing it, though it took them a while to get it to me. I first saw them the same night I first saw Franz Ferdinand at the start of the year in a genuine Glasgow 'art space'. I liked the Franz, but I *loved* The Mars Hotel. It is a pretty good time for Glasgow music. Although I don't listen to much I like to see groups play live, and I prefer to catch them early on. My favourites over the past while have been Lucky Luke, Scatter, Franz Ferdinand and The Mars Hotel.

While I'm on the subject of local talent, I've got to mention the tea shop that's at the centre of many musical 'happenings' at the moment. I have to mention it because we shot the cover pictures for *Dear Catastrophe Waitress* there, but I forgot to thank them on the sleeve. Ironically, they were the only people who stressed to me to give them a mention — I think they were banking on some indie traffic. Ken, I hope I can make up for it a bit. Tchai-Ovna. That's the name of the magic tea shop in a lane off Otago Street in Kelvinbridge, Glasgow.

"Kelvinbridge, that's where all the bohemians get off," I heard an elderly woman say to her husband on the tube, and she's right. They get off and go straight to Tchai-Ovna, a little slice of San Fran circa 1967 in the heart of the west end.

Snobbyburger and the Rotten Fruit Girl
Today I want to tell you about Snobbyburger and the Rotten Fruit Girl, a short tale that will probably involve John from The Yummy Fur and Douglas Coupland twice, in an obtuse sort of way. Before I explain where the term Snobbyburger comes

from I should stress that if anyone reading this is in the throes of forming a group, or is inspired today to do so, you could do worse than calling it Snobbyburger. Steal it, it's a good name. You wouldn't be stealing from me, you'd be borrowing from John and Lawrence, ex-Yummy Fur. I nicked *Le Pastie de la Bourgeoisie* from them and they didn't seem to mind, so go ahead. When I saw that graffitied on the wall of Greggs shop on Byres Road in 1994 I thought it was the work of a random drunkard. I liked it a lot, but I found out a year or so later that it was planned and executed by those two.

So Snobbyburger, that was the name they gave to Joanne, the girl on the cover of *Tigermilk*. It's a bit unfair though — she wasn't a snob, just shy. John and Lawrence thought she was aloof because she once pretended she didn't know them or something, but we've all done that. Then one time they saw her go into Burger King and they figured she was going in for a Snobbyburger. She's a lovely girl, Joanne. That's her on the cover of the fake jazz mag Marisa is reading on the cover of the *Fans Only* DVD.

The reason I got to think of her has to do with the current record sleeve. I wandered into the fruit and veg shop and got chatting to Oliver from Scatter. He was talking about the record and said he recognised Shantha, the waitress, because she used to come in there all the time. She used to root about in the box that was full of the rejected fruit and veg. She didn't like the waste. Oliver agreed with her, but mentally called her The Rotten Fruit Girl. He was alive to her charm though, as were many people by this time.

For some reason I was talking to Marisa about nicknames last night. Hers were of the standard Half-Pint and Pea variety since she is rather tiny. Or Spic because her school was pretty white

and her mum was Italian. She asked what mine was and it made
me laugh, because I used to get called Murdy. And that changed
to Merdy and Le Merde when we started learning French. The
Shit — cheers for that, boys.

OCTOBER 25, 2003
Glasgow, Scotland — Newark, New Jersey, US —
Atlanta, Georgia, US

 I've had a pretty rubbish two weeks in Glasgow. I don't want
to go into it, I just hope I'm going to emerge unscathed. I'm in
a timid mood. This will translate to the shows, at least to begin
with. I hope that's OK.

   I've been thinking fondly of the peaks in the last 14 days. I've
helped myself to a few intimacies, and it's left me wondering
how I was planning to get through the next six months or so
without such pleasures. I guess I was going to lean pretty hard
on the old concert experience. I guess I can guess again.

   It's a bit of a cliché, but it's true that life will confound you
and send you an ugly little surprise at times, or it may send you
an elegant love interest wrapped in pick ribbons, or it may lead
you by paths steadily downwards until you have to jump, leap-
ing away with your pulse racing and your plans in tatters. I'm
not sure which category I'm occupying just now.

   So I'm up here thinking of some of my buddies back home,
and some of my buddies scattered around the place. I'm thinking about the World Series too, of course. I'm thinking about
a pal who I watched wend her way up the steep hill towards her
house the other night. She told me that the previous night she
had to zig-zag exaggeratedly just to get up the hill, her long
dress not affording her enough leg movement to master the gradient. I wish I could have been there. I would have given her a

fireman's lift without too much effort, her being a skinny soul.

I'm hoping my office cohort, Miss House, is recovering from her bug. I think she timed her collapse to coincide with the departure of the group and the return of Big Jeb Brewster to the office after a year away, such a slave is she to the band's follies and ambitions. I cooked dinner for her a few times while she was on the wane and she didn't turn her nose up, bless her. Chances are it was blocked up.

As I continue my cerebral tour around the isles, my thoughts turn to Emma back in Cardiff. A stalwart of the B&S touring line-up for the past couple of years, she's got other commitments and is missing this tour. Never mind. I got a new sleeping bag, Emma, so we can go somewhere hot and camp. That sounds like we're going to a gay club. I meant somewhere hot *to* camp. Emma is quite game when it comes to camping. This summer her and some mates camped for two weeks on the Welsh coast while they were performing and rehearsing. Imagine performing Mahler in an evening gown and then groping your way back to your tent by the shore.

OCTOBER 26, 2003
Atlanta, Georgia, US

After the flight I wake early in Atlanta. I curse my luck that I'm here to work and not to drift. I love the job, of course, but right now I feel I don't have the ammunition. I don't have the qualifications. Tonight I'll be an undergraduate standing in front of an esteemed gathering of intellectuals who know more about the subject than me. I'm like the only kid at a hippie camp who isn't out of his mind on something.

What I mean is I've been sick for the past fortnight and don't much feel like singing. While it's nice to be away from my room in Glasgow, I wish I could slip to the back of the organisation, take my turn in the middle of the peloton, away from the jostling for positions.

It's raining here but warm, of course, so it's like a summer's day in Glasgow, the kind where if you were a kid you would stay in and play with Lego. You'd be as snug as a bug in a rug.

(I made my French tutor, Isabelle, learn that phrase the other day.

"Learn that," I said. "It's a really handy thing to know. You should say it a lot."

"Snoug … as a boug … in a roug," she said.)

It might be Sunday but I'm not going to attempt the search for a church. I'm going to be lazy, God. You'll have to accept my pitiful offerings from this suite, with a view of building sites and skyscrapers, water towers and air-con outlets.

NOVEMBER 3, 2003
Austin, Texas, US

I ended up going to church that morning in Atlanta after all. I went out for a stroll and walked past a church that was about to begin its early service, so I stepped in. The same thing happened here yesterday—I was up really early and went to the 8am service at the United Methodist church.

It was All Souls' Day, and they embraced the fact by allowing us to light a candle for a chosen saint or saints. I can't remember if they meant a saint or someone who had meant a lot to us but was now dead. So I got up and took communion. I got my little hunk of bread then went to the woman with the chalice. I waited for her to lift the cup to my lips and when she didn't I nervously put the bread in my mouth.

"You're supposed to dup the bread in the *whine*," she said.

Then I got my candle, lit it and knelt at the fence, praying for Lewis and Tolkien, Saint Jack and Saint Ronald. I hoped that was what they meant but didn't really care — I'd been up since 4am, ripping through a popular Tolkien biography.

I love Tolkien. It's only recently that I've come to think about him in broader artistic terms, with *The Lord of the Rings* films, his books topping polls and the way he divides the critics. I've felt that split myself. It still feels as though *The Lord of the Rings* is a guilty pleasure. When people asked me about the books in the past I would always hesitate to recommend them. I'd be quicker to suggest *The Hobbit* because you were on a surer footing there. It's a marvellous children's book that can also be read by adults and enjoyed because of its sheer quality.

But its big brother? I read it a few years ago before the first film was released, to get myself in the mood. I didn't expect to enjoy it so much, but I've now read it *five times*. Tolkien *must* be on to something. Like my list of favourite films, where I use how often I'm inclined to watch a movie as a mark of its quality, *The Lord of the Rings* has to be pretty high up on my list of favourite books.

And in light of recent debates that have forced people to take sides, I unhesitatingly say it is a great work of art. It's immature, it's escapist, it's even got its weaknesses, but what book hasn't? And would its strengths remain intact if the male/female relationships sparked with sexual energy, or if some of the characters were painted with a subtle watercolour instead of hefty broad strokes?

I'm in Dallas now waiting on a connecting flight to Kansas. I was ticking along behind the others, enjoying the walk between flights, when I realised I'd lost my boarding card. I got in the queue anyway, and when it was my turn I told the security official what had happened. He was stern.

"You'll have to go back to the ticket desk."

"Will I still make the flight?"

"There's no chance of that now."

So I scribbled a quick note to Dreads, who was already on the plane. He'd have had a heart attack if I hadn't told him. I didn't have time to register my carelessness with the others, so as far as they were concerned I'd pulled off a classic Hitchcock victim move, like in *The Lady Vanishes*. Something told me it would be OK, so I'm making the most of my time working on the set list for tonight's show in Lawrence, Kansas.

Once you're on tour you have a basic set that you mess with every night. We're five shows in from what is basically a new set, and still there are things not flowing right, songs that haven't found their niche within the show. We haven't been as adventurous as I thought we might be because I've been off-colour. There haven't been too many covers floating about, and we haven't played anything we didn't practise before we left.

I'm drawing a blank thinking of what to play tonight. At times like this I ask the group what they fancy playing. Their usual response is something like this:

Sarah: "*The Model*?"

Stevie: "I don't mind. I'm happy to play anything."

Bob: "A wee bit of *Me and the Major*."

Richard: "I'm easy. Whatever you like."

Beans: " … "

Mick: "How about *Roy Walker* or *Step Into My Office*?"

We always play *Office* and *Roy Walker*! They're permanently installed in the set. We're not playing *The Model* or *Me and the*

Major just now, and I don't fancy putting them back in. So my virtual inquisition has come to nothing.

We've been starting with *Passion Fruit, Expectations, Step Into My Office* and *Wrapped Up In Books*, and I see no reason to change it. I usually like to shift to the piano at this stage, and I quite fancy *Seeing Other People* tonight, so that's an angle.

NOVEMBER 5, 2003
St Louis, Missouri, US

Suffice to say the set was written, I made it to Lawrence, we played the gig and it was OK. I must be feeling better because I was edgy after the gig. I tried to watch *The Player* but the sound in the tour bus was all wrong and the cold air was blasting, so I turned in. I slept pretty soundly on my back.

I'm still edgy this morning. Part of the reason for my sprightliness is some new esoteric medicine I'm trying. I think it's going to drive me nuts, but good nuts. Stevie Dreads arranged for me to see an acupuncturist in Austin, when I was starting to feel a bit better. Dreads knows the right buttons to push! I liked the needle guy right off the bat. He was an anti-hippie, anti-hokum kind of practitioner, but after a while I found out he was a bit of a demon diagnostician. He understood my problems.

He came to the show, then the next day he dropped off some new stuff for me to make tea with. It turns out it's a fungus found on the underbelly of rare Chinese caterpillars. You couldn't make it up. I think it's going to work though, or at least I'm going to give it a ruddy good go.

I wish Ciara could see this guy. I'd be fascinated to see what he would make of her. She's been really sick with ME for 15

years. Maybe he'll come on holiday to Scotland some time. Hey
Symon, if you're ever in Europe, stop by and work your magic.

NOVEMBER 29, 2003
Glasgow, Scotland

It's 4am on Sunday. I've been lazy; I ate too much chocolate;
I've wasted too much time; I sit thinking about my exes; I sit
thinking about my wannabes; I forget to pray; I indulge myself; I don't phone anyone then get annoyed that nobody
phones me; I don't contact anyone; I want to race to intimacy
without the in-between stuff.

Like Truffaut, I can't be bothered talking to other men after
6pm, especially about records, or lists, or politics, or football,
unless we're playing football, in which case we communicate
with grunts that rival whales for beauty and economy.

I'm racing through the week and coming down ungraciously,
annoyed at not having things my own way, annoyed at having
to run to schedule, cold from the boring video shoots of
Monday and Tuesday, stressed by preparing the new EP, *I'm a
Cuckoo*.

I don't want it to be the wee small hours of Sunday morning.
I want it to be 8pm on a beautiful and placid Sunday without
my youth club, buoyed by the minister's talk of *The Scottish
Paraphrases*, excited by the vacuum of the week ahead which will
be filled with writing, writing, writing.

I dragged Num Num away from a party for an hour or so. I
was going to have the night in, but when I returned to the
church hall it was bursting at the seams with annoying late-
thirtysomething BBC workers having an early Christmas party
complete with a Proclaimers covers band. The smoke and booze
were coming up through the floorboards into my flat, so I

listened to Kirsty MacColl's *A New England* at top volume, then fled to the art school disco.

I talked about the beauty of ex-girlfriends in your memory. I talked about the salvation of song while waiting for Saturday cabbies. I talked about the line of a skirt, and I thought about the vaunted prevalence of lesbianism among the young, and whether this is a crafty male wank myth. I thought about moving the speakers in the disco because they sounded funny, and I was glad Num Num had made it out to accommodate my doubting and gossiping. She reciprocated with grace, but I know she could trump me for real gossip, easy.

I looked for the graffiti in the toilets, 'PUSH BARman TO OPEN old wounds' doctored as 'plEASE don't put YOUR FEET IN THE SEAts', but it had disappeared, and I felt old like I always feel old these days. I ranted against the blokes who stand in the middle of dancefloors supping pints, surveying all, like frigging lighthouses, sucking up space, making it impossible to dance.

Num Num went back to her party, Tony Doogan approached me at a silly time of the night and Beans showed up. Waves of young students painted the art school walls with Gap blandness.

Thank God for my niece and nephew. They are so nice, funny and well behaved. I visited my parents this afternoon and the kids were there, bright as buttons. I sometimes feel I should have children by now, but then I have the band. I wouldn't change it.

NOVEMBER 30, 2003
Glasgow, Scotland

I've calmed down a little today. Ciara and I have been on a beautiful drive to Luss on the shores of Loch Lomond, where we lunched royally and listened to the water lapping the shore. The scene was so pretty that I was fantasising wildly about lodging with a loved one in the hills and roaming like a wild deer.

Now I'm in my bed, the last night in it for a while. It's the best bed you could have. I wasn't happy before I got it, but I am now. Is that all it takes? I don't even have anyone to share it with. It's ironic that I eventually got round to getting a bed and a mattress, and then I became single.

You know I told you about those caterpillar tablets the acupuncturist gave me? Well, the box says they have another effect: they increase your sex drive. The trouble is I've got nowhere to drive to. Consequently I've been a little *focused*, shall we say, but I'm trying to steer clear of it and get back on the straight and narrow.

DECEMBER 2, 2003
Sheffield, England

It was a bit of a strange show at the City Hall tonight. It feels as if we're continuing the US tour, but the audience is of course quite different. Stevie was a nervous, and I understand why. There's a feeling that the audience is British and we're British — there's culture in common and nowhere to hide as far as music goes. We can't hide behind the veil of cross-continental exoticism.

Is it worth getting nervous? Emphatically not. It feels like we've been around the block a bit, and we approach things in a different way now. We perform confidently; we perform where we previously didn't. I want to take things to a higher pitch though. I want to feel the audience move. I guess we have to move them.

London, England

Tonight was the second of three nights at the Astoria in London. Due to a technicality, some kink in the acoustic of the hall perhaps, my stage sound was such that I couldn't enjoy the show much. The same thing happened in New York last month. This wasn't as bad, but it was more annoying because it felt like the stage was really set here.

You could tell instantly that the audience was a good one. I was in the mood for shaking hands with people before we played, but by the middle of the gig I felt like shying away. As Beans pointed out, this is stupid and in future should be avoided. It's looking ever more inevitable that I'll have to wear in-ear monitoring. I hate feeling like I've missed out though. I *know* folk enjoyed it, and I'm glad, but I want to be at the party too.

I'm back at the hotel and it's late. I don't even have a decent book to read. I tell you, though, my two favourite moments of the tour so far have occurred off stage, off road, off *out*. I went running before the first London show. I hit the Thames eventually, but I was trying to hit the extravaganza of St James Park, Green Park and Hyde Park. I got a bit lost, and was going to head back, but when I hit Hyde Park in the dark I was so glad I kept going. I traversed it diagonally, out to Notting Hill, surrounded by darkness.

There was enough light reflected by the clouds to see where I was going, though. I had the park to myself, and the feeling of being out there was heightened by the fact I was anticipating the show, thinking about new records and situations, about the set, checking off lyrics in my head.

The same thing happened in Sheffield the night before the gig. It's a great town to run around on account of the hills and the plentiful network of meandering rivers and canals, and quiet industrial roads. In addition that night, I had a song playing in my head. I wish we could have played it for you, but it has to be *just so* before we do it. The trouble is that when I imagined it on the run, it was sung by a twentysomething female with a piercing, matter-of-fact Ronnie Spector/Belle Star type voice. My conundrum is whether to write it for the girl, or whether I should sing it, or whether I should sing it *as* the girl. Oh well, it'll come.

My eyelids are heavy. I keep putting off going to sleep. Music, music, music. Thank God for breakfast, Tube trains and the myriad of cute faces on those trains. If it wasn't for such blessings I might turn into a sequence of notes, like in *Fantasia*, and be carried off in a dream.

DECEMBER 5, 2003
London, England

Stevie Dreads was funny last night. He's superb at his job — sincere and conscientious. I phoned him from the hotel, and he reminded me we were on at 8.45pm, and that I ought to be back at the venue at 8.15pm. I said I would be for sure, and then out of nowhere, to the tune of *I Surrender* by Rainbow, he sang: "We believe you! We believe you!" down the phone at me. Completely sarcastic, but pretty funny. It was then I realised I usually turn up much later and nearly give him a heart attack every time. Sorry about that, Stevie.

Another thing I was laughing at was a chance remark in the dressing room. Mick was commenting how chilled out a certain member of the crew had been recently.

"Have you noticed?" he said.

"Must be getting his Nat King ..." remarked Bob nonchalantly as he left the room.

DECEMBER 6, 2003
London, England

We've got a day off, so it's bath night. Dreads, Sarah and Katrina are going to see The Strokes at the Alexandra Palace, but I don't know if I can be bothered. They're a bit cutting edge for me. I feel like Sarah's man Sean, who used to worry that if he switched TV channels and landed accidentally on some crap soap or something, his channel hop would be counted in the viewing figures. He was terrified of being used to endorse cack programming, however anonymously.

I'm such a wanker that I'm wondering if I should try seeing The Strokes. The others are out to have a good time. The chances are I'll have a bad time, but the only options are to stay in and wonder how they got on, or go and see some boring arty film on my tod. *The Anatomy of an Art Scrooge.* (That refers to me, not the name of the film, but it may as well be the film.)

Earlier I said to Katrina:

"I'm going to have a bath and watch some porn."

"I've checked the programme and they all look rubbish."

"Did you look at the porn, you dirty bitch?"

"No! I just looked at the brochure."

"I've only seen one porno, and it was when I was 12. It was rubbish."

"I only saw a bit of one when I was 15. I can't remember much about it."

The film I saw had Bernie Winters in it, minus Schnorbitz. He was judging a nude beauty contest. All I remember is that the women all looked a bit pale against the flocked wallpaper of the 1970s social club it was filmed in. Cold as well. Their nips were up like button mushrooms.

I saw it at Mossy's house. He was the big pal of my pal Brian, and the big Thin Lizzy fan. Gus was there too — he was the big AC/DC fan. Brian was the big Quo fan. I was the little plastic AC/DC fan. I used to get my bootleg tapes off Gus, who got them off of some guy in Jersey. Those photocopied lists Gus and Mossy had were manna from nirvana. I remember there was a backstage pass for sale too. I wondered if it was still valid. I thought it meant you could visit AC/DC in their dressing room wherever they might be playing.

The idea fascinated me, though at the same time I could feel an acute sense of creeping embarrassment as I imagined standing there like a spare prick, getting in people's way, not even gormless enough to be spotty yet, while Angus and Malcolm picked out which groupie they were going to sleep with, and Phil Rudd told jokes I couldn't begin to understand. Pretty much like our dressing room, then. (joke).

DECEMBER 7, 2003
London – Bath, England

I went to see The Strokes after all, and they were excellent. At first I was going to recommend never going to a big rock show, because the build-up is ridiculous, cold, alienating and boring. To their credit, though, when the band came on I forgot about the surroundings, and forgot about trying to get back to the hotel quickly. The singer was funny — he knows how to handle things.

"We're just five faggots. Enjoy!" he said in a resonant New York accent, and his voice kept things interesting during the gig. I like it best when they slow down a little and the songs get a bit more Todd Rundgren. It's always hard to make out words in a place like that — I would have liked to get off on the stories, but I didn't get bored. Compared to the Yeah Yeah Yeahs these guys are geniuses.

We're on the tour bus and Mick is talking about the Museum of London. I've just heard him say: "They had a well laid-out Roman section." After 24 hours apart, everyone has stories about what they got up to. *Chitty Chitty Bang Bang*; the British Museum; food; pubs; walks; dinner with family; swimming pools; saunas; massages. I went for shiatsu on Friday before the gig. I was scheduled to meet Trevor for tea at his studio at 5pm, but I had to send a message to Sarah telling her my shiatsu had overrun. Only in London could you stand up Trevor Horn because your shiatsu took longer than expected.

As ever, I challenge everyone to a game of Scrabble. As ever, there are no takers. Murray tells me I could learn from a friend of his who used to go to the pub and play darts with himself. He'd play right hand against left, calling them Dr Jekyll and Mr Hyde. It's not such a bad idea.

DECEMBER 8, 2003
Bath – Brighton, England

We're on the bus again. I throw Stevie a bottle of water, and immediately think of the kid in the 1970s TV show *How* who asked: "Why, when I throw something up in a moving car, can I catch it again?"

It was a programme for swotty kids, and this particular swot went on the programme where you saw him throwing a tennis ball in the back of a posh ITV motor. The kid probably knew the answer already, but just wanted to ask so he could look good when he came up with the answer. It's not hard to imagine 1970s programming when you throw a bottle of water to Stevie, because he hasn't really grown up since then.

We have to double-check the answer with Beans. This is the usual drill unless, funnily enough, the question is in the area of sphincters, and then it is clearly Mick's territory. That's what he did his dissertation on when he was at university. To be fair, if it's a chemistry or biology query, it goes to Mick. And it's amazing how many times we need the answer to a biology or chemistry question.

According to Beans, when the object is thrown it is already travelling at the same speed as the vehicle plus or minus whatever speed has been applied to it within the atmosphere of the vehicle.

I'm playing Scrabble at the same time as writing this. Beans is doing well, as is Charlie. I'm having a dog of a game; there are too many vowels. I did get 'Aeolian' on a triple word score. I don't know what it means, but I got my bonus, as did Beans for 'beetling'.

Last night's gig at the Pavilion in Bath was better than the London shows. It's a rocking little place. I know it was Sunday night, but my sound was better, so I wrote the set as a bit of catharsis, and it sort of worked. There wasn't a subtle moment in the set! We sent the West Country kids home with their ears ringing, or at least that was the idea.

DECEMBER 9, 2003
Norwich, England

Tonight's show was good for everyone except Bob, who had a stinker, but we all have them from time to time, especially me.

112

There was a fellow called Sam who looked like Rod Stewart at the gig. He came up to say hello, and it occurred to me that we could have a go at *Maggie May* but he wouldn't sing it, which was OK in the end because I wanted to sing it. So we launched into the tune, albeit too soon for Sarah to get comfortable with the mandolin part on the violin, but it bowled along fine.

Again, there weren't too many subtleties at the gig. It's hard to keep the sound in check because the lad in all of us rises up, while the strings, piano and finely balanced loveliness of the soundcheck are buried in the rush to impress. That's just the nature of the show sometimes.

I had such a nice time in Brighton yesterday. It was refreshing just to knock a football round the hall during the soundcheck, like being at school again and getting out of class to practise for the school concert. Allen, Beans, Charlie, Murray and I were like Holden and his two friends who were throwing the football around in *The Catcher in the Rye*. We were moving around, digging the soundcheck vibe, skiving off, pulling off some good moves, loving the ball and the yard of polished floor.

Bath was a cracker too, with plenty of room to stroke the ball about and a rockin' little village-hall feel to the place. I asked: "So what happens on a Sunday night in Bath?" and some kid shouted: "Incest!", which was pretty funny.

DECEMBER 10, 2003
Norwich – Newcastle, England

We're en route to Newcastle, and all the stuff I was writing about yesterday — about music and sounds and laddishness and joy — doesn't seem to matter. This is dull. While we don't have a gig tonight, and I'm glad, I have nothing better to do: no squeeze, no drink, no smoke, no nuthin. Festive lunch at a Little Chef was the highlight of the day, and it was only festive because there were Christmas songs playing.

DECEMBER 15, 2003
Glasgow, Scotland

I was looking for Christmas lyrics before the end-of-tour show in Edinburgh last night, and I found an old letter I sent my brother Fraser. It's good timing, because I wrote it on the day the first B&S gig happened. I was quite the cocky wee shit. Sorry about that.

January 11, 1996

Dear Fraser,

How's it going man? I hope you are still sane from being at sea. Seen any good films, heard any good music? You're probably more in touch than me. I don't have a telly in my new place, and I don't want one either. I like the peace.

Did you know that I am the hallkeeper at Hyndland now? I live above the church hall, and I keep everything in order. I like it pretty much, except I have a lot of work to do on my house before it becomes comfortable.

I've been getting a lot of action since the New Year, which is nice for a change. Apart from my hall duties, I'm making a single for Stow College, which I think you know about. I think I'm going to have to step into the real world of The Biz shortly, and I don't know how I'm going to put up with all the hassle. It should be a laugh. I'm recording at the end of February, which is not too far away. I decided to use the name Belle and Sebastian for the project. I know you think that's daft, but it just happens to be the mode of thought that I'm occupying at the moment. I'm still thinking about the short story I wrote in the summer. I might put a copy

114

in for you. But the funny thing is that I met a girl called Belle, short for Isobel, at a party. And she's going to be playing cello and singing backing. Fucking crazy, huh?

Yeah, so you should be home for the launch party of the single at least. An extravaganza of (local) celebrities, my pals there for the free booze and scran, and Mum and Dad. Should be a laugh. Except for Dad nipping outside to let the dog go for a pee. While we're on.

Is there anything you want me to send you? I'm putting in a tape and a CD assuming you have the chance to use them. So what else is happening? That's rhetorical. I'll answer myself. I've been keeping away from _____ very goodly. I don't like it too much, but that's how it has to be. I think she would go back out with me if I indulged her, but she's got to get over it. Actually, she's probably having an OK time, because I know for a fact there have been a lot of people chasing after her, even if most of them are 'morons'. (Her word, not mine.) Meanwhile, it's the celibate life for me. The hall is Celibate City Central. Too many net curtain twitchers near me. I can't take a dump without it being discussed at the Congregational Board.

So the fellow in charge of Electric Honey Records at Stow is Alan Rankine, who used to be in chart act The Associates. He says to me the other day, "So Stuart, do you know what songs you are going to record?" I said, "Yeah, I just wrote a lead track called My Wandering Days Are Over, and everything's fallen into place after that. They're all new songs." He's like "…?" I said, "Don't worry about it, Alan. They're great!" But actually, they are quite good. He's just worried because he likes the songs on the demo. Everyone seems to like The State I Am In. I do too, but I have to move on. See, I know the new songs will be just as good when they are recorded, but no-one else has an inch of faith in you. You have to prove yourself constantly. I don't mind that.

It's not as if I ever want to do anything second-rate anyway. At least the band know what's good 'n' that.

Anyway, I've got a wash on down at the Union. Better go and put my

gear in the dryer. It's Saturday, and I think it's going to be hectic. We're
playing at a party in a wee room. A tidy wee seven-piece. The four boys
plus Mick the trumpet, Belle the Cello ... aah, only six after all. I'm
playing down the Halt Bar this afternoon, I think. And at lunch we're
meeting a madman. This geezer's got his own indie label, Jeepster, and
he's coming from London to see us playing in a room! Ha ha. We're meet-
ing him at The Grosvenor Café to laugh at him. OK, I hope you get
this pronto. Love to the seagulls.
  Stuart

DECEMBER 16, 2003
Glasgow, Scotland

The Ever Arching Vacuum of the Night

She is the jewel
At the encrusted centre of this town
I spend my evening looking for her
My suitcase, just touched down in the hall

I look in the tiered park
While the city mooches into darkness
I leave mulled wine and the company of smoke and noise
To follow my preferred thread of conversation, with myself

I look in the bored park
Where the new moon lights me up like something
Odious, studious and vulnerable
Ready to be picked off.
The trees give way, the cowards

The city rolls over like the family dog
Happy to see me
It knows the game I am playing
It's too dumb
And fearful of me leaving
To warn me against folly

The girl is ambivalent
Unaware, lovely
She doesn't know of our collaboration
The city and I

She's falling in gladly with friends
Cushioned from my sad games
The scribbling in doorways
The New Years flitting by
The constant awareness of trees
The life of freestanding buildings
The midnight bird's bewildered song

The jewel remains a mystery to me
But knowing it exists is all I need
It takes me and it leads me on in love
And gets me out of tight spot after tight.
The ever arching vacuum of the night

Glasgow always works its tricks on me after I've been away. Even though I'm still sick from the tour, I'm getting enough of a buzz off the place not to want to run away just yet. But the town faces its biggest challenge — Christmas.

I always feel like such a loser at Christmas. I've said it before, but there's no avoiding the feeling, which I've had since I was

18 or so. If there's one thing this time of year does afford, though, it's the possibility of time with people, cosseted in the darkness, with the turn of the New Year and booze promoting philosophy and confessionals.

Years ago, Christmas always meant concentrating on music and writing while people downed their tools and rested. I did next to nothing for the rest of the year, so I liked the feeling I got from being personally busy. Now it's more difficult. Out of necessity I have the band to help me realise my ambitions, but maybe I should take a step aside and think about doing something else. The trouble is I can't leave music or the possibility of it for very long. It goads me. Every time I hear a *great* tune it's like a gauntlet being thrown down.

I heard the new Franz Ferdinand single on the radio today, and it's terrific. They blow their peers away! They've got words, action and groove in all the right places. They deserve to be bigger than The Strokes. I was half kidding when I said we'd be supporting them 'at a venue near you next year' at one of the gigs, but it might come true. If there's one guy it ought to happen to it's Alex, who has served the longest, hippest apprenticeship of love and the underground that I know of. That boy was running two clubs a week, four bands a night, for years in the early 1990s, besides playing in his own band.

Back then, when I was starting to play, I quickly got used to the muted response most aspiring songwriters garner from the promoters, pub owners, other bands and magazines. I played some of my first shows at The Kazoo Club and the 99p Club, both of which he ran. I couldn't believe he actually wanted me to play — it meant a great deal. He said, "Whenever you want a gig, just give me a call." So good luck to the Franz. It'll be great to tune into *Top of the Pops* to see a terrific band playing again. Plus they're from Glasgow. Send it on!

Glasgow, Scotland

Every year we have a Christmas dinner, and every year we invite Bel. Well, this year she is threatening to turn up, according to Katrina. I'm not too bothered about it, but it probably ruffles me a little more than the rest of the group, and I'm not usually like that.

Katrina asked if I was taking anyone to the dinner. She needed to know for numbers.

"Is Isobel coming?" I said.

"What's that got to do with it?"

"I'm just curious. I might have to get a partner."

"*What*? I don't understand."

"I just want ... Well, I'm just thinking I might need some sort of ..."

At this point I cast about for the word while signalling roughly with my hands what I'm getting at here.

"*Force-field*," said Allen, most helpfully. I pointed to him mutely, finger on my nose charades style, signalling the right answer. We both delighted for a second in this triumph of male empathy, rising to the top for once in a matter of delicacy.

Och, it's fine. I guess I'm used to our bunch being easygoing. Also, after she left the group it took me quite some time to get things out of my system. There was a delayed reaction. I must have been struggling when she was around, having to be someone I'm not, and when she went, *things* started spilling out — emotions and modes of behaviour. I was free, I could shout, jump, sing and play. And this period of adjustment always elicits change, so change I did, and perhaps I'm concerned I might have to squeeze back into another skin for the night. We'll see.

Right on cue they've started playing her LP in the café, and right away I recognise it, getting the thought I used to have a dozen times a day at one point: 'Why couldn't that be a Belle and Sebastian record? It's not a great leap of the imagination.'

I guess she had other reasons for wanting to go off on her own.

DECEMBER 22, 2003
Glasgow, Scotland

We had our Christmas party yesterday and it was absolutely fine. It was nice to see Bel — I'm glad she came. In retrospect it was quite a *big* thing for her to do. I mean, I didn't speak to her loads or anything, but she was pleased to be able to catch up with Bob, Beans, Stuart David and his wife Karn. It was a really full house. Nearly all the string players made it.

Every year members of the road crew wish you a happy Christmas and thank you and stuff, and I'm always bashful because of course we should be thanking them. In my mind's eye they are all cartoon superheroes and sometimes I wish we could be one big gang hanging out for ever.

DECEMBER 26, 2003
Glasgow, Scotland

How was your Christmas? Gruesome? Good. So was mine, until I watched *Lost in Translation*. I'll probably watch it again soon, for one reason and one reason only: the lips, the tits, the join-the-dots gaze. I know that looks like three, but it's really only one — Scarlett Johansson. There's not too much else happening in the film, is there?

Funny, I've had some similar experiences to the characters in the film. I know you're *meant* to feel that, but hey, we can testify, can't we Marisa? Now if I write a scene for a film where the girl busts her foot and the guy has to *carry* her around the city for three days on his back because she's alone in a foreign land and has no one else to help, they'll think it's ripping off *Lost In Translation*. The guy takes her to the hospital and she's scared of what they might do to her because she can't understand the lingo, and he has to give her shots because she's too scared to do that too. And it hurts. Sorry.

I sang a Sex Pistols song in a private karaoke joint when we were in Tokyo. Mine was *Pretty Vacant*, though. And the video that was playing along with the tune, showing the words, featured a young woman *knitting* on a park bench!

We had so much fun on that trip. We seemed to be in Tokyo for ever, in a fancy hotel. We were doing press but it felt like we were doing nothing. I loved it but I don't want to go back. I feel the way the girl in the film feels when she says: "Let's never come here again because it would never be so much fun."

I must admit that a lot of the good times involved drinking and socialising. I get bored these days about 1am. I would've missed the karaoke had I been sober. I'm looking at new options though.

I was so sick yesterday that I had to call Katrina.

"Can you get a taxi round? I need help wrapping presents."

So she wrapped, I did the tags, and we made it down to the family gathering without too much ado. I wasn't up to amusing the kids too much, so we came back later that day, blethering about friends, passions, secret notes, the turn of the year and domestic colour schemes. I said I would dance at her wedding in return for her getting me through the day. She said she would rather I sang. How can I refuse?

Glasgow, Scotland

So today, after acknowledging my lack of vices, I chose to indulge in my drug of choice: acupuncture. After all, I need to get my shit sorted if I'm going to be fit for our tour of Japan next month. In that sense I'm a pro at this job: total collapse on Christmas Day but back fighting and scheming two days later.

The acupuncturist today was the real deal—I truly *felt* it. I hope he knows what he's doing. He's the first Chinese guy I've ever visited for the needles, the others having been strictly indie. You know, loveable, friendly, empathetic. This fellow today didn't mess about. I felt like Eustace Scrubb getting his dragon skin ripped off him in *The Voyage of the Dawn Treader*. I think the word I'm looking for is 'purged'.

Sticking the needles in quickly, he had me looking like a magnetic desk-tidy within two and a half minutes. And he stuck them in deep. He *screwed* them in. Friggin' masonry nails. At least that's what they felt like (you can't see them going in because you're flat on your back). For his pièce de résistance he disappeared and came back with an electro pack which he proceeded to rig up between points along my arm. He sent a signal and my muscles started twitching away. I lay there for 25 minutes feeling like an airport runway with its landing lights flashing. I tried to think of lingerie and the secret song that was hidden in a box in my dream last night, but I couldn't get past the feeling that I was an airport runway at night.

When the plane finally landed, and he told me to turn on to my stomach, I was numb, aching in places. Then he screwed some needles into my back until it spasmed. I'll be back on Monday to do the same, just so I can get my voice back. It'll be worth it. It always is.

I feel like a stuck pig now. If you filled me with water you could suspend me over your roses and I'd give them a nice even sprinkle. I've got more holes than Blackburn, Lancashire. What's worse, someone in this place has got BO, and I'm wondering whether it's me. Perhaps the acupuncture has made me smell like a sailor's sock drawer.

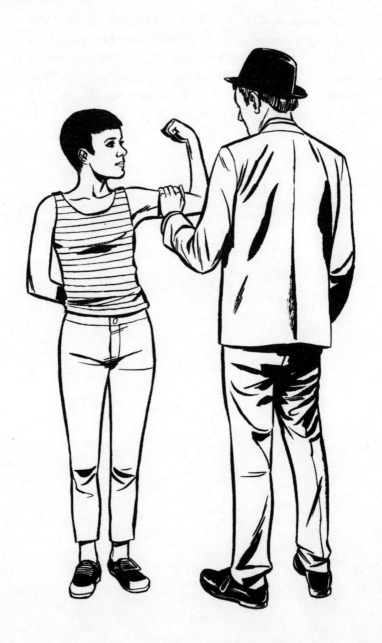

THE MINISTRY FOR
STRANGE AFFAIRS

Glasgow, Scotland

I was at the piano in my parents' house when I suddenly recalled an occasion when I was sitting there about 13 years ago. I was living there because I had been unwell for a couple of years. I'd mess about on the piano when I had enough energy to concentrate.

This one afternoon, shortly after lunch, I came in, sat on the stool and it suddenly occurred to me that there was life after death, that there was a place we would go, and God would be calling us, and in fact he was already calling me. For a second I saw that this life is like a holiday or an *assignment* to endure, enjoy, appreciate or denigrate; I knew I would be heading *back* to somewhere else when it was over.

I remember writing a short entry in my notebook about it. My outlook had changed at this point, and I felt myself slowly waking up after illness had shut me down. As a consequence, little revelations like this were coming to me fairly regularly, so it's easy to see why I simply noted it down and moved on. But, crucially, I never forgot it.

As I sat on the very same stool today I wondered why the idea of a place beyond this life came to me. It was an unbidden leg-up on the road to faith without which I doubt I would have remotely the inclination towards religion I do now.

When I was even younger, I had what felt like a recurring dream. I was at the bottom of our street on a sunny early evening in Clarkston, Glasgow, which means I must have been aged six or less. While I was playing I heard my mum's voice calling me in. (This was in the days when kids were safe playing outdoors and mothers were allowed to call the length of the street to inform their child that it was his or her bedtime.) When I heard her, everything else was still. Her voice calling my name was like a crack in the sky, a whisper in my ear, a voice inside my head. It echoed like a shout in a cave, and in the dream I would not have been surprised if the shout had the power to lift me by the collar and transport me home bodily.

The feeling I had on the piano stool was like this. Less vivid, but more profound and grown-up. It was as if the feeling in the dream was a rehearsal for a feeling years later. In essence that's what I'm getting at, that things on this earth might be a rehearsal for something to come later. Maybe not a *rehearsal*, actually — the performance has already begun. Let's call it an overture in which some of the themes are hinted at, the orchestra limbers up and the audience settles in.

JANUARY 8, 2004
Glasgow, Scotland

It has been a bit frantic in the office the last couple of days. Katrina kept shouting at me and telling me off, saying things like: "Well, you've had three weeks to think about it!" and then slamming the phone down. But I prepared myself to forgive her because she called last night to apologise. It's all because we had to change the front cover of the *I'm a Cuckoo* single, and nothing throws me more than that. Neil did warn me a few days before that I better have a plan B if we couldn't get permission, but I buried my head at the prospect. I'll explain.

When we shot the video for *Cuckoo* at the end of the year, I took the chance to take pictures for the cover on the set. It went smoothly and we had the sleeve done to my satisfaction within minutes of transferring the pictures on to the computer. It even became a fold-out digipak because I thought it would suit the colours more.

The front sleeve features Shantha, the waitress on the LP cover. She's wearing a gold suit with a quiff, pictured in profile in front of a picture of Phil Lynott from Thin Lizzy. I liked it. Unfortunately, over Christmas the Thin Lizzy people decided if we wanted to use the picture in the background it would cost us £5000.

So Neil wrote to Phil Lynott's mother. She was very nice, happy for us to use the picture, but it wasn't up to her, it was up to the lawyers. The upshot is we had to use a different picture. I mean, the photograph of Phil is just an old Decca record sleeve. It's not as if you can't go and look at the picture in a record shop.

JANUARY 11, 2004
Glasgow, Scotland

This is a sad day. Our minister John announced he was leaving back in November, and it came as a bit of a shock. Then Christmas was, well, Christmas as usual, and suddenly it is his last day today. I think sadness and emptiness will start to roll around the congregation in waves.

He's a great guy. He was my gaffer. He presided over the past 12 years of my life. He can't begin to understand what effect he has had over me, but it's only when something like this happens that you begin to understand it yourself.

At his final service he ran through some of the events of the past 15 years since he came to Hyndland, and it was emotional for everyone, especially as those years had been particularly tumultuous for John and his family. At one point during the sermon he asked us if anything he had done had upset us, or if he had somehow wronged us, and if so could we forgive him. Then he said that if we'd ever fallen out, or if we had ever done anything to upset him, he certainly forgave us now. It was so sad. It prompted my mind to jump back to a time around Christmas 1997.

The band were getting ready for three gigs in Manchester Town Hall. Our preparations were disorganised as we tried to get lots of new songs together for these concerts, which were fairly ambitious. Relations within the band were tense and I was a wreck. Back then, there was still a lot to be done around the church hall. My duties included keeping the place clean and tidy after various organisations had been in, and I was trying to balance that with planning shows and being away.

It wasn't working. I'd been letting the hall go a bit, but it wasn't until I got back exhausted from Manchester that I realised John had been in the hall and cleaned it up himself. I got it in the neck from the head of the board and I felt ashamed. Afterwards I was shy around John for months, though I wrote him a letter of apology. It didn't take long to parch things up, but that was what was running through my head during his sermon. I bet everyone in the congregation had their own feelings that were just as warm, sad and important to them as mine are to me.

It's not that they were sad times — far from it — but it's like the feeling you get at the end of a book you love. Maybe the characters are saying goodbye to each other, unsure of whether they're going to see each other again. They've shared a big adventure and have come to mean a lot to one another — that kind of thing.

The minister knows what he's doing. If it's time to go, it's time to go. Everything John's ever done has been all right by me, no question. Hand on your heart, how many people can you say that about with no debate and no second thoughts? Not many, I'll bet. Not even parents, because traditionally most people grow up questioning and protesting against much of what their mother and father say. That's just the way it goes. I wandered into John's church around 1992 of my own volition, and immediately knew I was in the right place. I never looked backwards.

He asked me today if I remembered the first time I came to Hyndland. "Yes, very well," I replied. It was at the tail end of the day, after a service and a big lunch in the hall afterwards. I remember so much about it all, and I love it. I could write a lot about all that stuff, and I imagine everyone who bade him good-bye today has their own volume tucked away inside them.

JANUARY 16, 2004
Glasgow, Scotland

It's quiet and beautiful and 1.40am. In little more than eight hours Sarah will come round to collect me and her cimbalom and we'll go to band practice. I just watched *Trust* again though I swore to myself I would never watch it again because I had seen it too many times. I dozed off at one point, but my subconscious woke me up for all the bits I had to see: the surreal beauty of the Long Island spring, car parks and dialogue as nourishing as oxygen. Hal Hartley writes like a dream.

My new piano is another happening thing. Playing it is like playing football on AstroTurf after gravel, the gravel being my dejected old honky-tonk thing in the next room. I am utterly happy in this flat now, just in time for them to build on top of me, which means I have to move. Dammit.

Now I'm halfway through my three score years and 10, I have the incessant thought to stop being mediocre, to at least try to do something worthwhile, pretty, artistic, ambitious, permanent. Time is running out.

Hartley, Altman, Woody Allen, Truffaut, Cassavetes, Mike Leigh — these men are kings. Leigh is the master. Beethoven and Bach stare down the years, crushing us with their genius and legacy, but these guys can stare back, knowing they've done their bit.

There's a new project starting to weave its way into my mind, and I'm quite happy to get on this particular train. It's going to occupy me for maybe a year and it's going to be tortuous in places, but there's nothing else to be done.

JANUARY 19, 2004
Glasgow, Scotland

I'm watching 10cc while typing this. *The Things We Do for Love* is a particularly great song of theirs. I had a good chat with Lol Creme in Los Angeles last summer after our show, where he was hanging out with Trevor. I think he was a *little* toasted, but I wish we could have the conversation again because I've been listening to quite a lot of 10cc since then. They wrote some terrific pop songs.

They're on a DVD Katrina gave me for Christmas. There's also *Up the Junction* by Squeeze, which they played at the

National Pop League club night a few months back. Initially I thought, 'I'll give it a go, but I don't know if I can dance to the whole song.' By the end of the song everybody was punching the air, shouting the words and pulling off some great moves. What a song, what a moment; perhaps the best dancing moment of last year. No, not the best. Stevie Wonder's *For Once in My Life* wins it for sheer consistency. We danced to that tune all last year, on the tour bus in particular.

Sarah by Thin Lizzy is on now but I've got to hide the video player, because the promo is a disaster. What were you thinking, Philip? The only good bit is when Scott Gorham comes in at the end of a long queue of girls and makes like he's trying to kiss you.

What else have I been listening to? I like the Dido single on the radio just now. The Phoenix tune in *Lost in Translation* is a great one. I've been listening to AC/DC too, and saw Lloyd Cole play an acoustic show tonight. I've also been listening to The Ladybug Transistor — that boy has a terrific voice. By your hip standards I've got terrible, inconsistent taste, right? I don't care.

Today I went to the caff with my accounts and stayed for so long that I kept feeling embarrassed about ordering more tea and juice. I keep terrible accounts. I don't keep any accounts, in fact. I think about them two days before the deadline. I don't keep any records — I just turn up at the accountant's office and throw myself on the mercy of the court.

It's worth it though. I know I miss out on money, but it's great not to think about it all year. Everyone tells you to keep receipts. I worked out a system whereby if I pay for *everything* with my bank card it'll show on my records at the end of the year. The trouble is I only remember the plan when it's time to do my accounts. I've been throwing cash around all year and every penny is accountable because I work all the time, but I've got no records. Just the ones the band make, and that's the important thing, right? Right on.

I ducked into town but the office was too busy, so I left them to it and went to get more acupuncture. I've perfected my technique. If you go really limp you barely feel the needles going in. The acupuncturist has started sticking them in the top of my head, which wiped me out, so I came home to watch 1970s pop videos before we went to see Lloyd Cole.

JANUARY 30, 2004
Heathrow Airport, London, England

After Japan, London is a drag. You quickly get used to the chipper nature of people over there, whereas everyone here seems sullen and dour. The fashion in Japan really appeals to me as well — I could spend all day feasting my eyes on the endless varieties of double-breasted jackets worn by the women and men. Their default city dress is so much more aligned to my aesthetic than here. And their taxis — shiny black and chrome, un-aerodynamic with the wing mirrors at the foot of the bonnet.

I didn't bargain for this four-hour stopover. The flight from Tokyo was good, flying directly over Siberia, taking a slice off the Arctic Circle, chasing the daylight. "I haven't been able to get the trivia machine to work," I said to Beans, an hour into the flight. "No, neither have I. We should just go round the plane asking everyone to ask us questions."

He looked out over the frozen tundra 37,000 feet below.

"Have you seen any wildlife yet?" he asked.

"Not yet."

"I saw a pack of wolves."

"You'll have to look harder if you're going to see the crafty arctic fox in his winter coat," I said.

"Ah, the reynard!"

I have a general feeling of slight dissatisfaction being back, though I can't put my finger on it. The concerts were terrific, the sound great. The acoustic was much more controlled than on the British tour, and, as I've said before, it makes *all* the difference. The acoustic is maybe my equivalent of the pitch in a cricket match, defining how the game pans out despite being of little interest to anyone but the performer. The pitch was playing real nice. I settled back to thrash a few fours around the ground.

I'm anxious to get on though. I'm in an ambitious mood. No disrespect to you, who may have been listening to us for a long time, but I want the band to start playing to a bigger audience. A new audience. I want us to delight and surprise you with every record we release, but at the same time I want us to break out. I may live to regret it, but you have to try it.

Let me illustrate my point. We were on our way back from playing a radio session in Tokyo and I was staring out the window of the van. I whined, rather randomly, to Bob and Stevie:

"When are we going to get a string of number ones, like Abba?"

"When you grow a pair of tits," said Bob.

FEBRUARY 1, 2004
Glasgow, Scotland

Being back home has left me feeling dreamy for Tokyo. My favourite moment was when we had just arrived, me and Stevie chatting excitedly on the way in about the general scene. I was

135

scheduled to do a couple of interviews that evening, but I was determined to taste a bit of the atmosphere before I went to the record company's office.

In the hotel I threw my case down and dug out my running gear. I headed out in the general direction of the park. There are so few parks in Japanese cities that I was desperate to get there, like a thirsty man looking for a well. I took my bearings from the Cerulean Tower in Shibuya, so I would know how to navigate back to the hotel.

I headed for the small streets to get away from the traffic. Soon I was padding past the public TV studios and into the park at the perfect time of the evening.

It was lighter than in Scotland at this time of year, Japan being much closer to the equator. So I was getting off on that, feeling a nascent spring vibe. I don't mind the oncoming dusk as long as I get out when there is still some light left. In fact, with the peaceful and at times beautiful people of Tokyo padding round the park with me, I felt at home, comforted by the strangeness, intoxicated by the smell of the trees, glad to be moving around freely.

I passed an elegant European on the path, and we shared a conspiratorial smile, grateful to be experiencing that particular time and place.

FEBRUARY 3, 2004
Glasgow, Scotland

BBC Radio 1 won't play our single. We're too old, too mainstream or something, though they'll play The Avalanches' remix because they are perceived as being cutting edge or something. They're the same age as me, I think.

I've been freaking out a little since I got back. In a good way.

In Japan I think I suffered 'green' withdrawal symptoms, so I've been wandering across Glasgow, breathing in the damp air, getting the town back in my veins and hanging out in the park at midnight.

Cops followed me last night, actually. In my head I ran through what I was going to tell them if they stopped me to ask where I was heading.

They've stopped me before. This time, I was miles from my house, so I couldn't say I was going home. But I was in a good mood from thinking about art and possibilities, as usual. I felt like Paul Simon. Got my poetry to protect me.

So I was going to tell them I was working on a book or something, and that I was working out the idea in my head. I was going to tell them I was working on a screenplay, quickly devising the plot and characters so I would have something to back up my claims with.

The story was about a guy who plays the clarinet. His girl finishes with him, so he vows he's finished with girls for a while, instead devoting himself fully to his instrument. He's going to give himself the summer to write a concerto for the clarinet, but to achieve this he'll have to quit his job as a swimming pool attendant. He likes it because it gives him plenty of time to think. He used to spend all day thinking about his girlfriend and pondering the various contours of the collected bathers. But there was no way he could get his reed out and start blowing it in the pool, so the job had to go.

Another hassle was that he needed a job where there was a lot of moisture in the air. The reason his girlfriend had helped him get the job in the pool was that he was badly asthmatic, and the warmth and moisture in the pool kept his tubes lubricated.

It was a simple task of finding a job that provided that kind of warmth and moisture, a Proustian silence so he could compose

137

and colleagues who didn't mind the odd caress of a clarinet outburst. The boy found a quiet spot and started making a list.

He quickly realised his ideal job environment was remarkably womb-like. He wondered what his ex-girlfriend might have to say about this, since she was always quick to use her fledgling psychology training on him, but he was alone now and had to work it out for himself.

So basically the film was a man's search for the perfect working environment. Would he find it? Would he write his concerto? Would he have to crawl back to his ex to borrow enough cash to get him through this experimental period? Would she have any pity?

"What sort of baloney is that?" the grey-haired sergeant said as he got out of the car and leaned on the top of the door. His sidekick got out of the driver's side.

"There's no real narrative drive there, not unless you count the stuff about him looking for his job. Not exactly scintillating stuff, is it, son?"

"Maybe it's a musical he's writing, sarge," said the constable, laughing.

"A musical? That would be a bit of all right. I like a musical. But it's got to be a proper musical with a chorus, pretty girls, plenty of songs and a good yarn. I'm not going to pay to see a musical about a guy playing the clarinet! He's like one of those buskers on the Tube. The guy sounds like a deadbeat!"

As I was racing round Park Circus with these ideas going through my mind I realised the cops had circled the circus, passed me and disappeared. I was a bit disappointed—I wanted to talk to them about my screenplay!

Glasgow, Scotland

As I got back to the church hall today I was drawn by its warmth and tranquility, so I went inside instead of going upstairs to my flat. I'm here fairly infrequently now I'm no longer the caretaker. Quiet moments like this are rarer still because the hall is well used these days, but it's striking how delicious and peaceful the place is. Just the central heating and a clock ticking. If you listen carefully to some of our records you'll hear the central heating in the background, though maybe not the clock. I think we remembered to take the battery out while we recorded. *You Made Me Forget My Dreams* is probably the best example of being able to *hear* the hall, or the little extra track at the end of one of the EPs, I can't remember which one. The tune that goes on rather awkwardly about 'songs for children'.

A place like this makes songs grow. It's a greenhouse for them. When you enter, your small voice becomes mighty and the chime of an out-of-tune piano sounds like an ensemble. I could write a song right now. I can feel it brewing. In fact there are quite a few I've written in here that I've overlooked for some reason and not bothered recording. One's called *Passion Play,* which begins, rather prosaically: "There's an echo in the hall around me."

Slow Graffiti started that way, me wandering in from a sun-drenched lane in the west-end spring. The title refers to a verse, which doesn't appear in the final recording, about the lazy, poetic graffiti some charmer had etched and I had spotted while out walking. It's my favourite source of the poetic moment, graffiti. To all those who partake in the sensitive defacement of mortar or bark, I salute you and love you.

Sometimes I would slip into the church hall to pray after coming home. I used to pray a lot more a few years ago, probably because I was more troubled and it was the way to peace.

I'm thinking about a friend whose mum's not well: how sad and harangued he must feel. Me and another friend talk about it in concerned but casual conversation, but it's him and his mum who are going through it. I pray you're on their case, Lord. Please be with them both.

The Ministry for Strange Affairs

It's later, and I'm sitting at the piano with a cup of tea in my hand. I'm thinking about someone I met last night. Impossibly cute, French-Moroccan, en vacances. I asked her what her job was.

"I am a professeur," she said.

"You are young to be a professeur."

"I'm not so young. I worked hard."

"Where do you work?"

"I work at the Ministry for Strange Affairs!"

"Ah."

"Feel my muscles," she said.

I felt her muscles.

"Very impressive!" I said.

She then proceeded to smoke everyone's cigarettes down to the last drop of loose tobacco.

I may as well try to write the song about her.

The Neutral Person

From time to time I go to the Glasgow Buddhist Centre to practise a bit of meditation. I'm poor at it — I always start where I left off, in the introductory class.

There are two types of meditation practice they take you

through, and it's down to chance which one you get. One, *The Mindfulness of Breathing*, is an exercise in focusing the mind by concentrating on breathing.

The other is called *Meta Bavna*. This is meant to encourage your experience of *meta*, which translates roughly as loving kindness. For part of the exercise you think of a friend, then a neutral person, then a person you find difficult to deal with. In turn, you spend some time thinking about them and wishing them health and happiness, hoping they will experience *meta*.

I've been thinking of one instance when I did the practice. For a neutral person I picked one of the staff at the sports centre where I play football. I've been going there for years. The fact I'm always in a rush and that the place is so busy means you never stop to chat with any of the staff.

The funny thing is, when I went to football that night, the guy happened to be around the entrance, cleaning up. For the first time, he nodded to me in recognition and asked me how I was! I didn't do or say anything different. But something *was* different. It's a small thing, but not the kind of thing you forget!

MARCH 4, 2004
Glasgow, Scotland

When I got into the café this morning one of the staff asked me to write a message to his girlfriend on a mix tape. I started thinking of inappropriate things I could write were I not an elder statesman of indie (that's why he asked me, right?), such as "I hope you have great sex on your birthday" (I think it was her birthday) or "This tape is terrible, you should date someone with better taste". But hey, I know the indie ethic — I wrote the friggin' book. Besides, the guy's cooler than me.

It's later now, and I've moved to the back clinic. I need to get my back snapped another time before our European tour next month. It went last Monday. I was reaching up for some vitamins at the time, which is fairly ironic. I couldn't tie my shoelaces or turn round from the waist up for a couple of days, so I thought I better get it seen to. It's funny, I had to craftily enlist a squad of people to rub balm into my back three times a day. Ostensibly they were invited round to drink tea, play Scrabble or watch a film, but then I got the oil out. You should try it some time — it's the slightly sleazier equivalent of walking a cute dog down the nearest hip street.

I once posted a list of my top 50 films but there were some movies floating about my head that I wanted to update it with. Suddenly the 50 became almost 100, so I just went with it. It starts with my favourite.

Annie Hall
À Bout de Souffle
Trust
Buffalo 66
Les Quatre Cents Coups
Pulp Fiction
Withnail & I
The Graduate
Mean Streets
Manhattan
Chung King Express
Kes
Performance
A Hard Day's Night
The Warriors
Life of Brian

A Taste of Honey
Shadows
Two Way Stretch
Kind Hearts and Coronets
She's Gotta Have It
Gosford Park
A Man Escaped
The Servant
Jackie Brown
Stolen Kisses
The Unbelievable Truth
Gregory's Girl
Dazed and Confused
Get Carter
All The President's Men
Amélie
The Killing of a Chinese Bookie
Star Wars
My Dinner with André
Lost in Translation
American Graffiti
The Apartment
Clerks
The Big Lebowski
Career Girls
In the Mood for Love
Slacker
Billy Liar
2001: A Space Odyssey
The Big Sleep
Easy Rider
I'm All Right Jack

The Odd Couple
Alfie
Stranger Than Paradise
Jesus Christ Superstar
Talk to Her
High Hopes
Jaws
It's a Wonderful Life
Five Easy Pieces
Paris, Texas
The Godfather
Crimes and Misdemeanors
Saturday Night, Sunday Morning
Chinatown
Goodfellas
The Loneliness of the Long Distance Runner
Pierrot le Fou
The Last Detail
Whisky Galore!
Life Is Sweet
Rushmore
Harold and Maude
Day for Night
O Brother, Where Art Thou?
Poor Cow
Taxi Driver
The L-Shaped Room
Au Revoir les Enfants
Shampoo
The Great Escape
Une Femme est Une Femme
The Breakfast Club

Les Cousins
La Dolce Vita
The Railway Children
Some Like It Hot
Trainspotting
Casablanca
The 39 Steps
Betty Blue
Saturday Night Fever
The Lord of the Rings: the Fellowship of the Ring
Broadway Danny Rose
The Sound of Music
The Italian Job
Dear Diary
Les Valseuses
The Double Life of Veronique
Fantasia
The Ladykillers
Surviving Desire
That Sinking Feeling

MARCH 6, 2004
Glasgow, Scotland

I'm in a spring-like mood today, and we're off to Paris tomorrow. Paris in the spring and all that.

It put me in mind of last spring when I met Marisa in Florida for a few days. She was down from Boston. I got in late at night, we hired a car and drove south, right down the coast, on a mission to take a few snaps, look around and catch up with the New York Mets at spring training.

The plan was to manoeuvre Mike Piazza into a picture, but

we couldn't get near the big man, such is his popularity with kids and housewives alike, so Marisa ended up buying a kids' Mets kit and she dressed up, hence the picture.

I wished I could speak French. The only phrase I can remember is one my friend Isabelle taught me, which roughly translates as 'what's new, pussycat?'. So look out for that.

It's funny, I got hassled by a bunch of wee neds today, so to avoid grief I replied to their brainless enquiry in French. The trouble is they wouldn't let it go.

"Whit are ye? Welsh or something? You must huv a pound. Give us a pound, big man, for the bus."

I kept it going for a bit but I used up all my French, and I think I ended up telling the kid I loved him. I had to lean on Gainsbourg, you see. I won't be sad to get out of Glasgow for a bit. Things are heating up for hipsters ...

MARCH 15, 2004
Bilbao, Spain

We've got a day off after a long string of shows. It's been a curious five or six days. Our first tour of Spain has been overshadowed by the bombings in Madrid, but I feel like I've been in a bubble, hearing most of the news from my parents or friends back home.

The bombings were on my mind during last night's show in Bilbao. The hall was beautiful and the audience had settled in. There was a rarefied, gentle atmosphere, as there was in the town when we went strolling in the early evening. You could almost feel people pausing with relief at the end of such a trying week. It was also election day, which added to the air of reflection.

I was tempted to say something during the concert, but I left

146

it and got on with the songs. What could you say? Since Thursday everyone has carried out their work with such grace — the people working with us, the promoters, press agents, journalists and local crews. The fact we were treated so well while it was all happening makes me feel a bit humble and useless. Never on a tour have the promoters been such fun to be around. It probably helped that there was a team of about six, including the press girl and translator. They always seemed to be looking after us, being unspeakably cool and cheery, each having a specialism besides being chummy and hard-working.

They're collectively known as the Sinnamon girls, Sinnamon being the name of their company. I can't believe we missed the chance to sing *Cinnamon Girl* by Neil Young or, even better, *Sally Cinnamon* by the Stone Roses as a loving tribute. Next time!

I so wish some of them were around this morning. I'm much more a morning person than an after-show person. There must have been about 40 people crammed into Richard's room last night. I get a little shy, not to mention worn out by the smoke, at that time. Mornings are good for getting to know someone, for chatting and being able to hear them without the accompaniment of loud music. There's usually coffee involved, and a background hubbub of sunlight and café noise; workers working, allowing us shirkers to keep on shirking.

Adam Green, our support act, was on good form last night though. I enjoy talking to him. He's so young! Twenty-two, and doing a similar thing to what I'm doing. I'll not tell you what I was doing when I was 22. It would depress you.

Whoa, there's some glamorous dame across the plaza checking me out. Castigate me if you will, but she has the air of a classy call girl, with lots of make-up and big hair. Maybe I'm way off; it would be funny if I got caught up in a *Belle de Jour* scenario, for you at least, because you'd get to read 'dot dot dot' and go on to fill in the comedy blanks for yourself! So if this paragraph goes dot dot dot at the end, you'll know what to think ...

MARCH 17, 2004
Milan, Italy

Milano 6pm

What people do at six pm
Is that they look for their loved ones
And their loved ones look for them

What people do at six pm
Is that they look for affirmation
From lovers and from brothers and from girls from tele-sales

I'm an eavesdropper
A tourist between seasons
I'm ignored, put up with.
The citizens are enjoying their own town in its prime
And without a foreign body to draw attention to
Its architectural clichés
They're taking joy in stone and glass
In the cut of slack and blouse
In the pealing of a ring tone
In the fashion of the season
And in the rituals of Lent

I know this town
The runner sees everything
It is his privilege to stagger

148

Through the six o'clock stroll
Picking up a scent from families
Leaning on the warmth of lovers
Stealing day-end joy from workers

I think I know this town
The runner sees everything
Thinks geography is power

I pretend to look at maps
But I really look in cafés
Like ships within a bottle
With transparent displays
Of coloured tile and vinyl.
The spectacularly modelled
Girl receptionists of Milan
Spill the gossip of the day

MARCH 21, 2004

Cologne, Germany

Sarah and I have decided to spend a night in a hotel to break up the trip a little, though I'm getting into life on the bus like never before thanks to little things, like the air con on the bus isn't insanely cold and there's an upstairs so you can creep into your bunk and be away from the action if you want.

Of course, the action is the football game on the PlayStation. I'm a late starter, but since I started playing as Italy I have felt national pride swelling, and have risen to every challenge Murray's Czech Republic or Beans' Ireland can throw at me.

I used in-ear monitoring for the first time in Cologne tonight, and everything sounded good. The downside is it's a bit like playing behind a glass screen; there's a degree of separation from the audience. Personally, I was happy I didn't have to screech and everything sounded musical and controlled. I enjoyed the gig vastly, which is a relief after the Munich and Hamburg gigs, where I didn't think we were firing on all cylinders.

Maybe because we've never toured Germany, it feels like the audiences have been nervous, even a little tentative, but the crowd in Cologne was really warm, and if they heard what I heard I'll be pleased.

This is such a nice tour, you really appreciate the way it sweeps through the countries on the itinerary when you've been on it for a few weeks. Bilbao seems a long time ago, as does Madrid. And as for Glasgow...

MARCH 24, 2004
Berlin, Germany

> *'Prawn population decimated by singer'*
> *'Man in Denmark devours whole village!'*

Those were the headlines in the Danish Prawn News I picked up yesterday after we visited a Mexican restaurant in Copenhagen.

I was so hungry yesterday. I always feel like that on days off. I have neither the time nor the inclination to eat properly on show days except for breakfast. Lunch is always a bowl of soup before soundcheck, and dinner is a case of trying to force something down after soundcheck while you're trying to write the set list, fending off questions and considering all sorts of issues verging on the technical, political and personal.

It's all good though. I may not have a strong appetite at the time, but one of my favourite things about touring is our conjugal meals. When the catering is good, as it was in Germany for instance, the kitchen becomes a bit of a hub, especially at dinner time. There's almost 30 of us once you count the band, crew, session musicians and drivers. Dinner time is when it feels most like a big family, a huge travelling circus. It's unrivalled.

I wish I could give you an example of the daftness and absurdity of some of the conversations, but I can't remember any. There are plenty of deft touches of comic timing, mostly from the crew and Stevie Dreads, and comings and goings that make us look more like The Muppets than The Muppets.

Take the other night in Berlin. We had soundchecked but kept going because we were trying a new number. I was a bit put out when we finished because we couldn't get the song right and therefore couldn't put it in the set. I forgot Dreads had said there was a woman coming from a German radio station to talk to me.

"Can't we do it after the show?" I said.

I was being a bit rude. She was already there, but it was the last thing on my mind. I had a sore throat.

"No, it's impossible," she said. "It will only take five minutes."

It turned out the reason Dreads had let her through was that he thought she was great looking and assumed I would see the bright side. She was pretty good looking, but more Dreads' type, I imagine. But then anyone is Dreads' type!

So we ended up in the production office where the woman said she was excited, *nervous* in fact, about meeting me. I *never* believe people when they say that. I bet I was more nervous than her!

On the way to the office along the corridor, even Mr Waddle, the stoical, work-wearied head of production, was seen to cast a couple of sneaky sidelong glances at the Germanic beauty leading me. "A great big barrel of sex!" as Dreads was later to proclaim.

I can't recall much of the conversation, but she did lean rather heavily on the question of *Dear Catastrophe Waitress*. This had been a matter between me and the Germans which had originated in October. The girl from Rough Trade Germany had the crackpot idea of running a competition to find the most catastrophic waitress in the country. As I say, a crackpot idea, but I like crackpots and the girl from the label had a lot of energy. So I gave her the thumbs-up and said I was into it.

Come March, the country had been scoured, nominations written and read, and waitresses spied upon by an expert team of café spies. I was a bit out of the loop but bluffing well during the radio interview and catching up with the girl's line of questioning. Once I was out of the interview hot seat, Dennis from the record company took me to where they had stashed the waitress! And there she was, Germany's most catastrophic waitress.

I had imagined her to be of the clumsy milkmaid variety, chucking knives about and gnashing her teeth. I was ready to take cover. But I was introduced to a petite and very pretty girl who looked like she couldn't smash an egg cup. I was relieved, because time was tight and my pre-gig routine in tatters. And to have to chaperone a real menace of the service industry would have been *too* much.

So we got chatting. Alex was her name, and we worked on a little sketch that involved me singing the song while she waited on me at a table on the stage, getting everything predictably in a mess. For a few minutes we allowed ourselves the conceit of imagining we attended some sort of school for half-assed drama. Allen helped out of course. Never try anything non-musical on stage without running it past the drum tech!

Once the sketch was written I bolted some food and escaped to the bus for a bit. When I returned, the group were jamming

Sound and Vision by David Bowie in the dressing room. I was given a couple of lines to sing, both of which I messed up when we performed it later in the evening. At least the waitress sketch came off …

MARCH 30, 2004
Brussels, Belgium

We've just done nine shows in 10 days, and I can't remember the last time I had this kind of breather. Maybe Bilbao, or Copenhagen, but it pissed down there. Besides, I had to do a TV interview on my morning off.

Don't get me wrong — the Danish capital is a hip place, I loved the venue we were playing and the concert was great — but when I turned up for the interview it was to take place in a café-bar that had been closed for us. A lighting rig was positioned next to a big window looking on to the street so that it would seem as though the interview was happening practically on the pavement. Every dozy citizen who walked, drove, cycled or rode on horseback past the café turned to see what was going on, and all of them were disappointed by the meekness and anonymity of the subject of the interview!

I'd assumed it was for student TV or something because their camera wasn't very big and the lone cameraman ate a full meal while filming. (He did it very slowly and very quietly, like a koala bear eating eucalyptus leaves.)

I talked candidly for about an hour and a half, telling the guy everything he wanted to know, even agreeing with some of his way-off assertions just to keep the interview ticking along. At one point I sketched a comical picture of the evolution of the Glasgow scene, simply because it seemed like the sort of thing he might be into. I mean, what do I know about the Glasgow scene? Nothing. We spent our formative years specifically trying to avoid it.

When we finished I asked the journalist who the interview was for.

"It's for DR1, the equivalent of BBC1 in Britain."

Shit. The Danish BBC1. Why didn't someone tell me? I hadn't even shaved, and still had my pyjamas on for God's sake (underneath my trousers, but pyjamas are pyjamas, and the nation would know!). What the hell did the Danish BBC1 want with me? And what would they want with extended musings about Orange Juice, how to cut your hair with a pudding bowl and how to cook leeks properly to impress a girl?

APRIL 1, 2004

Utrecht, Netherlands

That's the tour over, and I should say it was favourite so far. I heard everything clearly thanks to the in-ear monitors — it felt like cheating but, hey, if it means you're going to enjoy the game, cheat a little — I could control my singing much more and the band sounded terrific. If the music is good, little else matters.

The songs from *Dear Catastrophe Waitress* are sounding solid, but it's some of the songs around the *Fold Your Hands* period I was really getting off on. The arrangements were sound, and if the album lacked zing, we're getting it right now. *Jonathan David* has been an absolute pleasure too.

I also managed to stay healthy for the tour, which means a lot to me. I can't believe I've come back punching like a bantamweight with lungs like Shirley Bassey's. As usual we were well looked after by Dreads and the crew, and our Continental compadres. Thank you, brothers and sisters.

After last night's show we gathered round the Steinway grand in the dressing room (it's rare to see a piano backstage but the Vredenburg is mostly a classical venue), and Murray, one of our violinists, got behind the keys and played every old TV and film theme we could throw at him. It was staggering. *Grandstand*, *The Horse of the Year Show*, *Bergerac*, *Grange Hill*, *Star Wars* (three different themes), *Indiana Jones*, *Knight Rider*, *The A-Team*, *Last Of The Summer Wine* (which Brian claimed brought a tear to his eye), *Black Beauty*, *Parkinson*, *Cagney and Lacey*, *Dallas*, *Blue Peter*, *Amélie*, *Sportscene*, *Coronation Street*, *The South Bank Show* ... I could go on. Every time the momentum flagged he would strike up the theme from *Dad's Army* and the chorus would rowdily rise up and sing 'Who do you think you are kidding, Mr Hitler?' as if we were the most patriotic Brits in the world, and old enough to remember the Second World War.

APRIL 3, 2004
Glasgow, Scotland

I'm testing out a new café tonight, having spent most of the day in a daze. I think I was trying to commiserate with myself for being back in Glasgow, because I promised myself last night that I'd get up and make a couple of T-shirts today. I did it, but it seems the experience had a dreamlike quality to it on account of me being tired.

Making a shirt has so many 1980s resonances that I'm faintly embarrassed to still be at it: the visit to the photocopying shop; taking your own scissors; the anticipated impatience of the guy working the machine, revealing the lameness of your idea to an unsympathetic world of Saturday shoppers.

That's part one. Then you've got to go to the T-shirt shop. You place yourself at the mercy of the T-shirt man! He's pretty unreliable. You have to shepherd him through the whole experience. You have to bring your own shirt or you'll end up with a scabby Fruit of the Loom job that's 56 sizes too big. If you want the T-shirt printed that's what you *have* to do. He's got the only machine in town, and he knows it.

I met Carey from Camera Obscura in the shop. I felt sheepish, like I was in the queue for free lollipops or something. I mean, I'm old enough to know better. I didn't even have the excuse of making the shirts for someone else like she did. I was making them for me.

I met Jason in the photocopying shop, then I met Patrick and Carey again in the café 10 minutes later. It's good to know nothing much changes — the Saturday hipsters aspire to greatness in their quiet ways, posting out their music, knitting in public, showing off their girly neck hair to the jealous middling class.

I just left my friend Vrnda's house round the corner. Before going on tour I'd agreed to play a small part in a film she's making, but it turned out one of the actors dropped out, so she called me yesterday to see if I would play a bigger part.

"Um, it's a bit of a *romantic* scene, but the girl's *really* beautiful," she told me.

"Vrnda, you sound like a horse breeder, trying to pair us off."

"I suppose so!"

I told Ciara what was happening.

"Just think of you snogging some girl."

"Snog? If it's anything to do with Vrnda it will be *positions*, and my arse going up and down in the moonlight."

So I told Vrnda I'd let her know tomorrow.

Hey, did I tell you I got a message from the Catastrophe Waitress in Germany? You know, the girl who won the competition. I got an email from her via the German label, and it sounded urgent.

"Get in touch — I need to tell you what happened after the show in Berlin."

So I gave her a buzz. I knew they were going to take her picture for the paper, so I thought maybe she'd landed a modelling job or had been proposed to by a German coffee baron or something.

"I got fired!"

"What do you mean you got fired? Why would you get fired?"

"My boss said he had to fire me because of the publicity. They said they couldn't be seen to employ Germany's worst waitress."

God, I didn't expect that. Suddenly it's like an episode from a Bertie Wooster story. We tried to fix it for young Alex, but it turned sour. Where's Jeeves when you need him? Her boss must have one of the worst senses of humour known to man. I mean, come on! Isn't any publicity usually good, in the long run at least? I'll have to think of a way to make it up to her.

APRIL 23, 2004

Glasgow, Scotland

It's Friday night and weird things are happening in my house. At 10.30pm I was trying to get the computer to connect to the internet. For some reason it kept telling me it couldn't detect a dialling tone but when I tried the phone it was fine. After checking the cables I tried for the sixth and last time only to find it still couldn't detect a dialling tone, so I closed the computer, at which point the stereo came on all by itself! The power was on but I hadn't gone anywhere near it, and there's no remote control I could have accidentally touched.

There's a strange atmosphere in the house. When the song

157

started to play, immediately the hairs on my neck started to bristle. It was a song called *Turn to Me*, sung by Monica Queen accompanied by me and her boyfriend Johnny, recorded in their flat six months ago. It's a pretty song and it was nice to hear the sound of their living room in the simple recording. We were practising before singing it in church the following Sunday.

Her voice is commanding in a country sort of way, and the words are clear:

> Turn to me, oh man, and be saved
> Says the Lord, for I am God
> There is no other, none beside me
> I call your name

By the start of the final verse I was almost crying, though I don't know why. I was thinking about how I've just heard about the final plans for the church hall, and how today I found out I've got to move out before June. Right when the song finished, I felt the house was saying goodbye to me.

After a few minutes I tried to connect to the internet and it worked, no problem.

HEAVY BALLERINAS

San Francisco – Palm Springs, California, US

The morning starts with a stumble into the roadside Iron Skillet for French toast. It's baking hot outside, but I'm still flying the black polo neck and dressy shoes. In southern California when it's hot I like to put on the air of someone who got lost on the way back from his brother's funeral. It's a little affectation I have.

Inside the breakfast place I'm worried the tour bus might leave without me. It's a pity I have to rush, because I'd like to enjoy the music they're playing. They seem to be concentrating on Glasgow bands circa 1984–85, playing *The Honeythief* by Hipsway, a group I had a soft spot for at the time, then *In a Big Country*. I almost thought of getting up and announcing to the sleepy cowboys: "These guys are from Scotland! I'm from Scotland!", hopefully inspiring a few empathetic hollers. "Yeah? Shoot, well so am I!"

Now we're heading to the Coachella Festival in Palm Springs. The gig in San Francisco last night pulled me out of the dreamy state of mind I'd been cultivating for a few days. I've been so busy back in Glasgow. Only when I got off the plane did I start to wind down. I showed some bravado and went for a run, but there was nothing in the fuel tank. I had to get the trolley back to the hotel.

MAY 3, 2004
Palm Springs, California, US

I've just got back to the hotel after playing Coachella, which was even more beautiful than last time. So pretty, so hot — I like that. I still feel like we're usurpers, or charlatans, as if we shouldn't be there, but I feel very comfortable. It's a curious job. I can't believe we have chances like this, but I want to do it. Sometimes I might appear blasé about the whole thing, but I feel completely at home in front of that many people on a sunny day.

I'll tell you a funny thing. I was watching The Flaming Lips afterwards, pondering their stage craft. I was sitting to the side of the stage with the rest of the suckers behind a barrier, thinking if I could get through I could have a seat and see the whole show. I could also see Christina Ricci on the privileged side of the fence, and I was anxious to have words with her. At least I was anxious to sit close to her for a while so I could kid on I belonged there for a minute or two.

The problem was the security guy wouldn't let me through. I wandered round the back of the stage for a while, thinking I might sneak out into the audience so I could at least see the whole show, but then I spotted a hole in the security set-up. If I could wait for this one guy to be distracted I could stride across the backstage area and join Ricci and chums.

So when the guy started chatting to a member of the stage crew I hopped up on to the stage and past him, joining Ricci and pals and feeling much better about the world. I also started to really get into The Flaming Lips' set. I hadn't seen them for a long time and could see what they were striving for. They had lots of people dressed up in animal costumes on stage, moving to the songs, swinging lights around and generally looking surreal. I wanted to join in, so I waved to their manager, Scott, and asked him if they had any more costumes. He was very cool, taking me to their backstage grotto and telling me to help myself. I chose a tiger costume. I couldn't find the head, but that was OK. I changed into the costume and padded back to the stage, where I joined the rest of the animals up the front.

I had been up there performing an hour or so earlier, but I was just as thrilled to be up there in my tiger costume with the Lips with Ricci sitting just behind me. I felt like the kid in the school play who feels good because he looks good in his costume and there's a cute girl looking.

When the show was cut short and everyone cleared the stage I followed the herd back to the grotto to change back into our civvies, but before taking off my costume I spotted Ricci and her friend standing outside the tent, so I said hello. (She called my house once to ask if she could use *Stars of Track and Field* in a movie she was making.)

"Hi, I thought I'd take this chance to introduce myself," I said.

I should have introduced myself as Tommy the Tiger. After all, I was standing in front of Christina Ricci and her friend — the kid who gets beaten up in *Dazed and Confused* — in my tiger suit. She was very sweet though, demure even. We had a nice little chat, then she hopped inside my suit and we went around the site on all fours, causing havoc and cuddling people to death.

Actually, I made that last bit up, but that was the way the evening seemed to be going.

Seattle Airport, Washington, US

"You're multi-tasking. I know it, I heard a ruckus."

"We made, like, strawberry margaritas. I think mine had more alcohol. I couldn't sleep, I was, like, wired."

I can't take much more of these mobile phone conversations taking place around me. Another couple just sat down and the first thing they did was reach for their mobile phones. That makes four separate conversations within touching distance.

"I just bought you a T-shirt at the airport."

Just give them the shirt when you go home! You don't need to phone them.

I think about looking for the chapel area so I can get a restful 10 minutes alone with my soul and its carry-on bag-load of mid-week sin. John Irving saved me yesterday. I started getting into *A Prayer for Owen Meany*. Marisa gave me the book a year ago but I lost it. I bought another copy and left it on the plane the day before yesterday. So, yesterday I went for a wander after playing a radio session. I thought I'd get a second-hand copy this time, figuring if the book had been read before it was more likely to be read again.

I went via beautiful pristine mountaintop routes to Broadway, Seattle. I came to the bookshop, the name of which I forget. There was a notice on the door saying: "Hippies, use the other door," and a notice beside it saying: "This is a joke. Please do not call us about this." I thought, why bother? Just take it down.

The customer-baiting scheme continued on the inside with a list printed behind the till entitled: "Mildly amusing things customers have said to us before we killed them." It contained things along the lines of: "Do you know who wrote *Dante's Inferno*?"

I was preparing to be offensive to the staff before they abused me or said anything smartass. Luckily, little happened, and I got my book. Later, after reading it in the bath, it took me from a state of tension, fatigue, unconnectedness and mild depression to … Let's just say I felt much better. My gig was saved.

After the show last night at the Paramount in Seattle, we were taking the lift up to the dressing room with the jovial backstage assistant. He was a mite too jovial for us after we'd given our all for two hours.

"You should practise running up and down the stairs and singing at the same time — that would improve your breathing!"

Mick, who isn't known for his comebacks, remarked:

"I'll not do that with my trumpet, then. I'd break my fucking teeth."

MAY 7, 2004
Denver, Colorado, US

Fifteen floors up at the rooftop pool, 80°F air enshrouding our bodies, we gaze at downtown Denver. The skyscrapers seem empty and useless. The strangeness of an average American downtown in the evening might not seem the most spectacular quality to mention, but I always find myself, having been spewed out by the airport minibus, wandering the streets in search of life and trying to work out what the deal is. Why do they build these edifices in the desert when there are endless acres upon which to build?

A mile high, in our elevated state, we play a game of blaming the altitude for every glitch of mood swing and performance.

"I dreamed about tigers fighting lions."

"I dreamed I was in Cheap Trick."

"I dreamed I got off with my sister."

"I'm going to lie down; try to cultivate some more haemo-globin."

"I think you had better."

On Sunday I'll be back in Byres Road. This schedule is giving me too much time to think. What are we doing in a swanky hotel on a school night? Swimming our lengths, improving our crawl, dreaming of faraway friends and the progress of deciduous trees.

MAY 15, 2004

Glasgow, Scotland

It's been the best kind of day in the studio. The reasons are threefold. Firstly we were in studio two, which means the door can be left open, allowing the fragrant air from Kelvingrove Park to come in. Secondly, it's been a beautiful day. Lastly, the track, *Your Secrets*, is mostly done. We're just throwing a few ideas at it and tidying it up, which allows me to nip off on errands when I get claustrophobic.

I challenge anyone to suggest a more picturesque walk to get a sandwich than the one I enjoy on a regular basis. I turn left out of the studio door and left again, then walk past the brothel and into the park. Then I take the Park Steps up to Park Circus. I try to lose myself in the mess of lanes in this hilltop warren of palace-tenements. I walk over the cobbles, down to the food shop for the hip and righteous, Grassroots. Having been bolstered by the smile of the checkout girl, I trundle back, dawdling in the sunny spots as hanging hawthorns go crazy over my head. I choke myself with pollen.

I've just nipped away for another breather, in fact. Tony is going to prepare the mix. It is already 10.30pm. After telling all and sundry that this is the final track on the *Books* EP, we bloody well better get it finished. It's been too nice a day to get stressed about it.

It's been one of those weeks when trying to finish off little arty projects has been a bit of a drag. Every day was alike, though it's my own fault. At the same time, I still found myself up at five on Friday morning not wanting to go back to sleep because I wanted the day to hurry up and start, such was my excitement at doing what I had planned. I got three frigging hours sleep and spent the rest of the day a bewildered basket case.

MAY 27, 2004
Glasgow, Scotland

It's been an endless day. I flew to London, cut *Your Cover's Blown* for the final time, attended the Ivor Novello Awards ceremony, got back to Glasgow for a little football and made it to the café.

I thought I was going to have a heart attack this morning. Neil had switched my flight so I could attend the final cut of the EP, but the airline never got the change, so I had to queue up and pay extra. I didn't mind the money; it was the endless typing I didn't need. I was still at the ticket desk 10 minutes before the flight was scheduled to leave. I thought the situation was so fucked that I was having palpitations. I knew that in the cutting room in London they would give me 10–11am and no more.

I confess I was rude to the woman at the desk, rude to the man at check-in and rude when I got to the plane. Sorry, chums. You could have said the plane was running late.

So I made it to the mastering and got out at 12.28pm. The Ivor Novello lunch — *Step Into My Office, Baby* was nominated for Best Song — started at the Grosvenor House Hotel on Park Lane at 12.30pm. We passed it at about 12.45pm and there was a huge crowd of paparazzi assembled. I didn't think it was such a big deal! Some glamour puss was standing like the Statue of Liberty getting her picture taken, the flashes firing off her dress.

I got the driver to let me off at the corner and walked back, dragging my little carry-on trolley with me. There was no sign of the group. I walked in between the clutches of the fenced-off paps and police, feeling them having a look at me. One photographer said to another "At ease" as I went in. Great. The security guy didn't even let me past him. I had to go round instead. Geez, so much for showbiz.

Once inside I caught Trevor and his wife Jill coming in, and we greeted each other keenly. I got sorted with my ticket and took my seat in the grand ballroom.

After all that, they had the prize-giving and we didn't win. Everyone in the band got pissed. They barely let us on the plane on the way back. One of our party was pretty sick at the table, leaving red-wine vomit everywhere. We left him in the bath-room and ran for the airport. By a stroke of fortune I made it out of Glasgow Airport like a rat out of a pipe, and told the taxi driver to take me straight to football.

I changed on the way, like Wonder Woman. I missed half the game but it was good to knock it about a bit, with everything back to normal and no-one asking me daft questions. Just the boys stroking the ball about, moving like heavy ballerinas. I kept running after the game was over, straight here, into the caff, over the hill, into the dusk, back in my home town.

MAY 28, 2004
Glasgow, Scotland

I'm going down to Ayr to see my folks. I haven't seen them for ages. Lard's phoning at 4pm to interview me for BBC6 Music. I can just imagine what will happen if my dad gets the phone before me — my father live on air talking to Marc Riley, ex-member of The Fall. It could work.

I really want to go for a run before the interview. I'm going to run along the old railway from my folks' house down to the sea, going past all my old haunts like an archaeologist investigating layers of rock: my primary school, the church, the shop where I worked in summer 1983, the farm I worked on the following summer, and almost to what used to be Butlins holiday camp, where I had a summer job from 1985 to 1987.

I'm still getting off on the same music I was digging back then. I was at the club last night, off in my own retro world. I swear, the most fun, the most intense burst of pleasure I've had in months was the ecstasy of *Brighter* by The Railway Children. It was the best dance I've ever had. I know every beat, nuance and chime of that record, and I probably haven't danced to it since the 1980s. Even during my time as a DJ I could hardly get away with playing it, nor Felt, nor The Blue Aeroplanes, nor The Servants, nor Momus, nor other minor concerns I loved. They surface now and again, and the with-it retro gang seem to know better. They must be archaeologists too. They've come across a seam of diamonds and they are sticking with it.

My other favourite dances last night were *Pulling Mussels (From the Shell)* by Squeeze, *Embarrassment* by Madness, The Woodentops, Steve Harley, *Sunlight Bathed the Golden Glow* by Felt. I was REALLY in the mood. I drank water at the end, and it was only then that my body told me how dehydrated I was, because I felt queer and had to walk out.

Hearing these records makes me want to go straight into the studio and record more music. I'm feeling the pull of being a producer. I want to paint the picture instead of being a boy in the picture. I can hear a sound and I've got songs lined up. I could sing them, but I'd be spreading myself too thin. I'm thinking of a girl group, maybe three girls splitting the leads, trying to outdo each other on the chorus, harmonising from time to time. The group would accompany them, Richard cracking the snare, Mick on bass, Bob, Stevie and someone else on guitars, maybe all acoustic round one mike. I'd put down strings and brass later. Woodwind and double bass. Harp and timps. I can hear it, I can hear it. But it's someone else singing.

It's later on now. I went running and got back in time to find my mum holding the phone. It was the lassie from BBC6 Music checking I was there OK.

The run was beautiful, so green. I'm going to keep running and let my mind wander until I get saddled with responsibility, after which I won't be able to move so fast. While I was out I was wondering why I should be allowed such freedom, but then it isn't everyone's cup of tea.

I eventually got to the shore, where I took off my shoes and socks and carried on running along the shoreline, splashing along for a mile or two. The sea was flat calm and sparkling, Arran rising like a fictional lost land on the horizon. I bawled out the verse about running over wet sand from *Everyday Is Like Sunday*. They played that last night as well.

Glasgow, Scotland

It's one of those nights you spend the whole year waiting for.
It's close, which means it's stuffy and warm. I like that. When
Scottish people say it's close it comes across as a complaint. They
pray for thunder and rain to clear the air. I pray it will stay close,
that I can walk without the wind hindering my thoughts, that
I can put one foot in front of the other without the rain taking
my attention away from the soles of my feet.

All of which is to say I am bored out of my tiny skull. The
days have been a house of cards; my mood has been trembling.
I set great store by today's football match. A football match! I'm
a man of almost 36. Anyway, I blew it. I left the house too late
to pick up Allen, who was going to take a turn in goal. There
was traffic chaos everywhere, the roads delighting in teasing the
leisure-starved inhabitants. By wily ways we left the car in Ibrox
and took the underground train the rest of the way. We made
it before half-time.

Allen took over in nets and the game was balanced. Steven —
the player-manager (ex of the pop band Bis) — and I swapped
notes, and the game was fine for a while. I was annoyed about
missing the start but it felt OK to be watching at least.

After the interval a striker, Alan, shouted to me to swap places
with him. For some reason I asked Ronnie to move up to striker
and I would go to my usual midfield position. Stoopid. Steven
came on too for his little brother John. The tinkering was
enough to signal defeat and collapse in the eyes of our team,
and we lost four goals in 10 minutes.

From now on I'm a striker, I'm midfield, I'm whatever they
want me to be. I'm just going to come on and play like a madman. I feel like a madman. I'm getting a madman headache

looking at this stupid screen. I want to get back out into the street but I'm scared because I know this particular Saturday formula, and it involves nothing more than wishing it were Sunday night.

My sole objective is to get the girl group together. The thing is, I want to be in it. I don't know if I want to be one of the girls or play bass. I know I said that I want to produce, but what about the gigs? I ain't going to be standing about in a cravat, smoking a cheroot. I've got to live it too.

I'm dodging homework. I can't do it right now. I want to disappear into my own dream world, but we've got to go back on the road soon. Fuck the road. Ha ha! I know I say that every time. My mood will improve and I'll be ready. I'm meant to be writing a thousand words for *The Scotsman* newspaper on my experience of outdoor gigs. Instead, maybe I should write a thousand words on what might happen next Saturday, when we play an outdoor gig at the Botanic Gardens in Glasgow.

I love the fact that, from the stage, I'll be able to see quite a lot of the places where I wrote certain songs. A bit higher and I would be able to see the view from the window in *Dog on Wheels*. I can see the bench where Isobel was sitting, writing, in the video for *Lazy Line Painter Jane*. She was cute.

I'm also meant to be writing a short drama based on a passage from the Bible for the Sunday school. They are taking the service the morning after the Botanics show. I should do it tonight but I can't get in the mood. Moan, moan, moan. It's 10.23 pm and getting dark now, so I'm going out for a walk before the day goes completely.

Glasgow, Scotland

My running has gone to the dogs recently. I simply haven't had
the inclination. I'm just back from London. I would usually run
but I was kind of sleepy, so instead I just drifted along the street
in training shoes, running when I felt like it. I was going to take
my Munich 1974 design checkerboard football out with me, but
I thought that would be taking things too far. I'm desperate for
a game. I've got a couple of engagements at the weekend, which
means I'm going to miss our 11-a-side match. I want to be in
central midfield, moving the ball out to the wings and occa-
sionally through the channels. That's all I want to do.

Last night we played a set in London for XFM to a few hundred invited guests. It was a lot of fun. At one point in the set
though I distinctly felt like a transit of Venus. It's rare that I feel
like an astronomical phenomenon during a gig, so it must be
noted. I think it was because there was a burning light right
behind me, and I must have looked like a black dot to the audience.

So I'm allowing myself to drift along. I have to leave my flat
soon so I'm going to look in the newspapers to see if there's
anything happening on the housing market. As ever, my timing
is impeccable. Even the Governor of the Bank of England is
warning first-time buyers not to buy. What the fuck does it
really matter though? I saw a news report about impending
humanitarian crises in Sudan. It seems like it's all kicking off
there. There are millions on the brink of starvation. It kind of
makes my moan about house prices seem very trivial.

I went for a night run. I felt like Mowgli skipping through
the jungle. Thing is, now I feel tired and let down. That wasn't
part of the deal.

I took a train, two trains in fact. They took me way out the south side, then I followed a small river that took me almost to the Clyde. I passed through the graveyard where I took pictures of Shantha for the last LP. There's an old road running through it which could be a Victorian country track. It was pretty dark by then. It was as if the white pedestals were ghosts. They kept catching the corner of my eye. Chasing ghosts. That's what I was doing there anyway. I worked my way down to Glasgow Green, and turned to face the wind for the final three miles home.

JUNE 18, 2004
London, England

I've been up and down to London all week. It makes you want to escape into a good book.

I like London, it's just this down and up business isn't any kind of living. The show at the Islington Academy was good but the ITV show we appeared on, *Weapons of Mass Distraction*, was rotten. I'm not saying the show was rotten — I never saw it — but the experience was. But hey, you try something once.

I was meant to be on a football show on BBC1 tomorrow called *In the Know*. I was looking forward to it. They asked me, then cancelled, giving no reason. I can imagine the conversation though.

"So, Saturday's show. Who have we got so far?"

"Gianluca's in."

"Good."

"Ray Winstone."

"Oh yeah, the daddy from *Scum*. He's got a new film out, right?"

"Yeah, and he's a big football fan. Very knowledgeable."

"Knowledgeable, that's good. Who else? Who's the music?"

"We've got the lead singer from Belle and Sebastian."

"Who?"

"Stuart Murdoch. Sings for Belle and Sebastian. Glasgow band. Got a single out next week."

"Never heard of him. This worries me. Whose idea was this?"

"Em, that was mine, Geoff. He's a big football fan. Very knowledgeable."

"How long have you worked here, Dave?"

"It's coming up on six months."

"Well, I've been here four years, and I say I've never heard of him. What happened to the geezer from The Hives?"

So we've only come down to do *Friday Night with Jonathan Ross* — one song then back on the plane. Maybe that's why people move to London. I can see why they do. Seriously, if you're trying to break into the music business, move to London. It's not for me though — I treasure my city more and more each day.

In between these trips to London we played the show at the Botanics in Glasgow. We might have been on the telly, we might have been on the radio, but I bet what actually affected people was the gig in the park. I kept bumping into people today who had been there. They all seemed to have a story to tell. It's like that TV show that begins: 'There are eight million stories.' Well, there were 10,000 stories on Saturday, all intertwined; I'm into it, I want to hear what people did. I love the fact the west end was the backdrop rather than a festival site.

For instance, I bumped into Sarah, who plays my disgruntled girlfriend in the video for *I'm a Cuckoo*. She was buzzing when I saw her in the park, looking like she was dressed for the French Riviera in a short red skirt and a tight black top. I told her to come to the party afterwards. When I saw her later on, she and her friend Almaya were dancing to our guest band The Johnny 7. I was in the mood to dance and Sarah was really chatty.

"I had to go for a pee when I was in the park," she said. "I went into the bushes and peed, but I fell down the bank."

Then she showed me the gash in her arm. It didn't phase her though. She went back to dancing. Almaya was leading, and I found myself dancing alone. There was quite a gang of boys round them. I wonder why? I didn't stop to wonder for too long, leaving them to it and finding solace upstairs at the National Pop League club. Everyone sort of dances by themselves there anyway, so you never feel left out.

Later I saw Sarah and a pal dashing down the stairs and out into the night. I wonder where they ended up? Two stories out of 10,000.

JUNE 22, 2004
Glasgow, Scotland

I've been nipping about today with no real plan; just the promise of two hours of football in the afternoon. I'm meant to be organising my house move before we tour again, but I can tell the week will get gobbled up by the pleasure Pac-Man, or better still Ms. Pac-Man! Jeez Louise, the girls ... If one day you read of my death, and it is bicycle/car/lorry-related, you will at least know I died doing something I loved: spying on girls in the street from the saddle of my bike on a sunny day.

So that's how the day started. I stumbled up and out, picking up my bike from my friend's house. She pointed out how tired I looked — *I'm probably just looking my age, honey!* — and I rambled on to the council chambers on George Square to carry out a protest.

Late last night I got an email to say Tchai-Ovna, the tea shop in which we shot the sleeve for *Dear Catastrophe Waitress*, was under sudden and calamitous threat from capitalist-inspired *progress*. Basically, the council wants to build there, it being on a patch in the suddenly glamourous west end. Yuppies want to live there. Yuppies got money. Money talks, hippies walk.

Tchai-Ovna is SO FUCKING COOL. I was astonished when it opened. It's only been there for about four years, but it's a hub for right-thinking poets and wrong-playing jazzers. It's the closest we got to real boho, *man*, and thus a blot on the landscape for the suits.

The irony is that the council are pushing this 'cool Glasgow' thing. It's only the hippies, the musos, the kids on the streets who are making it cool. It's the youngsters with no cash who *do* stuff. If you're going to sweep out every little hip initiative with your capitalist broom, Labour, then you're going to end up with Dullsville.

What's especially irritating is that they tried to sneak it through at the planning stage. I mean, it's gone, it's sewn up, the plans are set. The council told the people in the tenements across the river but it didn't tell any of the residents or businesses in the lane where they are going to build — it's simply going to start building on top of them.

So, in 12 hours, to beat the signing of the final documents the proprietors of Tchai-Ovna organised people to protest at the council offices. I turned up on my bike and was immediately handed a banner which said: "Save our tea shop!"

For a small group, they made plenty of noise and spectacle. All the jazzers were there, and they each had an instrument. This was good. There was a giantess made out of wicker and papier-mâché with someone inside. This was very good, if a little scary. There were flighty girls with summer frocks and slightly unkempt hair. This was particularly heartening, so early

179

in the morning it was. A little breakfast for the eyes, a foxy
bonus for the soul!

Glasgow, Scotland

Here is a list of things I've thought about since I got up an hour
and a half ago. (I'm writing it to ease my brain of conflict and
to arouse sympathy for my plights this addled morning.)

- A new bridge section for a rambling country song I've been
  writing.
- Which songs we might consider playing at the forthcoming
  European shows, so I can give the session musicians advance
  warning.
- Meeting Ciara for an early lunch, thus ensuring my lunch is
  suitably digested upon entering into the arena of football at
  3pm.
- Getting her to pick me up in her dad's car so we could drop
  my not inconsiderable pile of washing off at the launderette.
- Writing to the property convener of the church to ask him
  to consider keeping my beloved gas fire in the kitchen of the
  flat when they renovate the hall. (The answer will be no, but
  you have to make your point for the sake of sanity and the
  greater good.)
- Warning the church board that, because I'll be away with the
  group, the builders will find me ridiculously unprepared for
  moving out when I return.
- Asking the builders to tread lightly on any unclassified docu-
  mentation they might turn over when they arrive. It'll probably be an unfinished song or an unrealised idea for a photo.
  The future of the next Belle and Sebastian record may depend
  upon it!

- The builders turning up with their boots and newspapers, making tea in my sink and circling a runner in the 3.10 at Haydock with the red pen Marisa sent me for correcting her screenplay.
- The list of records I could post to the BBC for an upcoming radio show that might feature me talking about some of my favourite records, and what I might say between songs without sounding ridiculous, laboured and pompous.
- Joy Division. I wonder why I haven't thought about their records for a while. The phrase 'a nihilist moaning over a bass solo' springs to mind. I consider the offence it might cause if that thought ever made the leap from my head to the airwaves.
- Neil and Katrina, and why there's no-one in the office. I'm not bothered though, they both work very hard. I can't help wondering what they are doing, though. Neil: something to do with his kid. Katrina: something to do with her bad back?
- Personal matters of slight social offence and social planning considering I'm going away for a while. Who I have to see before I go; who I might I run into while I'm away; provision for the friend who's going to look after my house for me, etc.
- Packing it all in and going to look for comfortable underwear. Expensive pants. I simply want to be unchafed.
- A demo my friend sent me. I thought about how great she looks on the cover, and how terrible the song is. I thought about how such a contrast could drive you to madness.
- The ominous and sudden presence of large industrial drilling equipment in the grass patch beside the church hall.
- The intricacies and general uselessness of the Glasgow City Council websites, and of fledgling web technology in general. I wanted to find out what the planning prospects were for a certain plot of land in Glasgow. I'm thinking about

moving near there, but I'll be damned if I'm going to move to another place that is just about to be developed, dishevelled, corrupted or polluted. The future of the next Belle and Sebastian record may depend upon it!

- The scene described in the following note sent to me from my friend Yoshi in San Francisco:

  "I had a funny exchange today with the cashier at Trader Joe's, the grocery store. I had on my Marisa/Belle and Sebastian button and he noticed it. He started the conversation by saying: 'You heard that Belle and Sebastian are supposed to be doing a cover album of Metallica's *Ride the Lightning*? It's going to be acoustic and I heard they were going to wear warlock costumes, all that shit.'" Ha ha!

- Why my cleaner never calls me any more. My kitchen still smells fishy from the meal I cooked last Friday. Everything is spilling out over the floor from my first attempts to prepare for my move. The floor has become universally sticky with a mystery substance! My laundry pile is growing and moving like something out of *The Thing*.

- The fact I've got to get out of here. The future of the next Belle and Sebastian record may depend upon it!

AUGUST 7, 2004

Benicassim Festival, Spain

It's strange the way things work out, yet not so strange. This is our last gig of the year. We were all looking forward to it so much because it was the last scheduled gig, the line-up was tasty, our friends were going to be there and the organisers made the bands v press football match official.

At this very moment different bands are lining up in a *stadium* just up the road, but instead of leading the charge from the centre of midfield I'm in my room with a bug. I can't go anywhere outwith charging distance of the toilet. Ach, well.

I took ill a couple of days ago in London. After returning from playing the Fuji Rock Festival in Japan we were detained at Heathrow for 24 hours because of storms in London. Everyone was desperate to get back to Glasgow for a couple of days, with me perhaps the least desperate. So I took myself off to a hotel to rest for this weekend, and that's when it got me. Have you ever noticed how often a bug comes in and takes over just when you take your foot off the gas?

I had such a brilliant time at Fuji that maybe the good times couldn't go on for ever. It might sound pessimistic, but in my experience it's hard to stay on the peaks without sinking into a few troughs. While all my friends are out there, running about on the beach, hanging out with the Pet Shop Boys and challenging Kraftwerk to a race on the go-karts, I'm going to be here in my room.

The nadir came last night when after almost five hours of sitting on the toilet I puked up the paracetamol I'd taken half an hour earlier, retching up practically nothing for half an hour. I thought I was going to die. I ended up lying on the bog floor, naked but for a blanket sweat, groaning.

It's been a fabulous six weeks or so. I can't remember when I was last home, it was so long ago. The music's been good; everything's been good. Australia was terrific. I've got a lot to tell you about Australia, and Japan, and Rome, and Dublin. I've been having such a good time that I've not had much time for typing.

I remember when I was 20 and working in Glasgow, my girlfriend and her pals took off for Europe with tents and train passes. Although I couldn't afford to go, I was planning to travel round Spain with them the following year, but I was ill the whole summer. I guess this is the pay-off for always missing out when I was younger. All this touring feels like InterRailing, but with music thrown in. Ah, the best times! I'm so lucky.

AUGUST 23, 2004
Glasgow, Scotland

This has been a very average day, but after a terrific weekend you must expect a modicum of stunning mediocrity. I'm terrible at settling down to a task, especially something as rigid as cleaning, sorting, tidying, packing, moving, organising. It's so easy to get stuck in a rut when you lives on your own. That's why I want to cast myself out into the streets. But are the streets of Glasgow going to throw up the answer? I like the fact things are quite lively here. I'm anticipating the buzz of the annual influx of students and newcomers to Glasgow next month. Although it doesn't feel like five years, it's 19 years since I moved to the west end of Glasgow and became a student.

And I'm moving to number 19. I think that's a good number, a prime number in fact. I've lived at a very divisible number for eight years: 24. Look at the factors of 24: eight, two, three, six, four, twelve, one. A busy little tart of a number, is 24. Do you think me moving to number 19 will be accompanied by a new austerity of thinking? Artistic posturing and three-piece suits? A paunch and a deepening of the voice? Who knows?

It was such an average day. I met a friend and went for a wander, but the excitement was too much. I found that upon consumption of a fishcake I became doubled up with cramp. I was compelled to retire from the excitement of the hip office surroundings to my couch, from which I watched the Olympics for hours.

I do love the Olympics. Funny, people think the Mercury

Music Prize is a big deal, but I'd give a hundred Mercury awards for one sniff of Olympic gold. We were chatting earlier, me, Patrick and Ciara. Ciara asked:

"If you could win a medal at one event what would it be? Mine would be the floor gymnastics."

"Oh God, the gymnastics are amazing. Those women are like cats, or little bi-planes or something."

"Mine would be gymnastics too," said Patrick. "I used to do gymnastics when I was a kid."

"What would yours be?" Ciara asked me.

"Oh, the mile. The 1500 metres."

"Why would you choose that?"

"I can't help it. I was hooked in the 1980s. There was a time when the British middle-distance runners were the best in the world. It started at the European Championships around 1980. I remember watching it on the telly and being excited at all the new British names and how well they were doing. Steve Ovett and Sebastian Coe in particular. They won the 800m and the 1500m between them at the Moscow Olympics. For the rest of the decade practically you were treated to the sight of British athletes poised at the final bend of Olympic finals, ready to waste the opposition with a last, unanswerable sprint. I loved it. Imagine being able to actually do it."

"You don't get many British athletes doing as well as that now."

"I know. We're only good at fishing and things like that. Darts. Cluedo."

"Cluedo's not an Olympic sport!"

"Well, you know what I mean," I said.

"How do some sports become Olympic sports anyway? Synchronised diving — who thought that up?" said Ciara.

"It's a bit random," said Patrick.

(This was when the conversation took a regrettable turn for the worse. Smut always comes to the fore on boring days, I find.)

"I know," I said. "They might as well have synchronised fisting."

"The asymmetric felch!"

"Indeed."

AUGUST 30, 2004

The Girl Who Slept

The girl who slept at François Truffaut's grave
Was in distress, but acting rather brave
She couldn't quite believe the man's demise
She had to see the gravestone with her eyes
He looked so young in later photographs
His peasant eyes could cut a girl in half
She sat down on the stone to rest a while
The god of clouds was watching, and complied
By letting shafts of sun embalm her face
The breeze conspired to leave the girl in peace
And so upon this sunny scene was set
A cradle for this interesting brunette.

SEPTEMBER 1, 2004

Glasgow, Scotland

I've been doing nothing so dramatic as continuing to wade through pile upon pile of stuff. God knows I hate packing for a tour, and packing for a house move is like packing for a massive tour. I'll feel good though when I get to my new place with only the belongings I really need to get me through the next year or so. I could live out of a suitcase, I really could.

Which brings me to a special offer. I was chucking stuff in a box, and thought I could keep a box of vaguely band-related stuff for one of you if you felt fanatical enough. I warn you it's mostly old clothes, stuff I couldn't even give to Oxfam. The odd trenchcoat, an occasional printed T-shirt, the best pair of trousers I ever had (with a little hole in the arse), my Glastonbury wellies, worn once and still caked in Glastonbury mud. There's also a cranky little squeezebox that Stuart David played on ... Actually, that can be the question. The first person to email with the B&S song that Stuart played the squeezebox on gets the dubious memorabilia.

So, I've been packing and that. It was nice to get out for a while to see Ciara. Not only had I been stuck indoors on a beautiful day when everyone else was out bowling and parading, but I'd been told off in a couple of emails. Someone was chasing me up about a demo they sent me a while back, saying it was impolite of me not to have responded.

"I mean, Ciara, I'm not a librarian, I'm a friggin' rock star! What do they expect?"

This turn of phrase amused her. I feel as much like a rock star as I do a woman, which is about 26%.

She brought in the roasted vegetables.

"There's something missing from this, by the way. I think it's potatoes. It's quite watery and insubstantial."

"Probably the potatoes. The noble potato. Do you know, if there was a tug o' war among vegetables the potato would be the anchor. Right at the back — sturdy, like a rock."

"You're right. It's dependable."

"Indispensable. No wonder it's our staple diet. You can't imagine the courgette as the anchor."

"No way. It would be up at the front, leaning on the rope, posing for the cameras."

"Precisely. And as for the mangetout, or the syboes!"

"Of course, the tomato would be sidelined."

"Wouldn't know what team he should be pulling for: fruit or veg."

"It's a shame really."

And so the afternoon went on, as we compiled the veg team for the tug o' war with the fruit. The team was mostly made up of the root crops, but we decided we'd let the courgette handle the publicity for the event and the syboes could do hair and make-up.

SEPTEMBER 7, 2004

One-Tone Lullaby

I always sleep with my head facing wind and nature
Helps me to forget that you have her, and I can't get her
Helps me to remember prayers and sayings
Makes me feel like I'm still moving
Gently rocks me with the sound of shushing
A one-tone lullaby
Helps me to shift on to dreaming plains
Then be dragged down, prostrate, head askew
Makes the six hours shorter, four, then two

Glasgow, Scotland

We lost out on the Mercury Prize, just like 10 other suckers. You should have heard some of the bull I spouted over the course of the last 24 hours. You'll never hear it, because we didn't win. History is always written by the victors.

I'm referring to all the interviews we did for television and suchlike. What I'd forgotten was that they would be rendered redundant as soon as we lost the prize, and we lost the prize.

I had an OK time though. It was something to do with the hotel and the lack of responsibility that a rock star enjoys. I wandered the sumptuous regions of Kensington and Holland Park, shopped for bowler hats and enjoyed an aromatherapy massage. Now it's back to Glasgow for some stabbings and a spot of shipbuilding!

Franz Ferdinand took the prize. For only 1.5 seconds did it occur to me that we had as much chance of winning the thing as anyone else. Like Charlie looking for the Golden Ticket, I waited while Jools Holland, the compère, and Dizzee Rascal, who was presenting the prize, kept us in suspense. I wrote the first line of my acceptance speech in my head ...

"Thank you, Mr Rascal!"

Then they announced the prize for the Franz.

The evening was a bit subdued after that. The only ones showing much lust for life were the cameramen round the Franz. At the very least they should have been made to go up and sing their number again like they do at the Eurovision Song Contest.

I spent most of the remainder of the evening making up imaginary compilation tapes with Geoff and Jeanette from Rough Trade and their friend Mark. I later found out he was almost controller of music at the BBC. I hope I didn't spout too much rubbish! I remember yelling "Reconsider Paul Weller! Reconsider The Style Council!" at him across the table.

After that I got bored because I didn't have drink or class-A drugs to distract me from the drudgery, so I went to noise the DJ up. Stuart Maconie sent me to find out if he had any Northern Soul records.

"Oh no, mate. I've left all my Northern at home."

He played all this unclassifiable funky stuff but I made the best of it, along with all the female staff of the Mercuries who were all having a good time now their work was done.

And thus I spent the rest of the evening, dancing too hard on an injured leg with Scottish Steph and Stuart Maconie, who has little feet but moves beautifully.

A funny thing happened today at the airport. We were in the BMI check-in queue, Bob and Stevie in particular feeling a little delicate after a very late night and duly cocooned behind shades.

A fellow came up to us. I think he sensed we were in a band.

"Are you … a band?"

"Yes, we're in a band."

"What are you doing here?"

"We're going to Glasgow."

"Are you Franz Ferdinand?"

"No, we're not Franz Ferdinand. What do you want?"

"I'm helping make a programme called *Airport* for the BBC. What's your band called?"

"Belle and Sebastian."

"Oh, I know *The Boy with the Arab Strap*. I was half expecting to see a girl called Belle and a boy called Sebastian! Ha ha ha!"

Silence.

Then the camera crew arrived, at which juncture Stevie pointed to them and said:

"Point that camera at me and I will fucking break you."

It's funny, Stevie's not really like that, he just has his moments. He's generally kind and gentle, but he can be quite changeable, as can we all. I like these kinds of traits. For instance, before the Mercury awards ceremony the organisers insisted on all the groups rolling up in Minis bearing the logo of the sponsor, Nationwide Building Society. There were three of them for us. We had to go out the back of the hotel, get into the cars, drive round the front and get out on the red carpet to face the press. Stevie was not impressed.

"Oh, this is the worst. We've gone too far. This is terrible. Fucking *Nationwide*. We've really blown it this time," he said.

"I don't think this is the worst thing that's happened," I replied.

"Look at us. This is ridiculous!" Then, to the driver: "No offence, mate."

"No offence taken." said the driver.

"We signed up for this as soon as we said we'd play," I said. "It'll be OK. Just enjoy the playing."

"I know. I just hate this."

Ten minutes later, after getting out of the cars, lining up for the banks of press and answering a few showbiz questions, he said:

"Actually, it wasn't so bad. I quite enjoyed it. It was fun! I was just worried we were going to get out of the cars and nobody was going to know who we were, as usual. I was scared nobody was going to take our picture."

He does have a point, though.

Glasgow, Scotland

I'm still sorting through the detritus of the past eight years in the church hall. An easy enough task you might think, but one I'm clearly not adapted to in this day and age.

Last night a friend and I took some shelves apart, then I dismantled the stereo. I decided I was going to throw the speakers out; in fact I decided I was going to get rid of the CD player too. I bought it in 1988. It's a funny size. I remember buying it so I could put it in a case and take it to the disco. I was DJing with a CD player in 1989 — pretty swanky. I'd go on the floor to dance then start the next track with the remote control. I hope there was a sensibly cynical clique at the club praying for me to mess up.

The speakers are even older. I bought a Sony separates system when I was 14 after working in a shop all summer. Such a beautiful thing, all stacked up in its glass cabinet. I couldn't believe it when I finally got it. It cost me £399 in 1983! That's a lot of dough.

The last track I played was *Red Light Spells Danger* by Billy Ocean. I've been listening to that track a lot this week. I emailed John at the National Pop League to request it for the next club night. He must have passed the request on to his colleagues at the NPL spin-off, Little League. When I paid into the club, a man I'd never met came up to me and whispered surreptitiously:

"We don't have any Billy Ocean with us tonight. We played that number the last two nights."

"Oh sorry, I was away."

They played a curious mix of tunes that night. The DJs work

in an Oxfam shop and had decided only to play records they had picked up while working there. Then they sold the records during the night. All vinyl, too. I hope the people at Oxfam know what sort of lengths their volunteers go to in order to raise money. They ought to get an Oxfam medal.

It made for an interesting night. The evening was held at the peerless RAFA club (it stands for Royal Air Force Association). It's an ex-servicemen's social club. You have to ring the buzzer at the front door to get in. You're greeted by a cheerful old airman and led through the pub, all Formica tables and brown dimpled glass, downstairs into a small hall with a bar in the corner, a small stage in the other corner and tables against the rest of the wall surrounding the small wooden dance floor. There's a large RAF logo painted on the ceiling. It's basically a mod target, so the place couldn't be more perfect. Model Lancasters and Spitfires hang from the ceiling and a portrait of the Queen takes place of honour on the far wall.

I think the Oxfam boys are fledgling DJs. Their choice of records was perhaps a bit limiting, and there were patches where they failed to attract anyone on to the dancefloor. I kind of liked it, though; they were feeling their way, offering songs that even the hippest of the hip hadn't heard in a long time, and perhaps had never considered dancing to. They would play a particular Sugarhill Gang or Haircut 100 record, sparking little debates about its merit within this very indie crowd. A consensus had to be reached before a particular table would take to the floor. By that time the record was half over. The whole night was disjointed and jerky, with highs and lows. I liked it.

James Kirk from the group Orange Juice was there. He was on fine form. A friend of mine came back from the toilets to report:

"When I went in, James Kirk was standing at the urinals. I went into the cubical because I sort of know him, but I didn't feel like striking up a conversation right then."

"I know what you're saying."

"When I was in there, I heard this ... Wo-oh-who! Wo-oh-who! WO-OH-WHO! He was singing the start of *Felicity*!" (*Felicity* being one of the songs James wrote for the first Orange Juice record.)

We'll not hold it against him, though. I'm sure if I'd had a skinful, you might catch me inadvertently humming the intro to *Stay Loose* while swaying and peeing. Just by accident. Still, strike me if you do! Strike me a blow that will bring me to my senses. Strike me, and I won't hold it against you.

Playing the Piano Well

Playing the piano well
Is like the ash outside my window
Is like the gorge of green which makes this view
Is something I would like to do

Purer I would try to be
Sit down at the stool with conscience clean
Ready for a day's work at rattling and tormenting strings
Coaxing, plucking, making up things

If you play the piano well
You need never go out again
You need never eat another meal
Your job becomes a meditation

Women come to bathe you
Men to upbraid you
Contracts are thrown at you
By idealistic radio programmers
By dreamers with graveyard shows
By ether painters, with swallows for pets

LOU REED'S MULLET

SEPTEMBER 22, 2004

Glasgow, Scotland

I've moved into my new place. It's lovely, though it's strange to be away from the desolation of the hall. I've even got neighbours.

This morning I thought I'd get up early, go to John Lewis and get a load of things I need for the new place. I got into a borrowed car. The street was down to one lane so I waited at the top of the hill for the traffic to come up. I took my turn when they had passed but then a taxi was coming towards me. There were two cars following me, so it seemed the easiest solution was for the taxi to back up. I figured he would see it that way too, but from 75 yards away I could tell the taxi driver was seriously pissed off.

I rolled my window down on the way past to explain. Before I said anything, he looked malevolently toward me and said:

"If I didn't have a passenger in the back, I would have waited all day for you to go back."

He said it as though he would have killed me for it. It was such a minor thing!

"I had already waited at the top for cars to pass," I continued.

"I don't care."

"Look, I'm just trying to be nice."

"Well, I'm not."

"Cheer up!"

"What, looking at you?" And then he drove off.

There's a lot of anger out there. Neil experienced an even more dramatic road rage incident on the bus today. A fellow driving a Merc took some offence at the bus driver, his rage culminating in him screeching his car across the front of the bus, getting out, shouting "Black bastard!" at the bus driver and trying to break his way into the cab.

Eventually he got back into his car, but the bus journey was punctuated by the fellow getting out to wave a knife at the driver and the bus in general whenever they stopped at traffic lights.

SEPTEMBER 23, 2004

Glasgow, Scotland

The days are thoroughly unremarkable. I could be taking a forward step on the road of life; I could be taking an attractive detour; but here I am, pondering in a lay-by.

I did an interview for the *Scotland on Sunday* newspaper this morning. The journalist was amiable, but we covered a lot of the stuff I've been talking about all year. *Dear Catastrophe Waitress* seems such a long time ago. I preferred it when we started talking about the novel he's written, a Russian epic with a humorous side to it. Good luck to him. It was nice to compare creative processes — I'm always slightly in awe of someone who has the stamina for a full novel.

So I'm just drifting along. The seed of my malaise could be

my boiler's broken switch, which is lying on the kitchen table. A couple of days after I moved in, the central heating gave up the ghost. I got some men out. They had a look at it, drank some tea, removed the burned-out switch and told me an entertaining story about how they played an essential part in the career of the fledgling Wet Wet Wet.

They must have been satisfied that the story was worth the call-out fee alone, because they haven't been back to fix the bloody boiler. I've called every day, but it's a game, isn't it? Workmen know they have the cerebral classes over a barrel. They're not in a rush. They know the hapless pipsqueak (i.e. me) will never roll up his sleeves and fix the thing himself. They might as well draw the whole episode out. It could be worth more.

In the meantime, I'm enjoying an ongoing series of cold showers. My new neighbour offered me her bathroom, which I declined. Cups of tea have to be offered and drunk before embarking on such an imposition. Careers have to be established; 10-year histories have to be explored; marital status has to be confirmed. Besides, I suspect that under her sweet and unprepossessing demeanour there lies the heart of a dominatrix. I want to string this fantasy out before I am disappointed by the pastel ordinariness of her boudoir.

Man, I wish I could have recorded my train of thought for you as I trotted home from football. I'm in the café now, but I had my momentum broken by stopping off at the flat.

I live a lot closer to football now. It's a beautiful thing, I can be home in 10 minutes and in the café in 20. I love my new flat. This afternoon Ciara and I sat out on the ledge with a beautiful 180-degree view of the west and beyond. You can see Arran, the top of Goat Fell and the wind turbines on Eaglesham Moor.

As the sun dipped and Ciara said cheerio, I stayed up there, angling the reflection of the window on to the houses on the other side of the valley. I sent secret Morse messages to returning students telling them to study hard. I sent flashed telegrams to lonely single mothers telling them to try night-classes. I flashed the incoming pilots carrying the businessmen back from Heathrow. "Safe home," I said.

I ran so hard during our football match that I was almost sick on the way home. We were a man down so we worked hard, but I lacked control at top speed. If you can marry speed and control, you've made it, but I kept falling over. A good striker like Thierry Henry will keep enough puff back to compose himself in front of goal. This is what I want my next little musical *divertissement* to be like. Sleek and fast, but with control in front of goal.

So I met my neighbour again. She asked a little favour of me and I was only too happy to oblige. It's funny how living in a flat among people can change you. I bought a pair of slippers so I can slip around quietly without disturbing the people below. And I find myself going to bed early. I used to stay up till all hours, picking my nose, watching the game, chewing chocolate. Now I hear the household preparing for bed. I can sort of tell when the girl next door is turning in, so I think to myself: if she's going to bed I better as well. It's going to be a big day tomorrow.

She's a journalist. She writes human interest stories. I told her about my friend. He's a human interest story.

He's called Ewan. I've been bumping into him twice a year since about 1990. He's always going somewhere on his bike, planning a trip. Apart from that I don't think he goes out much. I wrote a verse of *Dear Catastrophe Waitress* about him, but it never made the final version. It started: 'Dear Catastrophe Grandson, Dear Catastrophe Grandson.'

The reason is that he was visiting his grandparents in Aberdeen or somewhere. They were out in the street and bumped into some neighbours. Ewan hung back as the conversation went on. Eventually his gran introduced him to the neighbours.

"This is our grandson. He's not very grand!"

Anyway, when I saw him the other day he told me he was planning another bicycle trip, this time to Prague.

"Cool. Well, good luck. See you soon," I said.

"Oh, I forgot to say. I was at the doctor's yesterday and he told me I've got four kidneys."

"Are you serious? Four kidneys?"

"Apparently."

"What does that mean?"

"I don't think it means that much."

"Does it give you any special powers? Can you drink and not get drunk?"

"I don't think so. I haven't discovered any special powers yet."

"Oh well, nice one. See you later."

"Bye."

SEPTEMBER 29, 2004

Glasgow, Scotland

I spent most of last night dreaming I was in a Cabinet meeting with Tony Blair. It wasn't really him, though. It was the prime minister all right, but it was a blend of Tony and his wife Cherie. I wasn't looking square at them the whole time, but we were having a good old discussion. It's funny, considering I had snuck in there, that I became one of the principles at the meeting. The rest of the cabinet were a bit wooden.

It pissed off the security guy, though. I can't remember how

I got in, but I remember thinking I was going to be in deep shit if I got caught. When they finally found me behind the sofa in the policy room, the security guy got a real drubbing. They pulled him in and ticked him off. He was going to beat me up on the way to the cells, I could tell. I was appealing to Tony, though. I said I was sorry. I think I hinted that another security debacle might not do his image much good. Better let it blow over. Sort things out from the inside. I think I started giving the security guy a few tips.

So they let me stay for the meeting. It was then that Tony morphed into Cherie — Torie, if you like, or Cheny! But that's when I started having a good time. At first I was just glad to be there. I was still shitting it. For a start, if they had examined my computer case they would have found the replica pistol we used on the *Legal Man* sleeve. It's the real thing. It's got a blocked-up barrel, but try explaining that to a room full of Cabinet ministers as you take it out and swing it in the air.

So I was aware the whole time of sitting on the pistol. I sat there listening for a while, but then I was interjecting from time to time like Warren Beatty's character in *Mickey One*, when he was watching his fellow stand-up comedian do his turn. I started making quite valid points.

"Yeah, but you know that everybody could be driving around in electric cars," I said. "You just don't want to piss off the oil companies."

The members of the Cabinet were looking round kind of sheepishly. They couldn't disagree.

Crashing in on people of power in my dreams is becoming a regular occurrence. I had breakfast with George Bush the other week. In his kitchen. I was squeezing his oranges. Literally. He was really uncommunicative to the point that it was clear he didn't like me at all. I thought I was being charming, trying my

204

best, but he wasn't having it. He wouldn't look me in the eye and wouldn't address me at all after a while. I got quite a bad feeling off him.

I also spent quite a long time in the corridors of Buckingham Palace the other month. I don't mind the royal family too much. They're probably a shower of bastards, but at least they're a pretty powerless shower. As opposed to the large corporations: the new power showers! I was hanging out with the servants. All the time I was trying to find out what you called the Queen when you met her. Your Highness. Your Majesty. Modom. Betty. I could never find out. When I came to meet her it was cool, though. I think we bonded over Galaxie 500, or Ealing comedies, or something.

OCTOBER 13, 2004

Clouds

Last night I couldn't sleep because I thought
A vengeful God was looking down on me from gaps in clouds
So I dwelt on one sweet moment, life fulfilled

I sat and listened to the girl
Who, with a plaintive voice, tries out
A new song, every note devout
To me, a sick, starved, restless soul
Who begs to be excused from rock and roll
To spend the peerless gift of time allotted to him
Listening in silence ...
For in silence moves a beat, a note, a tune
For darling friends to transmit to the four walls of a room

Up above the city roofs are strewn
Puddles of the sunset, playing in kitchens,
Lighting up the girl, her frock, her elbow
Rendering her collarbone in shadow
Picking at her lips as she formed words
Tripping over tricky bits of phrasing
Trying hard in earnest, lost in doing.

I look out
The same clouds that will later
Pull apart, revealing vaults and potholes
Of the darkened high lands, now are tethered
Gathering and thoughtful
Heavy weathered

OCTOBER 15, 2004
Glasgow, Scotland

All Existence is Ecstasy

I keep meaning to put online the section of *The Screwtape Letters*
by C S Lewis I try to quote to people. It puts romantic love in
perspective as an encouragement for people who are in it for
the long haul. Men and women, sticking together. Mating 'for
life, like pigeons or Catholics' as Woody Allen said.

I'll do it when I finally put my books on the shelf and call my
home a home.

That's just a thought. Here's another: all existence is ecstasy.

It's a tricky one to pull off, that. I read it in a book of eastern
mysticism that my friend Alicia gave me. I believe it, but it's
hard to get a feeling for it all the time.

I was trying to think about it today. I've had an extremely
lacklustre day, one that might have inspired a *complaining* sort of

diary entry. But I'm going to make like Pooh, and try to avoid a *complaining* sort of a song. I'm going to think more about existence and ecstasy. Because he's right, that dude. Existence is ecstasy.

Late-Blooming Autumn Flora

Yesterday I enjoyed an ecstasy of existence for a while. I wasn't thinking of it that way, because I hadn't read the passage from the book yet, but when I think back, it was very nice.

It was a beautiful day and I tried to think of a task that would match it. I remembered I had some A4 posters that I hadn't put up, so I gave myself the afternoon to do it.

I was going to be snobby about it, though. I wanted to enjoy a leisurely, twisty stroll at some of my favourite stopping-off points in the west. I wanted to use the Kelvin Walkway as my motorway; I wanted to pop up from the riverbank to my chosen bastion of hipdom and post my notice, then disappear down into the foliage and late-blooming autumn flora.

I started in the fruit shop. I caught Oliver standing outside, guarding the fruit with a squashed aubergine.

"Oh, hi," he said as he batted the veg into his palm like a truncheon. "The kids from the school across the road have been nicking fruit. They've started bussing in kids from the east end of Glasgow for some reason."

At least it's better than nicking chips, I was thinking. Maybe the only way the city council is going to persuade children to start eating more fruit is to park tempting fruit barrows across the road from schools.

"A drunk guy went off with one of the plants yesterday," continued Oliver. "I caught up with him at the bridge. He said: 'Ah wiz fuckin' gonnae sell that.'"

I bought an apple, a russet, and went on my way.

I went into the overpriced second-hand clothes shop. They wouldn't let me put up a poster, so I went into TChai-Ovna, then Voltaire and Rousseau bookshop. Such poetic names! I walked up to Grassroots Café. My friend Andrea was there with her guitar. She was killing time before she had to work. We killed time together.

When we had killed that crazy old time, I asked the waitress if I could post my notice.

"You can, but it will cost you 30p a week."

"Oh! That's going to eat into your tip."

I didn't mean it to sound mean, but that's all the change I had.

"Oh no, he's saying it's OK, you don't have to pay." She was looking over at the man in the kitchen. "Because you're regulars."

Damn right I'm a regular.

Next, I went into the Grassroots shop. A svelte woman was writing notes at the till. Her hair fell over her face as she wrote. I stood there for quite a while.

"Excuse me," I said.

"…"

"Em, hello. Do you have a noticeboard?"

She looked up, uninterested.

"It's at the back."

"Oh, I've never noticed it before."

"It's 30p a week."

"Ah…"

I looked over at the board. The notices were of the esoteric wheatgrass and reiki type — 'does something that happened in your childhood still affect you as an adult?', that kind of thing.

"I'll just leave it," I said.

So I just left it. The woman didn't look up, so I leaned over and planted a wet kiss on the side of her face. Kidding.

I skipped up to the art school and CCA then I jumped a bus back to the office, where Katrina was being nice to me for a change.

"Does Neil know you've put his phone number on the notices?"

"Yes, of course he knows. Do you think I would do that without telling him?"

"Yes."

The phone rang.

"That'll be the first one," she said. But it wasn't.

I left and went through the park. I had two things I could've done that evening, but I think I let myself drift too late in my task so I wouldn't have to decide which engagement to go to. I kept putting those notices up. One at the university. One in Relics, pretty much my favourite shop. I hardly ever do a record sleeve without a visit to Relics. I usually pick up a prop, or at least something to inspire me. I chatted to Steve, the proprietor. I know Steve from way back because I used to work in a record shop in the 1980s, and he used to supply us with rare 1960s stuff. He got me into Nancy Sinatra and Lee Hazelwood and The Beach Boys in a roundabout way. I stared at those records so long that I ended up playing them all. He also lent me the priceless Orange Juice fanzines that fuelled so much of my daydreaming around that time. I've still got them. I used one of the pictures as the cover for the *Modern Rock Song* EP.

I popped into Boots before it shut. I went home. I skipped my 1950s dance class. I missed a birthday dinner. I heated soup for a friend.

Later on she said that when it came to relationships, women reasoned like chess champions, while men thought like footballers. I claimed my game had always been Cluedo, took her into the study and choked her.

OCTOBER 27, 2004

Glasgow, Scotland

I'm sad, but happy sad. It's been a privilege to share in some
small part the life of John Peel, who died two days ago. We were
lucky to have him. It was a shock to hear of his death. So many
people were in love with him! He felt like one of the family,
didn't he?

I'm sitting here thinking about all the great music he got me
into. The essence of Peel, the epic swathes of ambition down
the years. That's just me! He must have got so many people in
the same way.

The Fall – *Mr Pharmacist*
Primal Scream – *Velocity Girl*
The Shop Assistants – *Safety Net*
Happy Mondays – *Performance*
Echo and the Bunnymen – *Pictures On My Wall*
Bradford – *Skin Storm*
New Fast Automatic Daffodils – *Big*
The Orb – *Little Fluffy Clouds*
The Wedding Present – *You Should Always Keep In Touch
  with Your Friends*
The Jesus and Mary Chain – *Just Like Honey*
Momus – *Hotel Marquis de Sade*
Felt – *Primitive Painters*
Prefab Sprout – *Faron Young*
The Smiths – *Well I Wonder*
10,000 Maniacs – *Can't Ignore the Train*
Cocteau Twins – *Pearly Dewdrops Drop*
The June Brides – *Every Conversation*
McCarthy – *Red Sleeping Beauty*
The Fall – *Lay of the Land*
Everything But the Girl – *Night and Day*

The Associates – *Club Country*
Joy Division – *Love Will Tear Us Apart*
Shock Headed Peters – *I, Blood Brother Be*
Bronski Beat – *Smalltown Boy*
New Order – *Blue Monday*
The Smiths – *Reel Around the Fountain*
Billy Bragg – *A New England*
Cocteau Twins – *Peppermint Pig*
Aztec Camera – *Oblivious*
The Sugarcubes – *Birthday*
King of the Slums – *Vicious British Boyfriend*
The Raincoats – *No Side to Fall In*
The Slits – *In the Beginning There Was Rhythm*
Kitchens of Distinction – *The Third Time We Opened the Capsule*
Suicide – *Frankie Teardrop*
New Order – *True Faith*
The Fall – *Hit the North*
I, Ludicrous – *Preposterous Tales*
Sonic Youth – *Schizophrenia*
Public Enemy – *Rebel Without a Pause*
The Primitives – *Stop Killing Me*
The Railway Children – *Brighter*
Buzzcocks – *What Do I Get?*
The James Taylor Quartet – *Blow Up*
Big Black – *El Dopa*
The Colorblind James Experience – *Considering a Move to Memphis*
The Teardrop Explodes – *Reward*
Talulah Gosh – *Talulah Gosh*
The Sundays – *Can't Be Sure*
De La Soul – *Eye Know*
Inspiral Carpets – *So This Is How It Feels*
Dub Sex – *Swerve*
The House of Love – *Destroy the Heart*

The Great Leap Forward – *A Peck on the Cheek*
Dinosaur Jr – *Freak Scene*
My Bloody Valentine – *You Made Me Realise*
Cocteau Twins – *Carolyn's Fingers*
James – *What For*
MC Buzz B – *How Sleep the Brave*
A Guy Called Gerald – *Voodoo Ray*
The Go-Betweens – *Right Here*
The Pastels – *Baby Honey*
The Woodentops – *You Make Me Feel*
Primal Scream – *Higher than the Sun*
Pavement – *Summer Babe*
PJ Harvey – *Sheela-Na-Gig*
The Beatnigs – *Television, Drug of a Nation*
Pulp – *Razzmatazz*
Tindersticks – *City Sickness*
Stereolab – *Ping Pong*
New Order – *Temptation*
The Clash – *Straight to Hell*
Scritti Politti – *Faithless*
Associates – *Party Fears Two*
Simple Minds – *Someone Somewhere (in Summertime)*
Joy Division – *Transmission*
Public Image Ltd – *Public Image*
Stiff Little Fingers – *Suspect Device*
The Fall – *How I Wrote 'Elastic Man'*
The Jesus and Mary Chain – *Some Candy Talking*
The Primitives – *Really Stupid*
The Fall – *Guest Informant*
The June Brides – *In the Rain*
The Only Ones – *Another Girl, Another Planet*
The Damned – *Smash It Up*
The Smiths – *Bigmouth Strikes Again*
The Weather Prophets – *Almost Prayed*

Cocteau Twins – *Love's Easy Tears*
Siouxsie and the Banshees – *Hong Kong Garden*
The Fall – *Rowche Rumble*
Magazine – *Shot by Both Sides*

He was a terrific guy. Very, very funny, and very good at his job. What a storyteller. He's playing Bogshed and Death by Milkfloat in heaven tonight.

God bless you, John. You brought us all up. We're your family. Stockbrokers and hippies, train drivers and car salesmen are shedding tears. They were creeping in to listen to your show but now you aren't there. What's Christmas going to be like without the Festive 50? It was the highlight of my year throughout my crappy youth. The Cocteaus chiming down the ether. The Mary Chain and glorious New Order. Sifting through the hardcore, the noisecore, the trance and the reggae for a gem, finger on the pause button.

I want to walk all night listening to your voice. I want to hear your theme tune, that little bluesy tune. It'll just make me cry even more, like you after Hillsborough. Nobody who heard you will ever forget that. You will never walk alone.

NOVEMBER 9, 2004
London, England

I'm in London today, starting to master the collected EPs with Frank Arkwright. We're listening to *Lazy Line Painter Jane*. Man, there's no lifting that track out of the hole! It's pure church hall. Sorry Stevie, there's only so much we can do with this baby.

We're going at this quite randomly, dipping our toes in where it needs it. We spent a long time mastering each EP in the first place, so I have to remind myself not to unravel any good work.

Memo to self: don't fix what isn't fucked.

OK, I'll remember that. It's funny, I never trust groups when they remaster their music. You always get the feeling they're tinkering where they don't need to; that perhaps they are applying new-found knowledge or philosophy to make their old creations *better, different, more dynamic*. For some bizarre reason I have a picture in my head of Lou Reed's mullet. What has that got to do with my reasoning? Quite a lot. It might take a couple of pages to explain the subtleties of why Reed's mullet ought to act as a warning sign to us all, but I think I'll just leave it hanging. Let's just say that during this mastering session I'm not planning any new haircuts ...

So how come we're in such a hurry to put out the EPs all of a sudden? I don't know. It just seems like the right thing to do. I thought I'd never want them compiled, away from their original jackets, confined to CD. People change though. I've changed!

Nobody's actually selling the original EPs now apart from a few speciality shops — probably the same shops that sold the original *Tigermilk* — so we're putting them together.

I was sort of dreading coming here. I'm missing football, but at least the music is sounding good; that makes up for a lot. I heard *Jonathan David* almost directly on coming in. It sounds *zowwee*! Sorry to use such a prickish term, but that's a bull's-eye of an A-side. *Carriage Clock* is straight after, which I love as well. Pity it's such a rip! It's a nice-sounding track, and I'm pleased with the words. It's a vindictive little *vignette*!

Frank's just gone back to the original half-inch master tape of *Painter Jane*. It does sound better, I must admit. It's going to be a long night, but I guess it's for the best ...

Back to the earlier EPs. He's going into the original tapes. Fair enough, they actually sound better off the original. They all sound good. *Belle & Sebastian* is a bit ... *ooof*! It's quite hard for me to listen to. It's out of tune; it's the first song recorded under the name Belle and Sebastian. Fitting, but rough.

I went to bed early last night, which set me up nicely for the day. Of course, packing for four or so days always gives me a heart attack. I'm meticulous about packing — I've got all these pills and potions to remember. Also, I've always got to salvage clothes from big piles of mixed laundry since I never put the stuff away.

We're on to *A Century of Fakers* now, to some extent the most representative track of the early band. It's another church hall recording. I've got so used to hearing it the way it is that Frank's going to have a hard job convincing me he's changing it for the better. I love Stu's vocals. Stevie's playing bass and Stu's playing the chiming guitar. I miss that about the band a bit. By the end we're all swapping vocals and it's soupy and delicate. Without Bel and Stu we would never have made a record like that. But that's what it's all about. It makes it more precious to me now.

I remember writing the song on the train back up from London, after cutting *Sinister* probably. Those interminable train journeys! I can't remember where it came from, but I do remember meeting Vikki, the girl on the cover with me, on the train. Her story and the story of the song became intertwined, I guess.

I was going to tell you about another dream. This follows on from my going to bed early. I crashed out before midnight for the first time in months and was bang awake at 6am. I dreamed I was playing a gig, a low-key thing. I was playing a nice old baby grand piano. Because we were in between records, I thought it would be an idea to play a cover of a song by an obscure Swedish band from the 1970s.

I got it going for a bit, but I messed up the lyrics and stopped. Stevie looked over.

"It's great, isn't it?" I asked, grinning.

"Well, it might be great if you could play it."

Undeterred, I had another go. I got snatches of the chorus out, and then my fingers started misbehaving, or the microphone stand started to droop, or something. It fell apart. The crowd were getting restless but I didn't care because I was so high on what I could hear was a terrific song. How did those guys manage to stay so obscure! The trouble was, what I could hear in my head was in no way going to give satisfaction to a real audience. It was no good me telling them how great it was going to be when it was finished!

So the attention drifted away from me, and I drifted into the audience. The crowd seemed still to be watching the group, or watching something. It was relaxed, like a crowd at a hip 1960s disco. I wandered over to some people who seemed to be having a good time. One girl was really smiley; she seemed full of energy. When she saw me she said:

"I can sing one. I'll sing the next one."

I was in a great mood, so I was all for it. I gave her the microphone. She stood up where she was and sang *Tainted Love* or *California Soul* or something. Whatever it was, she sang it beautifully. Tunefully, with feeling. Of course I was thinking, hey, she can be in the girl group! Like a shot! I wonder how I'll get around to it. Somehow I felt she wouldn't be interested. She was too full of goddamn beans!

(*Put the Book Back on the Shelf.* Still a bit of a shambles; the hall is really inappropriate for this type of pop record. It's funny, if you listen to our records in sequence, including the albums, they start to fade away by the end of 1997, like a fog is coming in. The sound gets more and more distant. I wouldn't want to change it though; we had to have our little sojourn into sonic wilderness. I love the bit when Bel sings 'Are you happy with yourself?' on her own. If I was a lonely boy pop fan I would sit up and take notice of that. Pretty, soft, comforting and sexy in a way.)

When I woke up I couldn't remember the tune written by the obscure Swedish group because the girl had sung her tune in between my attempts at playing it and me waking up. That's annoying, because I know it was a great one. The chorus felt so good. It's funny to think that it would almost certainly have ended up on the next B&S LP if she hadn't got up to sing. Darn it.

NOVEMBER 12, 2004
Glasgow, Scotland

I just got back from John Peel's funeral. I'll give you the low-down on that tomorrow, but I feel like talking about something else.

I'm feeling flat, calm, cold, empty; not surprising maybe after the last few days. The heating's broken again. That'll explain the cold bit. I haven't really spoken to anyone since I left Sarah in Colchester to catch a bus at 3pm today.

"Man doesn't live by bread alone." I can testify to that. What does a man need to live? What can he lean on? What can I lean on? Let's not be too sweeping here! I'm talking about me … God, women, the arts. That's what I feel like when I feel this way. Friends are good too, of course, but sometimes you pass the point where you don't want to talk about it. And when things get real tough there's God and only God.

217

Glasgow, Scotland

It was a good funeral. Does that sound crazy? On the whole I like funerals, but then I've not had to bury any close family recently. Once you've got over the shock of someone's passing and felt sad, it's good to gather in the sight of God and see someone off. That's the way I look at it. It was a good send-off.

It was an honour to be there. Sarah and I were privileged. If I hadn't made it with the music, I'm sure I would have stood outside with the even-greater masses. I know it was a funeral, but it was still a better show than any I've been to this year. The music was good, the speeches were funny and touching, the place was packed, the guest list was immaculate and God added the spiritual dimension. I was just hoping that the burden of organisation hadn't been on John's wife Sheila and the family.

When we took our seats we were fairly close to the mixing desk and sound equipment that would later broadcast bits of Peel and bits of source music to the congregation and the people outside. It was nice to see Peel's usual crew, Andy Rogers and his team, stationed there, in their mourning dress. The last job they'd do for the gaffer: broadcasting Their Master's Voice at his funeral.

The tributes came from Paul Gambaccini (who worked in Peel's office for some years in the 1970s), Peel's brother, Alan Ravenscroft, and a friend of the family, Charlie Bell, on behalf of Peel's children. One of the fascinating stories Gambaccini told about Peel was that he once stood on President Kennedy's car bonnet so that he could get a better picture — at the president's invitation. This was in Dallas just before JFK was shot. Peel remarked:

"Either Harvey Oswald was the best actor I've ever seen, or he didn't do what he was supposed to have done."

Peel's brother was funny, a very good speaker. He fondly remembered constantly playing in goal as a child, defending against John's ferocious right-foot shot. It put him off football for life.

Peel was of course mad for the game, and mad for Liverpool. His brother remembered that he had a framed picture of Kenny Dalgleish above his desk at the BBC. The caption Peel had put there read: 'God – A Likeness.'

Peel sent his brother a letter from America once when Alan was at an impressionable age. It was about sex.

"Remember, girls enjoy it too," he prompted.

The loveliest part of all the reminiscences came from Peel's children. They commented on their father's unusually good sense of smell, which led him to ban deodorants from the house, and the fact that it wasn't until Peel was 55 years old that Sheila allowed him to have a bank account! He immediately bought a large American car, a Thunderbird I think it was.

Afterwards I remember nipping out and finding a lot of people milling around. We headed for the train station and got the hell out of there, taking our thoughts and memories with us on the road back home.

NOVEMBER 15, 2004
Glasgow, Scotland

I was listening to *Heaven and Las Vegas* by the Cocteau Twins on the way down here to the office. I've been listening to it constantly the last couple of days. What a record! Come on, Liz, be in my girl group! Go on, go on, go on, go on. (Actually, you're all right, hen. I don't know what I would do with you and *that* voice.)

There's one song on that record, *I Wear Your Ring*, where you can start to make out what she's actually singing. The range of tones Liz displays on that one song is amazing. Half the time she's up in the clouds as usual, the other half she's singing with this warm, warbly, Karen Carpenter sort of a croon. It's gorgeous. She's gorgeous; I love her for it. I wear *her* ring.

I spent the weekend acclimatising to Glasgow again after being away. I had the beginnings of a cold, which has blossomed somewhat today. I was singing scabbily today at rehearsal, but it was great fun nonetheless.

We're toying with the idea of a concept LP that celebrates the lives of not only great philosophers, but great mathematicians too. The other morning, when we ought to have been playing, we spent time naming our favourite mathematicians through the ages. Among some of the more recognisable names, like Pythagoras and Fermat, Bob and Richard volunteered Johnny Ball (from BBC's *Think of a Number*) and Carol Vorderman.

Today it was the turn of the philosophers. Hegel, Kierkegaard, Descartes, Plato. We're thinking about calling the LP *Immanuel Can!* in homage to the great German moralist. I started to explain how the history of philosophy was like a river, and how the earlier philosophers weren't wrong, they were just further upstream, but it was basically the same river that we were seeing. At this point Stevie pointed out that if life was a river then we were 'up shit creek without a paddle'. That seemed a pretty good cue to pick up our instruments and do some work.

Glasgow, Scotland

We lost hopelessly at football today. I'm glad the game went ahead, though. We started at 4.30pm when the light had finally faded, meaning it was a floodlit game, with the temperature dropping down the Kelvin scale like an experiment in atmospherics. Ice formed. Legs were in danger.

The referee took me aside at the start and asked if there was a chance we might play a benefit at the Maryhill Community Halls. He pointed to the building, the old Methodist church where we played hard-fought warm-up gigs many years ago. He's the caretaker there. I told him I might have something for him in the new year. It's a beautiful hall.

I rushed to the wholefood store after and stocked up. I've been eating shit for a week on account of rushing about and being single. I suddenly felt like I needed broccoli, and I needed it bad. I drained a smoothie in the store as the fellow put through the rest of my messages [groceries].

I came home and made dinner in a rush. Simple fare, lots of new potatoes. I turned on the rest of *The Big Lebowski*. Now that is a smart, funny movie with two of the best characters ever committed to the screen in The Dude and Walter. The film totters hither and thither, but wins. You don't have to puzzle over a plot. Just embrace it.

Writing to you now implies that I'm taking my feet off the gas ever so slightly. Commitments are waning slightly. As with every end-of-year layoff can I state again my categorical commitment to making music and whatever else comes to mind? I am your servant. I am, however, your servant who does exactly what he likes and takes no notice of your opinions and desires.

I know best. I love you, but when it comes to our music you're going to have to take the rough with the smooth. You're going to have to accept the limits of our talents. You're going to have to accept that we must go forward, never back. You'd miss us if we were gone, but at the same time, you'd like us to go for a while so that you could have something to talk about. Change is good. I think we'll change.

DECEMBER 21, 2004
Glasgow, Scotland

I had a nice time last night. I went to watch Snow Patrol at the Barrowland. I drifted in, watched the crowds celebrate, felt not quite at the party and was happy to wander out into the welcoming east end. It was funny to see my football team-mates up there being lauded. I wish them all the best.

I walked a perfect arc on the map back to my house, taking in the Necropolis, Alexandra Parade, Sighthill Park, Port Dundas and the canal. It was one of those quiet nights preternaturally lit up by the moon, casting shadows of trees on frosty ground. I plotted stories and tunes, content in the knowledge that I was, with my limp, bowler hat and black leather gloves, probably the scariest thing walking that particular Glasgow night, and that I had nothing to fear.

I'm in a funny mood today though. It's kind of predictable. You get what you ask for, and find it's not quite to your taste after all. Peace to run and play footie; a clear schedule to write, to sing, to celebrate the solstice! What happens? No firm agenda arises. Your sense of achievement is zero as you mop up the tail-end of the most trivial tasks. Football takes on mounting salvationary proportions but it's cancelled after hardly anyone turns up.

Glasgow, Scotland

On the walk here the sun had just disappeared over the faraway Fereneze Hills. The university and surrounding minarets were doing their best to look like a Tony Hart composition from the 1970s.

There's still a dusting of frozen snow on the ground. Nonetheless, when the university bell struck the still evening air, and the bird twittered suddenly, the mind of an optimistic young lad looked to the spring, and the remembrance of springs past leap down the years to comfort and cajole.

I passed the Queen Margaret Union, and from the top of Hillhead I can see the view depicted, pretty much, on the back of the *Fold Your Hands* sleeve. You would have to go to the laundry on the top floor of the QM to get the exact view, because that is where Laura stood when she depicted said view. Because I sent her there with her pencil and expensive paper. Because I used to stare out at that view while waiting for the drying cycle to end.

That's one of the tasks I miss, going to the laundry. At least it's one of the tasks I think I miss when I fondly ponder the nicer moments and the reveries. The odd encounter with a revolutionary girl and her underwear, the endless letters written to the accompaniment of the spin dryers.

In reality it was probably just about twice out of all the years I did my washing there that I achieved a state of detergent bliss. It was satisfying to come away at the end of the morning with everything washed and folded, socks already paired, nothing shrunk, even the odd shirt ironed. What happens to the time now? I guess we're much busier. For all your pleading for us to come and play in your backyards, I bet there's some of you who wished we kept our 1997 work-rate up and kept hitting you with loss-making, unwieldy, four-track EPs. Please consider our sanity, though.

By 1997 or so I was increasingly embarrassed about sneaking into the union. I always wondered if I still looked enough like a student to get away with it. There was a point when I realised that perhaps I couldn't pass for an undergraduate any more. What about a post-graduate? Or a mature student? And do postgraduates still have to do their own washing, or do they have a fag to do it? Did the fagging system still exist at Glasgow University, or did it ever exist? Could I even pass for a fag?

All these matters would flit through my mind as I made my way perilously past the caretaker of the building, who was meant also to be checking your student credentials. I even composed elaborate reasons for still being there, giving myself imaginary BScs and MAs, and had complex ideas of theses to hand to satisfy the curious janitor.

What was more of a beamer was that the caretaker damn well knew me and probably knew I was not enrolled any more. He knew because I also worked in the building for years. That still didn't qualify me to use the laundry, but I had to get in there. There was nowhere else so cheap, so cosy, so ... right on! It was there that I easily composed *Marx and Engels*. I can't remember if there was a real-life subject of the song. Perhaps not. She was probably an echo of Communist Party meetings attended in rooms very close to the laundry.

Glasgow, Scotland

Today has been more organised, chilled and productive. I cleaned the kitchen, humming new kitchenesque tunes of longing, picked Ciara up and stole into the university swimming pool for a half-mile swim before dropping her home. Then I went to acupuncture. I always like seeing my acupuncture man. I am in rude health compared to this time last year, thanks to him. He's even reducing the ringing in my ears.

I spent a lot of time in the office this evening playing the piano, trying to become a better player. I don't think I'm going to have time to learn, though I really want to. I also spent quite a while trying to get Alex the German waitress a flight from Berlin. She's coming to Glasgow to try out for the little vocal ensemble I'm putting together. It's a long way to come. I'll have to make it worth her while and organise something fun.

So I took a pile of your letters to the café to try to answer them at last. Some of them are from a comically long time ago. You may be surprised to get a response. I like to send postcards out, but I just missed the vintage postcard shop. It closed, so apologies if the cards lack charisma.

Marisa's coming back from Florida tomorrow. I've got to get up early to pick her up. I hope the plane's not late, hen! I've got a football match to play. I've got to focus.

There's terrible stuff going on in the world and all I can do is write about my ordinary life, but I'm thankful for this warm flat, the bowl of soup I'm going to have and the lamp-lit sky over Glasgow. Say a little prayer for folks who are struggling tonight. I hope *you're* OK though. Night, night.

THE SCOTTISH PARLIAMENT

JANUARY II, 2005
Glasgow, Scotland

I feel sugar-shit sharp today. It must be a continued plunge into the gusset of this new year! Personally speaking, the further we march away from the festive time, the better. I love it when things get back to normal. The street clears at appropriate times, you can get a table in the café and, hey, *Another Girl, Another Planet* comes on the stereo. What could be better?

I'll tell you a couple of daft things that nearly happened to me in the last 24 hours. I nearly lost a testicle, and I nearly lost my eyelashes. I shall explain. At football today I took a terrible one in the groin. It's an occupational hazard, but it seems to happen to me rather a lot. I think it reflects upon the gung-ho way I charge into challenges. Perhaps the opposition panic and just boot the ball away as hard as they can. Unfortunately, on this occasion, I caught it full in the worst place. It sent me staggering to the dressing room, almost puking.

I can report that both patient and testicle are doing well, though I may have to pay a visit to the doctor to confirm the orientation of said nut is in fact normal.

The other daft thing was my own fault. I was enjoying a bath, and had lit candles to enhance the mood. After drying myself I sprayed my foot with an aerosol, being constantly on the alert against the dangers of athlete's foot. I thought I would extinguish the candles with a puff from the aerosol but this merely resulted in the sort of billowing flame of which an oil rig might be proud. I kept my eyelashes, you'll be glad to know; some of the hair on the back of my hands didn't fare so well. I smelt like a school chemistry lab for a while. What a knob.

So school started again today. We got off to a slightly faltering start because everyone seems to be sickly. Also, Neil is still on holiday, so as a ship we are rudderless.

We ran through a pretty easy number that I had. A nice enough tune, it jogs away chorusless for six or so verses.

"Pitch it somewhere between Richman and Springsteen!" I cried.

"Peter Buck 1982!" was the response.

Trouble is, without a chorus there was no real title jumping out. I thought if we could give the girl in the song a great name we could call the song that. So I asked everyone for their porn names. You know how that works, right? The name of your first pet coupled with your mother's maiden name. This is what I got.

"Corrie Wilkie," said Richard. Pretty good.

"Jim Jackson," said Sarah. Wrong sex.

"Timmy Graham," said Stevie.

"Jaws Stiven," said Bob.

Good, but pretty butch. Mine was Cindy Massey, a bit glamorous for the girl in the song.

"King Crimson Pay," said Mick. I don't think I could make that work. And Beans' was Brian Merit.

I might have to think again.

Glasgow, Scotland

We rehearsed today. It snowed, so everyone was late, but that was OK. We had a meeting to talk about the year ahead and all that — we need to make good on some of our wayward promises, so a plan is overdue.

I was in the bath earlier, and it occurred to me as I sat in the half-light that it's amazing Beans and me coexist happily in a band. Most of his favourite records seem to eschew lyrics and melody, and that's the direction I reckon he'd like to explore, whereas I'm all about lyrics and melody. it's merely an observation. We'll work it out. We always do.

We started working on something Bob had started, and that I'd written some words for. After a while Beans said:

"It's a bit like Parliament. The Scottish Parliament. "

"Good name for a record," said someone.

"Oh, you don't want to call a record that," said Stevie. "It would come in years late…"

"And £250 billion over budget!" added Sarah.

I went for a run last night after the snow had calmed down. I was drawn to scouting round the town while I could see everything clearly. When it snows in Glasgow and the clouds hang around, the 'sky is like a yellow balloon', as Felt once said. What with the white bowl of the Clyde Valley and the yellow sky above, everything is clearly illuminated, the street lights bouncing around with no means of escape.

I scooped up some snow in the cathedral graveyard and ate it, then jumped over the wall into Dennistoun. Suddenly, the batteries went in my legs, like the distributor going in a car. I knew I must be getting ill, so I made for the nearest train station. At Queen Street I got on the Tube, and while I was waiting I looked back up the stairs to where a girl was on her way down. It occurred to me that Marisa might be getting on the Tube some time as she was working late in Edinburgh. Then she came down the stairs just after the girl! I like it when reality and imagination merge like that. I imagined Marisa and there she was.

I cooked her dinner. Her mother would be glad to know that I'm participating in a scheme to make sure Marisa eats at least one hot meal a day. She moved into a new place and the gas isn't connected yet; four weeks and counting. That's harsh! No hot water, no cooking. Come on Mister Gasman!

I told her about the dream I had just before I went for my run. We were married and I was content with my new responsibility. I was trying to write a song, though. I can't have been paying enough attention to her. The song was *really* good. I was going to stick it on a tape when she thumped me — pow! — right on the shoulder.

She's pretty strong. The pain seemed to grow and throb the way the sound of a gong grows after you hit it. She was laughing at me but I couldn't help myself and gave her a little flick on the nose, just a prod with my mitt, but her nose bust all over the place! She went round to see Ciara. I was now a confirmed wife-beater.

Later in the dream I was organising a trip to a park above a city for my family. Most of my aunts and uncles were there, and my cousins. I was specifically accompanying my folks up the path to the inner gate of the park. There seemed to be some trouble getting through the gates. It didn't help that there were kids running about, plus I was looking after a cute but boisterous chihuahua.

The thing is, the purpose of the trip I was so busily organising was a termination of sorts. My folks, about half of my uncles, aunts and cousins and I were going to die. I was OK about it, simply trying to get everybody there in good order and on time.

My dad was last to the gate with his stick because he moves pretty slowly these days. What with me getting tangled up in the dog lead, greeting relatives and trying to get some people through the gate, the situation became rather fraught. I looked back at my mum, who was trying to get through the gate, and could see she was upset. I rarely see my mum upset, so it pulled me up. It was only then that the gravity of the moment struck me. Even though we were both very likely going to the same place, it felt like a parting of a kind. It still felt like the time to tell someone you would miss them very much, and how much they meant to you. I went to give my mum a hug.

When I woke up I was sad. Luckily, my dad phoned soon after and I spoke to both him and Mum. I didn't tell them about the dream, but it was nice to speak to them. I suppose I take my mum for granted sometimes. She's usually so together. I should spend more time with the pair of them. That's what the dream was probably telling me.

JANUARY 19, 2005
Glasgow, Scotland

I'm glad I got up early this morning. It afforded me a few Billy Liar-ish glances at alternative life paths. I went to the university chapel this morning for the short service. As the pastor spoke, I imagined I was rector of the whole place. I imagined the pastor greeting me warmly, perhaps taking me aside to discuss a small matter of business I should attend to.

Then I imagined retiring to my office in some quiet corner of the quadrangles, where my secretary would inform me of urgent business as I swept past the line of young men and women waiting for me, clutching papers, petitions, causes close to their hearts. I would attend to them as soon as someone handed me a strong americano and I had scanned the latest copy of *Rector Today*.

As I left the chapel, my mind took on another flight of fancy—I was back at university as a physics undergraduate. At the time I was passing the old physics building, where I would attend a lecture every day at 9am. It's a vast old lecture theatre, curving upwards in a perfect parabola so that the pleb might get the best vantage point from which to examine the maestro, his scribblings and explosions.

I was alive to the glories of Faraday and Newton; the aura of Lord Kelvin was palpable in this varnished woody chamber. Equations jumped around, but I found I also spoke the language of the equation, that these complex sentences of maths that the lecturer said to me were perfectly comprehensible. In fact they were as sweet to me as hearing an unheard hour-long Smiths' opus, or a poem by Coleridge when you're in the mood.

The subject I actually studied at university was chemical physics, or physical chemistry—I can't quite remember which. I didn't get to specialise in this topic as I never made the third year. It amused me, then, the other day to be having a conversation with someone where the phrase 'physical chemistry' popped up a couple of times. We were avoiding the whole area of chemistry at the time, and physics. Ironically we were closer to the subject of biology…

Imagine waking from your gloomy sleep to be ushered into a vestibule only to be entertained by someone drawing a map of the universe for you, someone explaining with chalk the unarguable laws by which we live. The secret forces to which we are all slaves. The possibilities of life beyond these physical plains. The hidden beauty held in an arc of white light. No moral grey

234

areas. No low human examples. Pure unadulterated science.

That's the reasoning that led me to the lecture room in the first place. The reality was very different. It was work, work, work in isolation. It was not understanding at all that drove the lab-coated colleagues around me. They all seemed at home there. They all spoke the language. I had hoped they would speak the language of dreams. I should have stayed in bed.

JANUARY 25, 2005
Glasgow, Scotland

I've just left church, where we had a meeting about upcoming evening services. I love being in the church in the evening, even for a meeting. I felt better as soon as the minister asked us to close our eyes for a short prayer before we began. It felt good.

I'm not at my best. I can't seem to shake off this cold and feel drained. I met a girl on the bridge last night who told me that yesterday was statistically the most depressing day of the year. She looked a bit depressed. I wanted to cheer her up, but I had nothing in my arsenal.

I thought about what she said. I usually have no truck with generalisations such as the above, but I did consider that I had felt rubbish when I got up, and that I was going to meet another friend who felt so rubbish that she couldn't even tell me what she felt rubbish about over the phone.

As I arrived outside the supermarket late, she thrust a small dog into my arms and ran into the store on a mission. I stood with said dog, not knowing whether to make a fuss of it, stare into the middle distance or watch people as they came and went, thereby running the risk of dog-appreciation interaction. I took to strolling up and down in front of the shop, but still managed to attract the attention of chatty well-wishers. At least nobody

235

threw anything, least of all a barbed comment. It wasn't until afterwards that I realised how I might have deserved it — I was wearing a tall fedora in the style of Chamberlain, black leather gloves, and black throughout in fact, apart from a Royal Stewart tartan muffler. Skeeter the chihuahua — for it was he — was resplendent in a Royal Stewart tartan jacket. It must have looked like an elaborate pick-up ruse on my part.

Thankfully, the friend wasn't in the shop for too long, and she heaped further woe on to what was becoming an inauspicious day. No matter, I can take it. What are friends for?

She remarked that her preacher had told her something that had stuck with her. He'd said that at times when we are at our worst — the sad times, the bleak times — God is closest to us, and shouldn't that be some sort of comfort in our sadness?

I've been thinking about this since last night. I looked back at some of my saddest times; I saw them happily now like scenes in a film, and I saw the palpable spirit of God propping me up from all corners. He saved me from dropping into the abyss. He saved my life. He must have thought it was worth saving. One reason I'm glad he saved my life is that I wouldn't have met all the people in my church.

I would never have imagined, back in the worst of times, the scene that was played out tonight. Me at the church meeting. We were sitting in a circle in the small chapel to the side of the church. One of the ladies, Janet, was late arriving. She has difficulty walking, so everyone shuffles round the circle to let her get a seat on the near side of the circle. Since there was now a full attendance, I found myself moving right up next to where the minister was sitting.

Jesus told a parable which I was reminded of as I sat there.

"When someone invites you to a wedding feast, do not take the place of honour, for a person more distinguished than you may have been invited. If so, the host who invited both of you will come and say to you, 'Give this man your seat.' Then, humiliated, you will have to take the least important place. But when you are invited, take the lowest place, so that when your host comes, he will say to you, 'Friend, move up to a better place.' Then you will be honoured in the presence of all your fellow guests. For everyone who exalts himself will be humbled, and he who humbles himself will be exalted."

Luke 14:7-11

It was an honour to be sitting there, even though we were just meeting for a blether.

As they talked and I listened, I had a look into the far, dark corners of the church to see if I could see any spirits fooling about, or any ghosts or manifestations. I didn't see any. Our sanctuary is a wonderful place, though, and I almost wouldn't mind seeing something, although it would scare the shit out of me, especially if I was there alone.

After the meeting I walked up the street for a short distance with one of the ladies until she went in a different direction. I carried on on my own under the low sky and the bare limes. I put The Clash on my headphones. Memo to self; to band; to Richard: must try to get the drums to sound more like those on *Death or Glory*. What a song, what a sound!

Glasgow, Scotland

I got up, wheezing badly from not enough sleep. This chest thing is digging in again. My Chinese man is doing everything he can to dig me out, but it might take time. Maybe that's why Neil sent me off to California.

I swear I don't know how it happened. When I went into the office this morning I was full of good intent, with a list of things battering my mental inbox. I kept switching subjects mid-conversation. I wasn't making much sense. I was talking about the record, artwork, accounts, my lecturing debut, a.n. other musical project, and how I was going to split my time up and be good and conscientious. I guess I was coughing quite a lot. Neil said:

"I think you should go to San Francisco."

And I said: "Yes, I think you're right."

So I'll be there on Saturday. Look out for me. I won't have my bucket and spade, but I will have a frisbee that says Haight-Ashbury on it. Maybe we could have a game of football while I'm there, or throw a frisbee around? Watch out for me in Golden Gate Park near the glasshouses.

It was a curious thing for Neil to suggest. He knows I'm broke, what with buying my flat and paying my tax. It's perverse of him to suggest I spend my last pounds on a trip. So perverse it couldn't be ignored.

Whoa! Cancel all operations—I'm sick. I guess my cute little cough virus got smart. He now has my whole body to ransom. I'm not going anywhere (I'm not holding anything in!). Normal service will hopefully be resumed after a few days of California Dreaming.

Glasgow, Scotland

I'm still hacking away with the cough so I haven't been singing.
I've got a nice tune in my head but I can't get near writing it
because I can't sing it. I feel like a mute trying to make himself
understood.

I's a curious way to work. I never used to be like that. I guess
it's being around the group for so long. My audio visualisation,
if you'll pardon the contradiction in terms, has become primed
to the extent that I can enjoy a song almost as if I was listening
to it from my Walkman, before it has been played or sung out
loud.

The method lends itself to a certain kind of a tune. A wispy
kind, a jamming kind rather than a folky one. For a band perceived as being folky in the past, there are scant few folk tunes
coming our way. Stevie is most inclined to lead with a folk bent,
but that's because he tends to write with his acoustic. He plays
well too; his pieces are often stylistically fully formed when he
brings them to the group.

So I've got this tune, a Big Star kind of thing. A bit boogie-
ish. But then I had the notion that we might strip it back with
the discipline of New Order-type drums and choppy guitar.
Then it might become something you could dance to, because
that's important. We want to take you from your bed to the
dancefloor. If there was a 10-year plan for the original fan it was
to take you from your bedroom to the dancefloor, no question.
But as with most 10-year plans you won't find much mention
of it at the outset.

So Marisa came round for tea. I made a stir-fry with sea vegetables. It smelt a bit like Ardrossan Beach. I was looking for
something to put on while I was cooking. I put on Lambchop

but took it off and put on a mix tape one of you sent me. A good thing no doubt, until we realised with a shock that it was Christian rock. Then we took it off in a hurry, like shit off a shovel.

"Listen to this," I said, holding up another tape. "Some guy made a programme for Radio 4. He sent me a recording. He said he used a lot of our music. I wonder what the show was about."

I put it on. The intro to *Expectations* played underneath a man's voice. He was summarising the topic of the documentary, the story of a kid who is disabled and having a hell of a time managing at school.

"Oh, it's about some disabled kid. How could I have guessed?"

"That *Pumpkin* film was about disability as well."

"Yeah, and the kid at the start of *Storytelling*."

"Well, they're hardly going to use AC/DC."

"Why not? I'd use AC/DC. Disabled dudes listen to AC/DC."

"I suppose. It's just that disabled dudes' documentarians listen to Belle and Sebastian."

"It's true."

I guess I should be happy. I like Radio 4 and wish they would have us on. You know you've reached the top of your field when you're asked to talk about it on Radio 4.

They have a long-running programme called *Desert Island Discs*. In Britain it has become a saying for things you would take if you were cast away on your own. It's the ultimate top 10, if you like, though the guests only pick their favourite eight songs.

It usually makes for great listening because you get to hear about the life of this person you've often never heard of. It's as celebrity as Radio 4 gets. The guest could be a civil servant, an explorer, someone who has served the country well and long. It's the radio broadcasting equivalent of a knighthood. They wheel them in, the guest and presenter gas away for half an hour and in between they play about 20 minutes of music (they edit the choices).

Most of the selections seem to be classical — Mozart, Beethoven, Schubert, Wagner. Gilbert and Sullivan is sometimes as pop as it gets. It must be said, though: the guests seldom lead dull lives. It's the perfect programme to listen to in the bath.

To be fair, the guests are getting younger and funkier, so you get a collection of classic rock, or contemporary folk, or whatever. Back in the 1980s I used to fantasise about what my eight choices would be. I don't know if I'd choose the same eight now, but I had these eight for so long. I thought about sewing them into the lining of my underpants in case I got run over and they could broadcast them posthumously.

The Smiths – *Reel Around the Fountain*
Wire – *Outdoor Miner*
Felt – *Riding on the Equator*
Young Marble Giants – *Final Day*
The Pop Group – *Savage Sea*
The Mekons – *Ghosts of American Astronauts*
The Left Banke – *Something on My Mind*
The Lovin' Spoonful – *Do You Believe in Magic?*

I like to think they take you to a secluded London club at lunchtime and get you pissed to open you up a bit. Then they push 'record'. They wouldn't have to get me pissed to get me to talk — I'd spew my guts all over the microphone.

A perfect place to talk is in the crow's nest, the alcove I fashioned in the window of my front room. It's like a crow's nest

241

because it seems perched on top of the good ship Glasgow. I've been spending quite a lot of time there this week; talking to friends and watching the sun go down over the spires of the university. The sunsets have been excelling themselves. I have never seen any quite so beautiful, but then maybe I never had so comfortable a perspective.

I had some of the choir over the other day. The youth faction in the choir, minus Max. That was Andrew, Andrea and Andrea. Sometimes we go for lunch after church, but this time we grabbed stuff out of the supermarket and went up to mine. As we drifted along Byres Road I heard someone call my name. It was my brother-in-law, George. He had just pulled up in a car with my sister and their three children. It was a nice surprise. They live out of town and I don't see them much. They were going for pizza but I was committed with the Sunday gang, so we rambled on up to the crow's nest. We ate cheese and salad and bread and hot-cross buns, and looked out to the far horizon where the wind turbines stood still again in the benign January becalming.

I got fed up staring at them yesterday. I still felt shaky on account of the bug and I didn't have a car, but I didn't feel like heading into the office and dealing with stuff. So I inflated my bicycle tyres and took to the road. I wanted to stand under those turbines, man, as the sun flashed around me and those blades sucked me off the ground. I got the train across the city, got off and started my journey in the direction I thought they lay in.

I couldn't see the turbines as I was in a dip compared to the view from the crow's nest; therefore I could only guess. I navigated tiny roads on Glasgow's southern boundaries but never found the turbines. I'm glad, though: they still possess the same allure.

I'm messing with your attention today, I know. This is the Grateful Dead of entries, like a 17-minute guitar solo in the middle of a song.

MARCH 14, 2005
Glasgow, Scotland

It was Bob's birthday today. It was just a regular practice day—we got together and started playing at 11am. I was up early, though, the sun having woken me at 7am. I drifted off listening to Felt for a while, then thought I might as well get up and see what was going on down at the chapel. They have a morning service, and if I shifted my butt I could make it down on time.

I shifted my butt and I made it down on time. The reading was from John. It was about a seed having to die before it becomes a plant.

> "Very truly, I tell you, unless a grain of wheat falls into the earth and dies, it remains just a single grain; but if it dies, it bears much fruit. Those who love their life lose it, and those who hate their life in this world will keep it for eternal life. Whoever serves me must follow me, and where I am, there will my servant be also. Whoever serves me, the Father will honour."
>
> John 12:24-32

I skipped out of there and listlessly down to the coffee shop to kill time before practice, forcing myself to deal with a few matters of business by email. Then I set out for the office. I was going to catch the bus, but I followed the river instead, through the park and into the office. The atmosphere was pure post-weekend. Subdued. Katrina was the only one there, exercising her eyeballs over the computer screen. I was the first of the band to arrive by quite some distance.

We got to work pretty fast, recapping a couple of songs we were working on last week.

"That's not quite the sound I had in my head," I said at one point.

"What do you have in your head?" said Stevie.

Pause.

"Oh, you don't want to know," I said.

"It's a load of women running about in bras, isn't it?" said someone. It might have been Beans.

"Thanks a lot. Thanks for that. Now all I can think of is *Carry on Camping*."

We continued successfully until luncheon was called. We decided to go out because it was Bob's birthday. Andy had turned up with the mock-up of the *Push Barman* booklet, so he came too.

After a civilised lunch we carried on with a song called *You're a White Collar Boy*. It's the story of a boy who falls slightly on the wrong side of the law. He gets caught fiddling the books where he works. He needs the extra cash to try to keep up with the lifestyle of his friends, but instead he lands up in court. He narrowly avoids going to prison, the judge handing him a fine and community service instead. The following weekend he reports to the city docks for some manual labour. They lock him up for the day and chain him by the ankle! Even more unlikely, they lock him up to a girl who's doing her service as well.

They are banging away at some rocks for a while when she says to him:

"I got to get out of here!"

"What do you mean? Where you going to go?"

"I've got to get away. I've got a date later on. I hate my Saturday getting wasted like this."

"Well, just go and ask the guard! I'm sure he'll order you a cab!"

"I mean it, I'm getting away."

"Don't be stupid. We're not in prison. They'll let us go home at the end of the day!"

"I don't care. I can't stand this. Are you coming?"

"No!" he says, with an incredulous chuckle.

Just then, before he can do much about it, the girl lifts her mallet and neatly brings it down on the head of the guard who had his back to them.

"What the hell d'ya do that for?"

But he doesn't get more time to moan. The girl grabs his arm, takes a step towards the edge of the dock, then jumps, taking the boy with her. She knew what she was doing. There was a barge passing by.

We got to the point where they are floating down river on top of the barge. We can't get it sounding the way it was sounding the other day, so we left it and did something else.

I've got this other little tune in my head that I showed the rest of them. It doesn't have any words. We chucked it around for a while. I like it; I'm just singing 'la' like a jazz singer scatting. So much for my theory about the words coming first, or at least arriving at the same time as a tune. (That's what I was claiming in a talk I gave a few weeks back.)

These days we often end up playing almost a whole tune before an intelligible word is uttered. You should hear Stevie sometimes — it's the singing equivalent of speaking in tongues. "Today I'm a Mexican bandit, and this is the song I'm singing to rouse my compadres." Then he raises his voice and sings in a nonsensical Spanish sounding vernacular.

MARCH 15, 2005
Glasgow, Scotland

I'm still pondering what the group said about what was going on in my head yesterday. I protest! I think that's quite a poor opinion, but then people will think what they think and nothing will stop them.

I think of a lot of things, though. As I got into the café this morning, I blew my nose and thought of Antoine Doinel, Truffaut's most famous character. He wouldn't blow his nose on paper. I will blow my nose on paper, but for once, this damp morning, I remembered a handkerchief, so I luxuriate in the cotton/nasal clash and think of Antoine.

I'm thinking about a funny incident that just happened. It was like a *Father Ted* episode, the one in which Mrs Doyle and her friend get into a fight about who should pay for the tea in the tearoom. They both insist on paying, to the point where they get in an all-out scrap and the police are called.

My episode was better natured. A woman stopped me and asked if I had change for the parking meter. She was holding a £5 note.

"I don't think I've got change for a fiver," I said as I searched in my bag. I pulled out a £1 coin and a £2 coin.

"How long are you going to be here?" I asked.

"Well, she's got an interview," said the woman, pointing to her daughter in the car.

"Just take this, then," I said, offering her the pound, which would pay for three hours' parking.

"Oh no, I couldn't. Give me the two pounds and you can take this," she said, offering me the fiver.

"No, just take the pound, really!"

This went on for quite some time.

"Take the fiver, and have a drink on me," said the woman.

Eventually I said, "Look, I'm putting it here!" and put the coin on the ground and ran off.

OK, I've got to drag my weary ass down to the studio. Yesterday it felt very much like a school day.

"Oh no, I've got science and maths this afternoon," I said to Stevie.

"That's my worst afternoon. A total nightmare."

"No — wait, I was wrong. Double music! Yes!"

"What about PE? It looks like we could all do with some exercise," said Beans.

"In that case I'll be seeing you," said Bob. "I'm going to nick home to watch Stones videos."

"And I'll be doing a lot of walking about aimlessly followed by a spot of smoking later on," said Richard. He wasn't kidding. I think that pretty much summed up his schooling. He probably got up to a lot of other stuff that he's not really letting on about.

Man, that's my trouble. I can't tell whether I ought to be a schoolteacher or one of the pupils. Some of the teachers I know are comically messed up — I don't know how they manage to pull it together and teach anybody anything. Some of them are good, though. You can tell they're teachers you wished you had had yourself. A friend who was a teacher asked me if I would be interviewed by two of his pupils for his school magazine. It was funny to hear them calling him 'Mr So and So' and 'Sir', but you could tell they liked him. And you could tell he didn't take any shit.

It was funny to think of teachers as human beings when you were at school. It was something I didn't do often. The teachers probably didn't like to encourage it, because it would necessarily expose a weak spot in their armour.

I'm reminded of one episode I'm not particularly proud of. There was one teacher who was pupil fodder to such an extent that even the tough nuts had given up taunting her. She was too soft. She sent me on an errand once, but for some reason I thought it would be funny to attract my classmates' attention by throwing stones at the window while I was outside. Although I didn't break anything it was still a stupid thing to do. When I got back to the classroom she pulled me up for it, keeping me back afterwards.

She was quite young, still a 'Miss', but she had the demeanour of someone defeated, someone old before their time. A classic spinster, I suppose. She shared a surname with the subject of a famous pop song with a character in the title, so she became known by that name. That was lucky, because much crueller nicknames were handed out randomly to much tougher teachers.

She sat on the desk and asked me what I thought I had been doing with the stones.

"Sorry, it was stupid," I said.

"Yes. I expect more from you, Stuart. You're smart; what's the problem?"

Silence.

"What do you want to do when you leave school?"

"Oh, I don't know. I don't think about it too much. I suppose I'll try to go to college."

Pause.

"Maybe I'll be a teacher. Is it a good job?"

"Hmph! Don't be a teacher. Never be a teacher. It's not a great life."

As she said this, she was looking round as if she was going to get caught, as if she was speaking out against a dictator, and the dictator happened to be teaching in the classroom next door.

"Why's it so bad?"

"Well…"

At that point I could tell she would have to tell me something about herself. I think then she realised it would be pointless telling a 14-year-old boy anything. I still wonder about her, though. Did she ever get a break, meet a man, get married? I can't imagine she'd ever want to have children. Brats like me probably killed the urge.

MARCH 23, 2005
Glasgow, Scotland

You know what I'm currently really into? Tea. Infusions, to be accurate. I'm having a camomile now; it's so fitting and civilised for this late hour.

My favourite infusion is Yogi Tea, specifically Himalaya Sweet Harmony Ayurvedic blend. I can't leave the house without slipping one of the bags into my back pocket in case of emergency. They do one called Nursing Mom which I nearly tried once, but stopped short in case I started lactating again. Always a bit embarrassing that, eh lads?

Decaf Earl Grey is a bit of a winner too. And the best black tea blend goes to … Yorkshire Tea. Available in UK supermarkets.

I was going to talk about my favourite hymns too. One of you asked me about that a while back and it set me thinking. I've got so many favourites. It's late, though. I shouldn't even be writing this. There's so much to tell you that I don't know where to begin, so I'm not going to. Instead I'll tell you this vital piece of information. It's VERY IMPORTANT.

If you have an enquiring mind and find yourself with a spare 45 minutes, go to Radio 4's *In Our Time* archive, find the programme called *Alchemy* and listen to Melvyn Bragg and guests exploring dark energy.

Man, that's the most head-splitting radio programme I've ever heard. I must warn you, though, it's three boffins talking about the latest ideas in cosmology and physics. What a trip though! 'Quintessence' indeed.

MAY 10, 2005
Glasgow, Scotland

I'm sitting here on a spring evening playing *When Love Breaks Down* by Prefab Sprout on repeat, although I don't particularly have love at the moment, and if I did I would see no reason why it should break down.

The windows are open and one bird is singing the theme music to *Tom and Jerry*. Just the one bird though. It makes me a little sad to think the cartoon made such an impression on the youngster that he took it with him into adulthood at the expense of grown-up conversation. I bet he doesn't have a girl-friend.

I had a simple dinner, thrown together. I like simple dinners thrown together, dinners that take no longer than a quick run through *Life in a Northern Town* or *Someone, Somewhere in Summertime*, and there you are, ready with an open copy of *Optic Nerve* comic and the radio switched to *Front Row* on Radio 4.

I can read and listen to the radio at the same time because *Front Row* reviews books, plays and music, and I can tune out anything I'm not interested in. While I was tidying up after dinner they had a piece about Chas and Dave, which did grab my attention. They were two blokes from east London who played traditional pub-type music and became popular in the 1970s and 1980s with their witty lyrics.

My position in the kitchen is perfect, but does not last long. The guy in the flat opposite starts blasting rock music. That seems to be the rule in the city. When you have a perfect moment, you only have to consider it perfect and it will be spoiled soon enough. Oh yes. But then I choose to live in the city.

Marisa calls for the third time in half an hour about some detail or other and I'm short with her on account of the fact the rock dude has ruined my perfect moment. I move that bad karma on like an Ultimate Frisbee.

I have my cinnamon tea here courtesy of the Yogi Tea company. They must have read about my affection for their product and sent a box of tea today, a big box that a child could hide in. I drowned myself in the stuff.

Be careful not to call it chai tea, though. Last time I did that, Bemused of Linlithgow wrote to say that 'chai was tea' and that in essence I had written about drinking a cup of 'tea tea' and 'didn't I think that was a bit silly?'.

When I came in from football today I had an altercation with a pineapple, and the pineapple came off worse. Ever since hearing a Radio 4 broadcast on the subject of pineapples and the high esteem in which they were held, particularly in Victorian society, the Murdoch household has never been without one. Marisa brought this particular one here yesterday. I ruthlessly stripped it and prepared it yesterday while pirouetting round my kitchen on the soles of my sandals. Little did I know how desirable those cooled and sealed chunks would seem after two hours of slog on an artificial surface.

I devoured the whole thing without a break, my stomach distended like a snake after snacking on whole armadillo. It was like the magic Turkish Delight the Witch gave Edmund in Narnia, though less wicked. I think it ranks as my favourite meal ever. One pineapple!

I'm glad to talk to you. I have been a little fraught of late, but it's good to have the energy to tell you my troubles and trivialities. I've been wrestling with a suite of a song called *The Act of the Apostle*. In fact the whole band have been. It's very good of them to have the patience.

At the minute it seems to me the most beautiful of possibilities, but I don't know where to take it. My trouble is that the girl to whom the slight adventure happens, the apostle in question, is young. She bunks off school and is lured to the city for the day. But she's too much of an innocent to have the kind of things happen to her that my normal array of wasters let themselves in for. It's weird. In the first verse she's a child, scared about her mother being sick, and by the end she's a young woman travelling through the city to find someone who she thinks can help her. I guess I'll finish it soon enough. It's almost like I don't want to because it is a treat to sing.

I've moved back to the kitchen now that things have settled down a little on the rock front. Marisa and Padraig are in the front room, setting up cameras and things. Marisa has taken it upon herself to make a documentary about the girl group project, and she's interviewing me about it. I might interview Padraig about it after that and then we'll both interview Marisa. Then maybe we can get some money so we can turn the idea into a concept.

I'm probably better back in the kitchen. I can still see Jupiter from here, just. Plus, in the front room I spend my time gazing out over the rooftops and get nothing done. I was speaking to a girl called Sally the other night, and she thinks she can see my house from her balcony.

"Oh God, I better be careful, I'm always walking about in the scud in front of the window," I said.

"Don't worry about it," she replied. "My neighbours have seen my baps about 15 times. I'm always sunbathing on my balcony."

So I've been on constant bap patrol since last Thursday. It was election night, as it happened. Not much changed. Blair got in with a reduced majority. At least that Tory wank Michael Howard didn't get in. A wank's always a waste of a good election.

JUNE 2, 2005
Glasgow, Scotland

I'm sitting in the herb border in the park near my flat. The wind's blowing from the south and the sun's nearly out, which is a rarity. I came by an overgrown path that led by the river, soothed by the green above and on all sides.

In the breeze the ash tree above sends the occasional tear down to the annoyance of my computer keyboard. Still not quite out, the ash tree is the last of the common deciduous trees to throw its lot in with the summer (apart from the misplaced plane tree). I think I've got something in common with the ash. It's not fooled by April sunbursts or May Day celebrations. It waits until the mercury hits 16°C before it makes its moves. Less than that and it's not interested.

It's ashes that hang near my back window at the house. I recently defended them at a residents' meeting. I had sat for a couple of hours saying absolutely, resolutely nothing. The talk circled around the matters of roof maintenance and Victorian plumbing.

I had sat through the previous meeting without opening my

trap either. I was fascinated to see my new neighbours in action. They were like a team of superheroes. Every household seemed to have sent a representative with a secret power, amazingly apposite for attendance at a testy meeting with contractors and architects.

Among the ranks were a journalist, a property developer, a financial advisor and a lawyer, each speaking up when their expertise was called on. It was like the bridge of the USS Enterprise, with Captain Kirk calling on them one by one. Sort of.

At one point someone suggested the trees at the back of the tenement were threatening the building, or at least becoming a nuisance. I had come to think of the tree at the back as a brother of sorts, even in a short space of time. I said:

"Ash trees often grow near buildings but they never pose much of a threat. They hardly ever fall down, especially with the shelter the building gives from the prevailing wind."

It felt odd to hear my voice after sitting there mute for so long. It seemed to come from someone else. It took a few moments for voice and brain to become aligned, like eyes that have long drifted off into space. The others must have felt the same way because they seemed to have difficulty ascertaining where the voice had come from.

I was winging it. I'm no expert, but because I had waited until then to speak, the initial assumption must have been that I was some kind of tree specialist. Nature Boy, they must have thought. It worked though, because someone said:

"Ah."

And then we moved on. So I found my place in the gang.

Tonight I came back in from football and thought I'd go out again and walk around so I could think about music and pictures. As usual I was dehydrated and headed for the pineapple juice. The trouble was that while I was drinking it straight from the fridge I had the distinct feeling that I was turning into part-pineapple. I have been leaning rather heavily on that particular fruit. You are what you eat, and I'm part-pineapple.

It started to rain when I stepped out, so I took my big, black umbrella. I never mind the inconvenience of holding it above my head; in fact it gives me an excuse to be out walking at that time, when often the only people you see are late-night stragglers walking dogs. If I needed any extra context for my walk it would be that I was taking my umbrella out for a walk. The thing is, if I bumped into someone I knew and they asked me where I was going, and I said I was taking my umbrella out for a walk, they would take me for a smart-arse and probably wouldn't be friends with me any more. The moral of the story is that in some situations it's better to keep your trap shut.

I walked around with the rain coming down heavily. Again, I never mind this as long as it's coming straight down. In fact, it feels like a godly embrace, so it's to be encouraged. I share in the warmth of yellow windows from under the soft canopy of my umbrella. And that's when the early summer blooms send out their finest smells.

THE CHEERLEADER'S HOMEWORK

Glasgow, Scotland

Another Sunday night, another bath night. It's a curious time, this. We're about to go off and make our next record but it has been slightly delayed, and the hiatus has led to some curious behaviour and feelings.

Recently, for example, I've taken pleasure in moving really slowly, not rushing to get out of the house. You often find that by doing nothing much in particular you achieve more, and get greater enjoyment from it to boot.

I'll describe the other morning. It was a Saturday, when I try to nurture the Saturday feeling by going slowly anyway. I thought about going for a long bike ride, visiting my folks in Ayr, getting hold of Stevie and busking down Ashton Lane (I went so far as to phone him but he wasn't answering), going to the practice room and playing the piano.

In the end I closed the kitchen blind and watched the 1979 FA Cup Final on my laptop. I mean, what a waste of time, but I did enjoy it. I'll give you a bit of context.

I've joined a film library called Lovefilm. It's like Netflix in the States. They send you films in the post, you watch them and send them back, then they send you more. I like it. I'll probably exhaust what I'd like to see fairly quickly, but I like it for now.

I was reading *Fever Pitch* by Nick Hornby again. It's terrific; my favourite book of his. It's not to be dabbled with, however, unless you're into football, or at least have a passing understanding of the obsessive possibilities of following a sports team.

In the book there are certain key matches described that were formative to the young Hornby's character. One of them occurs in 1979 when he finally gets to see his team, Arsenal, win the FA Cup against the mighty Manchester United.

So I rented the match from Lovefilm and watched it while the current Arsenal team were playing the current Manchester United team. I was more interested in the 1979 game. I knew pretty much all the players too — it's funny what you pick up when you're a child. I think it helped that there were so many Scots in the big English teams in those days.

All I wanted to see were the goals Hornby describes in the book, but I ended up watching almost the whole match. It was fascinating to compare the pace and the look of the game to the pace and the style of the game today. I'm not going to go into it, though, for fear that I might bore you. I fear that already. But then at least you have an idea of what we are dealing with here.

I've a good mind to ask what you do, or what have you found yourself doing in those drifting hours, those times that you finally have free to yourself. Or they might be times you'd rather not have free, and you find yourself filling them in the most ludicrous and wasteful and annoying ways; times where you might actually end up saying to yourself: 'What the hell am I doing? How did I get here?'

OK, do it. Send them in. I haven't set homework for you for a while. And it's Sunday night, so it's time you were thinking about school or work tomorrow anyway. Send me a short description of a lost morning, a wasted afternoon, a blissful pocket of escapism, or a lunatic show of extreme sloth!

JUNE 7, 2005
Glasgow, Scotland

Sometimes it comes down to something as simple as loving the day and hating the night. I want the day to go on and on, never wanting to go to bed. I don't know why — it's not all bad. The light in the sky always remains, dipping down to a deep purple at 1am then returning two hours later. It makes me want to cycle around, looking for action, but I think other people have better things to do.

Some people might ask why I am resisting growing up. 'You're like a big kid,' says my mum, and she's right. My brother and sister have three children apiece. My folks know they won't see any more grandchildren from me in the near future, but they're cool about it. It's stupid, but I feel like I'm married to the band, and that the people who listen to our records, the people who come to our shows ... well, if pushed, I would admit I feel like a *collective guardian* of sorts. Can I be your guardian?

I do love our group. Everyone has substantial relationships outside it, especially these days. It goes without saying — nearly all of us are in our thirties. I'm perhaps the only one who doesn't.

A few days ago we had a practice, very much at the tail-end of our long writing/arranging sessions. I don't know about the rest of the group, but I'm a bit fatigued by it. We're like boxers.

Songwriting boxers. We're in the 10th round, leaning against each other to stop ourselves falling over.

In the middle of the contest, Stevie, Sarah and me were flipping harmonies around while the others looked on. Sarah is usually the guide on these occasions since her ear for harmonies is probably the best, and her memory for parts and visualisation is certainly the best. Stevie challenged her on something:

"Are you not singing my part?"

"No, you changed your part halfway through," said Sarah.

Stevie thought for a moment.

"Ah, yes. I see. Sorry about that. Yes, let's try it again."

Everyone was tired, and you know how easy it is to get narked when someone points out where you're going wrong, especially when you're tired. As usual, the politeness of Stevie's response was immaculate, and it led me to say aloud what I was thinking.

"You know, if you weren't all so polite, we probably would have split up years ago," I said. "Manners maketh the man, as my old Latin teacher used to say."

"Manners maketh the band," said someone.

"Write that down," said Stevie, so I did.

I read some of your responses to my request for a short description of a lost morning, a wasted afternoon etc. Here are a few excerpts from the first batch. Apologies if that's all I end up posting, but I shall certainly read the rest.

I would skip my classes, walk to the other side of town and look for somewhere to do some contemplation, like a park bench or a football field. The bus is a good place for it. It's like a house on wheels. All it needs is a recliner and a discussion group.

David

I've found myself wasting many mornings before work enjoying doing nothing more than dreaming up stories and business ventures, watching my cats go about their business of napping, bird hunting and sunbathing while I get ready and clean up.

Talia

Last night I declined the invitation to go out because I was too tired to move, but after 30 minutes of lying on the couch I noticed a stack of photos waiting to be put into an album. Next thing I knew the sky began to clear. It was 5 am! I lost my sleep time, and my bum was sore from sitting on hardwood floors all night.

AF

Getting out of the house for walks feels like you are being painted on an urban canvas. You've got train tracks, ugly houses, parking lots and strip malls, and you're painted in the background like Mary Magdalene in the shadows of a religious painting.

David

JUNE 10, 2005
Glasgow, Scotland

I'm buzzing after a fantastic day. I had to get out of the house because there are workmen putting a new roof on the building and it's driving me nuts, so I got up early and took my bike to the train station. I caught the train to the sea, and then the ferry across the sea to the island of Bute.

I was feeling uncertain about it all until I got on the boat. When you feel the tender embrace of the Caledonian MacBrayne ferry company, you know you are home. I think I even dozed off in the downstairs lounge for a while.

It was still pretty early when I arrived in Rothesay, the main town on the island. I cycled out of town to the north, my plan being to catch another ferry to the still more magical land of the Cowal Peninsula. There was a light headwind but it was nice to have the water beside me and to smell the heather and ferns. The highland air in June is a meal in itself.

I nipped over to Colintraive on the short ferry crossing and almost immediately I was cycling through some of the nicest scenery I've ever seen. I think my feelings were heightened by the fact I'd just set out from Glasgow by bike that morning, and now I was in the wilderness, where the wild rhododendrons fight each other for supremacy. I took great pleasure in stopping at burns to drink the fresh water.

My idea of heaven is a deserted country road on a balmy day, sitting up, no hands on the bike, drifting through the greenery and glens with the gradient in my favour. Thoughts turn to songs and other nice things. I can't imagine such peace anywhere else. I think it's my new drug. Scotland in summer. It's a pity you have to wait so long for it to happen.

There was quite a pull over the hills to Dunoon. Some of the descents were a little hairy. I tried not to touch the brakes, but you couldn't tell where some of the twists were going to take you. As the road flattened out and it grew warmer, I considered the Calippo. I pondered allowing myself to be sponsored by the company that makes Calippos. (They are long cones of flavoured ice, by the way.) I wondered whether it would care to make a healthy option, like a frozen pineapple on a stick. All this was mounting in my mind; my mouth was like the Gobi Desert.

I drifted along the coast road to Dunoon and was reminded that the last time I was here was when Sarah, Stevie and I took a day out of recording *The Boy with the Arab Strap* to go and look at a vintage car holed up in someone's garage. It was a Rover

P6, my favourite boyhood car, but this particular one was in really bad shape so it was a fruitless adventure. I needed to get out, though. The LP wasn't going well at that point. I think I left Tony to mix something. It happened to be Beans' birthday, I think. When we eventually got back, work had long been abandoned and the boys had given in to the attraction of absinthe, which was the new buzz drink. Beans was hallucinating and Tony, I think, was in his underwear. You'll have to ask them for more details; my recollection is hazy.

If this was a nadir for the group, a couple of miles round the bay I came to a spot that hosted one of the peaks: the Queen's Hall in Dunoon. It was the start of everything that went right for us. That Scottish tour in June 2001 was when everything fell into place.

So I hung out, had my strawberry Calippo, bought some postcards and waited for the MV Saturn to come into port and take me back to Gourock, from where you get the train to Glasgow.

JUNE 14, 2005
Glasgow, Scotland

I'm up late; I'm scared to go to bed because my bedroom is open to the sky. All that's separating me and the rain is a board of wood and a light sheet of plastic, so I think I'll hang around the kitchen for a while. They're a good bunch in general, the dudes fixing the roof. They know me pretty well now; in fact I think they saw me in the bath this morning.

One of the neighbours sent a *complaining* type of email to their office. Here's a bit of what we got back:

Further to our telecon with the writer of last week and your subsequent email of yesterday, I confirm our company's position in respect of same.

On Monday of last week the adverse weather did not allow progress and we aborted the operatives going to site.

On Tuesday the weather turned unusually fine and progressed exceptionally until today, where, as you will be aware, it slipped to wet again.

On Wednesday we progressed the front wallhead cappings which the joiners had relined the week previously. These works went on till Thursday.

Given the extent of the fine weather we commenced on Saturday at the oriel roofs and completed the covering by the end of the day.

Our tradesmen were discussing issues with your neighbours during the weekend, and it has been confirmed that an offer of fruit melon was granted and accepted during Saturday by one kind owner.

We were not on site on Sunday given the very important football match that was being played.

We returned to site on Monday and worked till around 2.30pm, when one of our tradesmen took unwell.

We aborted the operatives from site this morning due to adverse weather and will return Wednesday, weather permitting.

Sincerely, etc.

The tone of voice I imagine the letter to be read in is straight from *I'm All Right Jack*, in which Peter Sellers plays the immovable shop steward. They're having a laugh, by the way. I must admit to being the neighbour with the 'fruit melon'. I never thought it would be mentioned in dispatches!

So, I was coming home tonight with the rain falling, a warm south-westerly breeze and the foliage out almost to the full. I love this town in summer! This is the only time for years that I've done such a stretch in Glasgow, watching the summer slowly moving in.

I feel like I deserve to stay here now and see it out — to see the students thin out; to look at the faces of the aspiring hip from

my bicycle as they endeavour to make little films, take up un-
fathomable art projects, swim in the old Victorian bath-houses,
let their wardrobes go to tatters, do no more than plan day-trips
to the Trossachs. It needs to be celebrated, this damp and delirious Scottish giving in to leisure and art and nature. I'm planning
some pictures ...

JUNE 26, 2005
Los Angeles, California, US

This morning at 7.04 am was the most magnificent I've felt since
I arrived. Up since 5.30am with the jet-lag still toying with me,
I decided to watch *Betty Blue*. I haven't seen it for a long time. I
have no love for it, but it maps out a time and a place for me, and
watching it escorted me right back to that time and place.

There was one scene in particular, with a shot looking towards a boat sailing past and a very 1980s guitar playing the
familiar theme from the film. The sound provided resonances of
Felt guitars from the mid-1980s. I was back on Woodlands Road
in 1986, when my town got really quiet in the summer and
there was nothing to do but try to figure out where the boundaries of the mystical West End started and finished, and to try to
circumnavigate it dutifully and thankfully.

The mystical West End was given a new annex in the shape of
my first girlfriend's house. I drifted out to unimagined suburbs
on the same faithful racing bike that carries me today. She was
brought up in the city, while I was a mere tourist and would remain so for 10 years. But while those closest to the glories, such
as she, were happy to live and enjoy, it took the tourists and
Johnny-come-latelies, such as me, to try to canonise the whole
thing.

So I romanticised all experience to the extent that I was

267

neither enjoying it nor living. Still, looking back, it was a pivotal time, a dreamtime, or so it seems now. Perhaps LA truly is the city of dreams. This dumb matrix of traffic is such a blank canvas for the visitor that they can't helped being pushed back into their past. Into the past I push and drift, while visceral experience evades. Songs become ludicrously important. To sing like Debbie Harry, to be Debbie Harry for my time in vocal booth. Why not? You can be anything here.

So it's not quite *37°2 Le Matin* (the French title of *Betty Blue*) at the minute, but it feels pretty warm. The first time I went to see that film in a packed Glasgow Film Theatre, I was with the girl previously mentioned. I think it was a Sunday night. We might have screwed already, but we probably screwed badly, as early daters do, so the opening scene of the film had me cringing a bit, sinking into my seat. It was a sticky love scene.

"So that's how she's meant to feel," I thought to myself.

I felt inadequate. Not for the last time. The girl worked in the BBC canteen. I felt proud to know someone who worked in the BBC canteen. I told her of her magnificence, and she told me it was a shit job, hot and underpaid. Nevertheless I loved to go and pick her up from work, locking my bicycle beside hers outside the BBC and going inside to wait for her, pretending I had some sort of business being there.

I worked in an independent record shop. Rebel Records. Though sometimes I change names of things and people, this I will record. Rebel Records, owned and run by a dreamer, Pete, who was still led by the hand of Phil Lynott in his everyday work and play, though he was married and soon to be a father. *Shades of a Blue Orphanage* was the west-coast rocker's *David Copperfield*.

I wanted to lift that shop up by the scruff of the neck. I wanted to give the indie kids around the best records, the best prices! We stuffed the racks with reverential fervour. I searched out records I thought could change lives, placing them at the front of the racks, playing them on the crappy shop stereo, watching the mystified eyes and feline movements of the girls dressed in brown suede. They circled and pawed and finally parked their twisted desert boots in front of the Monochrome Set or the Violent Femmes or the fledgling Sugarcubes, and gave their cowlicks one last tweak before deciding.

We heard about the Stone Roses and what they were doing in Manchester. My girl and her friend had seen them, though they were more enamoured with the support act, King of the Slums, who were indeed terrific. There was talk of the Roses' early single *Sally Cinnamon* and how it was a legend of beauty and whispered vocal. It was reissued and, on the day, I leapt on my bike with the big 12-inch single flapping about my front forks all the way to the suburbs. I damn near put it through the spokes so many times, but it was worth the look on her face, like the look on Betty's face when Zorg, her boyfriend, lets her move in. A big, toothy, lippy, beautiful smile.

JULY 24, 2005
Los Angeles, California, US

I'm sitting naked on a Yellow Pages. Naked because the flat is so warm, and on a Yellow Pages so I can reach the keyboard without straining. I'm sorry if I've given you an unfortunate mental image, but there you have it. I'm worried that when I get up I will find myself attached to the shiny surface of the Yellow Pages.

All work and no play makes Jack a dull boy. It's 3.17am and I'm feeling dull. I had to force myself over to the table to type this. That's the trouble with making records. They take over your life to such an extent that at the end of the day you're in tatters.

It would be nice to have a late-night chat over cups of tea, or to be taking someone to lunch tomorrow after church. I could take one of the congregation to lunch, I suppose, but typical me, I ended up walking though the door of the gayest church known to Christendom. Don't get me wrong, I love the gathering and I adore the service like a dog loves a bone, but I want to flirt a bit, pry into the life of, or at the least sit back and bask in the presence of, a member of the opposite sex. 'Hopelessly heterosexual' my good friend Steve called me once, and he was right.

(Oh God, someone in our hip courtyard has got a guitar out. Thankfully my flat is double glazed. I'll just have to cook on top of the sheets.)

I'm not letting this magnificent mess of a city get me down though. No way. Its secrets can be conquered with a car and a mobile phone, and for the first time in my life I have both. I just don't have the time. I'm not moaning; we finished the live backing tracks for the album yesterday. It was the most focused and rewarding piece of studio time the band have enjoyed since 1996.

I wish now that we'd spoken to Chloe Sevigny in the thrift store the other day. But then, what would you say? It was Bob who spotted her. I didn't really know who he was talking about, but we had little else to do, so we did another lap of the shop so we could get a better look at her.

"Ah, you're a film star. Jolly good. We're a pair of idiots from Scotland."

What was I meant to do — invite her to church?

We did have a chance with another film star a few days later. We had been to a friend's for some dinner, and the group were quite far down the road to social drunkenness. Back at the apartments we decided to go for a nightcap. We piled out and into the lift. There was a very beautiful girl getting into the lift with two male friends as well. It was quite a crush, and Bob insisted on jamming his foot in the door and yelling out:

"Where's Beans? We gotta wait for the Beano!"

"Bob, the Beano is standing right in front of you! How many drinks have you had?"

Beans was in fact two inches in front of Bob, and had been half deafened by Bob shouting his name. We finally got going. One of the strangers said:

"So, what are Belle and Sebastian doing in LA?"

Any other time we would have been polite, delighted to answer an astute enquiry. On this occasion, the question was met with what was probably a series of smarty-pant answers. I think someone managed to say we were there to make a record.

The beautiful one said: "*Fold Your Hands Child* is my life."

I never heard her, but Sarah told me later. We also figured out that she was an actress called Eva Mendes. So now she thinks we're a loutish band of miscreants.

Give me another chance! I'm listening! Tell me about your life!

Sarah's in her element here, being surrounded by a troupe of delightful studio dogs. We couldn't have planned it better. The moment Abby, the docile dalmatian, loped out to meet us at the studio, I knew the gods of recording karma had smiled upon us. Everything was going to be OK.

As Sarah made her obsession clear to everyone at the studio, we were introduced to Abby's pal Stella, a dalmatian pup, and a beguiling spaniel called Captain, also belonging to one of the engineers. I was delighted further at the prospect of being introduced to a parrot belonging to the technical support chap.

"Does he talk?" asked Sarah, excitedly.

"Well, he can only really say one thing," replied the parrot's owner.

"What's that?"

"'*You never, never know!*'"

Can you imagine that thing perched in the console in the studio?

"Oh, Mister Parrot, is our record going to be a hit?"

"*You never, never know!*"

"Should we jump on the New Wave bandwagon, or stick to our more traditional sound?"

"*You never, never know!*"

"Are we really going to finish within the budget?"

"*You never, never know!*"

That's what we need. An eternal optimist with a succinct saying in times of doubt.

JULY 25, 2005

Los Angeles, California, US

Beans and I have spent the past couple of hours trying to find Richard, Mick, Bob and Bob's brother. It's Richard's birthday and they've all finished their work. They're not where they said they'd be. I looked round four bars, then we got a message that they were up the street at a bar where the music is good, so Beans and me went there.

There was some confusion on the door. The dude didn't want to let us in, but in the end we gave him the name of a dude that the dude's friend knows, so we got in. Beans showed his ID; I floundered around looking for mine. After a while the dude grew impatient.

"What age are you?" he asked.

"Thirty-six," I replied.

"Yeah, right … you can go in."

Inside, Beans was laughing at the guy's reaction.

"He thought you were telling such a whopping lie that he just let you in."

It was like that bit in *The Catcher in the Rye* when the 16-year-old Holden is trying to get a drink, and the fella asks how old he is.

"Fifty-three; what the hell does it matter?"

Or something like that. Except that I am 36! Nearly 37. On top of that, everyone in the bar looked like a kid and the boys weren't there, so we hung around until they played *Young Americans* then left.

JULY 26, 2005
Los Angeles, California, US

I didn't sleep well last night, so I was drifting off in the bath, tripping out on visions and contingencies. It's getting to the stage of the record — and I don't wish to jinx it, especially as I've not listened to any of it back yet — where we're on pretty solid turf. Of course, that's a cue for me to start tripping on sleeves and videos, running orders, etc. That's what I was doing in the bath.

It's quiet. Last night was a bit more noisy. We've split the studio into two, with Todd Burke, the chief engineer (just like my faither!), handling the instrumental additions and Tony Hoffer, Captain Kirk, guiding the vocals.

Stevie came in this morning waving *This Year's Model* around. Last night he came in waving *Blood and Chocolate*. The boy does-

273

n't need much encouragement. I picked up a new biography of Elvis Costello, and I've been fighting to get first read of it ever since.

Last night, I wandered in from my vocal booth and quoted from the book to anyone who might care to hear. This is on Nick Lowe's production techniques for Costello's first album:

Most of the album was recorded live, in first takes, with Declan (Elvis) singing and playing to the band's backing. There were a few overdubs of backing vocals here and there, but very little polish, to the extent that the backing band were originally a little concerned by the rawness of the final takes.

If any of the band came to him wanting to redo their bass part or have another go at their guitar line, the standard Lowe response was:

"Ach, nobody will hear it in the morning!" And he was right.

"My kind of producer," I pronounced.

"Would you get the fuck into the vocal booth and sing this," Tony then pronounced.

I had been procrastinating about only wanting to go back and do an overdubbed vocal for a song when everything else was in place. We had a song on the desk called *Another Sunny Day* (nothing to do with the Sarah Records' band, by the way, so put your mitts back in your duffle coat, little twee spotter).

We had recorded it live, with everything in except Stevie's vocals. So while Sarah and Stevie were sticking down their backing vocals, I was to have a go as well. (By the way, overdubbing is the term for anything that gets put on a track after the live track is recorded. This LP will be the least overdubbed since *Sinister*.)

I wanted to hear the violin and the mandolin guitar working at the end, but it wasn't technically possible at that point. Still, we went in, the three of us, and sang through the song a few times, and it was very nice. I was in the mood for it. From that dimmed hole in the back of a small LA studio I was racing through the backroads of Scotland, playing football and kicking about Glasgow, all with the subject of the song for a while. In fact, the subject of the song came and sat in the corner of my vocal booth to listen for a while, scrunched up, knees to chin, not overly impressed, but simply enjoying the story, the story about her.

JULY 27, 2005
Los Angeles, California, US

It's quiet. The boys are going home tomorrow. I don't know quite how we did it but I think we're in good shape for mixing, with 18 songs in the can.

Earlier in the evening everyone went out for a meal. I skipped out because I was tired and I wanted to save energy for singing later. I moved very slowly. That's the nice thing about LA, it's so warm you can move very slowly if you want. I moved slowly into Borders and bought *The Prime of Miss Jean Brodie* and *The Big Chill* on DVD. *The Big Chill*, for God's sake. I moved into the elevator and went up into the apartment. The warm sofa in the warm apartment engulfed me and I tried to get into *Baseball Tonight* despite all the fricken adverts.

"I could eat some Japanese food," I thought to myself, slowly.

There's a Japanese restaurant in the building as well as a Borders, so I phoned them, ordered the special, and got comfy again. I started watching *The Big Chill*. Twenty minutes later I sauntered down to the restaurant to pick up my food. I came up, had my dinner and watched more of the film.

At 11pm I went back to the studio and sang *Funny Little Frog*.

Stevie sang along to the backing track with me. It's about the only time of the day when I feel useful, committed and alive. Perhaps that's the secret: make everything else so dull that you want to live inside the record. I'm living inside the record.

Los Angeles, California, US

Today slid from the sublime to ... nothing. I got up pretty late, looked up to see what the Dodgers were up to and found out they had a game on in LA starting in half an hour.

So I had a wash then ran out. I was going to try to catch people this morning, but I thought they would understand. I took the number 2 bus toward Downtown LA, and I meditated badly on the way.

I was late for the game, arriving in the fourth inning. The crowd was mostly bussed-in schoolchildren because it was a noon start. I didn't mind; I felt like I was on a field trip.

The ticket office was shut, said the dude on the gate.

"But I've got a ticket here," he added. "You can give me $5 for it."

I tried to fish out $5.

"After the game! Go ahead, go ahead."

So I went ahead.

Now, Dodger Stadium is a beautiful place. It's a nice enough stadium, just like my flat in Glasgow is a nice enough flat. What makes them both beautiful, however, is the view. The view from the stadium is of parkland, palm trees, a hint of the desert, then ranges of desert mountains and the most 'drawn on' cumulus clouds I have seen outside of a Ladybird book. How they organised that view, when the stadium resides just on the edge of Downtown, is a triumph of environmental architecture.

It's a pity the view of home plate wasn't so hot. An uninspired team went down 6–1 to the Reds from Cincinnati. I didn't mind so much — I was feeling good, letting the nice bits of the last few days roll over me.

What I like even better than attending ballgames is walking away from ballgames. I like the way the crowds dissipate. And I like to find myself walking down increasingly silent streets. In Glasgow, or Ayr, this would be more drawn out and palpable, but in a big American city it's a bit of a joke because *everybody* gets into their cars. I'm the only sucker walking home. And it takes me three goes to get out of the parking lot because all the pedestrian exits are blocked, so I have to jog alongside the cars.

Eventually I take a left into a quieter street that seems to go up into a park. I let myself meditate as I drift, enjoying a traffic-free quiet that is rare. This time the meditation is not about people but about songs, about the record. I'm trying to imagine the running order, but it's not really working.

I look at my new cords. I can't help looking at them because they seem to me to be on the perfect cusp of blue and green and grey. But then I am colour-blind. Maybe Barney Sumner is colour-blind as well, and that's why he came up with the words to my favourite New Order song: "Oh you've got green eyes, oh you've you've got blue eyes, oh you've got grey … eyes. And I've never seen anyone quite like you before."

While I looked at my cords I wish that fashion had given in to practicality that morning. Sweat trickled down the back of my knees.

Echo Park, Silver Lake, Thai Town, Los Feliz — those are the names of the places I thought I might hike through to get home. I want to give this town the same chance as I did San Francisco. I got hotter, however, and the roads became twistier, so I didn't make it all the way.

Eventually I jumped back on to a busy bus on Sunset Boulevard, but it broke down. Whoa, the passengers were pissed off. I didn't mind. I sat in a launderette to cool down and missed a couple of other buses while I read *LA Weekly*. I watched pretty girls load the machines wearing clearly the few scraps and patches available to them, everything else being in the wash.

Launderettes are snapshots of public domesticity. Women in curlers, men wearing vests, girls waking up for the back shift, boys just in from the early shift, everyone looking grumpy, unapproachable, unkempt and beautiful.

When I finally got home I was thinking, like I always do, that something good should happen tonight. It's my first day off in weeks, I want to go somewhere that's happening, and talk and fool about and dance, and wear something new. C'mon, you owe me something, city.

Nothing's doing. Jackson's gone to ground, the boys have left, Bob and Sarah have gone to pick up their respective spouses at the airport and it's too late to phone any of my fledgling LA companions.

So I loaf and watch the Mets score on the internet while the game's taking place. I sit and watch the score! (Funny how, like in *Fever Pitch*, when football becomes extra important to the author in times of extreme non-happenings, my baseball concern surges in the vacuity of this Southern Cal apartment complex.) The Mets lose. It's midnight. Everything seems rubbish.

That's the danger of living in a record. When the music stops you fall off the turntable.

Los Angeles, California, US

I don't have anything to say to you, diary, or at least I think I don't. But then I should approach you like a prayer.

I don't know how many of you are in the habit of saying your prayers regularly, but this applies equally to meditating, or going to the gym, or practising clarinet — something that requires a degree of discipline. What I'm saying is that if I simply start, even though it's against the initial will of my body (which wants to flop down and switch on Turner Classic Movies), perhaps I'll find something worthwhile to say.

Which raises the stakes somewhat. I might have to try to make in-roads into a subject deeper than the here and now, or deeper than even my day was (as deep as a summer puddle, as it turns out).

A long time ago I read a book called *Dangling Man* by Saul Bellow. I think the protagonist and narrator was waiting to be posted in the army. He was in the midst of a hiatus, where everything seemed to be paused. He could do nothing but tread water, seeking pleasure in whatever was immediately to hand.

Obviously I'm going to draw a comparison between the premise of the book and the situation I find myself in. I was in a terrific mood this morning. I'd had a good weekend away from the songs, but at the same time I felt a sense of accomplishment from knowing all the parts have been played; pretty much all the singing is done too.

You know as well as I do that terrific moods, while they can be enjoyed, cannot be bottled and stored. No matter how much you position yourself, the mood will slip away by a natural process called 'mood osmosis' and you will be left to make your next move. Which, unfortunately for me, was down to the studio.

I packed my running shoes because I had a plan to look in on proceedings, then head down the Freeway to the Santa Monica beach, whereupon I would change into my shorts and jog off along the shore. It would be dark by that time, but the thrill of being where the land meets the water would be undiminished. In fact, as the stars above the water came into play, there would be the interaction of those three elements — a rich canvas indeed.

As long as I could avoid the shady side of Venice, I could enjoy myself. Eyes steering toward the infinite and away from the city, it would be just the spiritual breathing space I desired.

As it turned out, there was work to be done. I toyed with the notion of driving down at 12.30am. I toyed, but didn't make it.

Hence, I'm telling you about something that could've been. There's a lot of that when you're trapped in a studio for the summer. One leans heavily on ghosts, fantasies and Mexican food.

AUGUST 3, 2005
Los Angeles, California, US

This is more like it. I'm in the piano room in the studio down the street, where we've moved to mix the record. We had a few things still to be sung and played, but now that we have sung and played I can hang out back here in this truly quiet room, free from the scourge of air conditioning.

We're very close to Sunset Boulevard, but I can't hear the street. If I step out of the door there's a courtyard, and through the leaves of the rubber tree I can see a Spanish-style church steeple. My typing is accompanied by the crickets.

Nothing too much to report today. I've mostly been singing and playing tambourine and keyboard on a song called *To Be Myself Completely*, which was written by Stevie. In fact, Stevie was singing with me most of the day as well as we tried out some new harmony and counterpoint.

I think I'm slowly being pulled away from the idea of a double LP (in the old sense of four sides of vinyl). We certainly have enough tracks to make a nice four-five, four-five formation, but is it really worth it? I mean, how many of you reading this are old enough to know what I'm going on about anyway?

I only have to consider how many of my favourite LPs are doubles to be put off the idea. But then, there maybe is the rare occasion, the rare justification of the long format. Let me expand.

In the beginning, the length of our LPs was suggested by the songs. The first two were sequenced with five tracks per side before they were recorded. It made sense. Hopefully they wouldn't be long enough to bore people. As we went along, things got more mixed up musically, with different singers and a wider musical palette. It seemed, especially with the different voices, that we could and should stretch to six a side, to make the best of what we had.

I feel quite protective about the current set of songs, proud we managed to get so many tracks to the finishing line. Is that not the record done, then? We acted out the script we wrote. All those winter weekdays practising. All those cups of teas and endless anecdotes about sex, spouses and the Stones.

Then I think about the all the doublers that stopped me dead, that were no-go areas. I love all The Beatles up to and including *Sgt Pepper*. I've had them all since I was a wee boy. I've never heard *The White Album*. I dipped into Dylan; love *Freewheelin'*, *Bringing It All Back Home*, *Highway 61 Revisited*. Couldn't be arsed with *Blonde on Blonde*. Never gave it a chance. I've never heard *Exile on Main Street* all the way through. I'm sure these are terrific albums, but I must acknowledge the fact they are 'serious' doublers put me off.

I gave up on buying 'new' CDs pretty much as soon as they started making them. I couldn't understand why bands thought they should try to fill up the 74 minutes available when it was clear they were stretching people's interest at around 45 minutes to begin with. Longer songs, 'tranced out bliss', more turgid verses, dark, interweaving bollocks. That was my experience of the CD in the 1990s, more or less.

There are, of course, exceptions. (May I reiterate that these are my grubby, late-night thoughts and I don't have the strength to be reasonable, so I'll just carry on regardless.) I always loved Prince's *Sign o' the Times* as a proper studio non-compilation doubler. That's the LP of his I listen to most. It seems his ambition in this case simply needed to spill on to four sides.

Then there's *London Calling*, of course, and Tindersticks' first two. Were they truly doublers? Or just longish albums stretched on to two platters because they were indulged by their label? Like us and *Dear Catastrophe Waitress*. (I mainly wanted a double-vinyl *DCW* so I could use two more pictures of the Waitress on the labels.)

I just thought of one more band who support my argument against doublers: Led Zeppelin. I loved all their records except *Physical Graffiti*, which I never went near. I even love *Coda*! When I was 13 or so I picked up the notion from seniors at school that *Physical Graffiti* was something special for the fans. But that's probably because it was the mark of the hardcore fan to stay with the group through four sides of black wax. I never went near it.

I want the next LP to sell, by God. If it don't, I'm changing tack. I'm going to be a lighthouse keeper, or have a big brood of kids, or drive a train. Now is not perhaps the right time to hit the public with 18 songs.

Los Angeles, California, US

I was just talking to Chris, the studio engineer. He seems to be a kindred spirit regarding the allure of waitresses. I can't remember quite how we got on to the subject.

"It's tough. I mean, they probably spend the whole night getting hit upon. I've got a line, but I've never used it," he said.

"What is it?" I asked.

"'Is it rude to ask somebody out when they're working?'"

"That's pretty good," I said. "I might use it."

"Use it," said Chris. "Tell me how you get on."

"Thing is, I would never make a move like that," I said. "I don't think I've ever straight-out asked anybody out in my life. There was one time, years ago. I had a thing about this girl who worked in this place we always went to. Every Friday night, and the rest. It went on for a year. I would never talk to her apart from putting my order in at the bar. We called her Attitude. Well, my ex called her Attitude really, and it just stuck. She had a kind of ballsy attitude, which didn't put me off to tell you the truth."

"So, did you get a chance to ask her out?" said Chris.

"Yeah, well this one night she was off duty," I explained. "She was sitting on her own near the door, sort of waiting. I was with some friends, and I could tell she was actually waiting for me to ask her out. I might be deluding myself, I might have made this up, but I'm pretty sure she was waiting for me to go over and talk to her."

Reflective pause.

"I just couldn't do it. I couldn't go over and give her the old chat."

"So what happened?"

"She eventually quit working there and moved away."

There was a thoughtful pause, then it was Chris's turn.

"I used to go into this coffee place on my day off," he said. "There was a girl who worked there. I think we were on nodding terms after a while. Well, one day she starts to talk to me, asking what I did. It was real easy. She was interested, asking questions."

"Did you ask her out?"

"Not really. We used to have quite long chats, but then she mostly asked me about my job. She was really interested when I told her I was a music engineer. She always wanted to talk about recording. She was getting songs together herself and needed some way to record them. I got a bit bored talking about it. I wanted to talk about something else."

"So you spent about $300 on lattes every day so you could get to record the girl's demos?" asked Tony from the other side of the room.

"Pretty much," said Chris. "I felt like I was back at school, doing the cheerleader's homework."

"You know, now I can see the situation from both sides," I said. "There's some girls I know, friends of mine. They befriended this guy who works in the Mac shop. They're friendly enough to him; they pop in and see him at work. You should see them if he ever phones the house, though! It's, like, big sirens go off all over the kitchen. It's not like they want to know him, or socialise with him or anything. To be honest, the girls just want to get their friggin' hard drives fixed."

"It's the way of the world. Girls just want to get their friggin' hard drives fixed."

Cue music: *You Only Love Me cos I Work on Your Car* by The Reverend Buck Naked.

Later that week …

We just got back from lunch. The waitress asked if everything was OK. I nearly stood up, grabbed her by the lapels and said:

"OK? OK? Look where we are. We're in this brilliant place, the food is good, the coffee is good, we're making a record, you look … *great*, and *Watching the Detectives* has just come on the jukebox!"

I nearly did it. I was pretty excitable at lunch. I was so excitable last night that I drove drunk. Shit, I don't drink, and I rarely drive, so I thought I'd go with the party LA mood and drive a little drunk. I mean, all the roads look like landing strips anyway, and no-one cares about pedestrians at the best of times, so what could go wrong?

I'd been to the opening of some club in Hollywood. Jolie the journalist invited me out, so I thought I'd pop out while Tony was doing a mix. The place was very Hollywood. There was a floorshow with a muscly couple climbing the drapes and doing contortions. Déjà vu, Brazil. I said to the girl next to me:

"I'm waiting for the time that the show finishes and they play Michael Jackson so we can dance."

The show stopped. They played *I Want You Back*! We danced.

Afterwards, a man told me he saw me on the dancefloor and that I had some 'pretty bad moves'. I didn't care. I went to get a couple more of those free melon cocktails, and we sat outside, where there was an artificial waterfall vibe going down.

The place was full of the so-called beautiful people. There were some pretty ones, sure enough, but I thought the cocktail waitress was the real cutie. I was going to put a tip in her tip jar, just while I was leaving. (I was a little tipsy.) I only had a dollar or I had 20. I mean, a dollar wouldn't have warranted anything but a wry glance from under her fringe, whereas 20 seems a bit sleazy. Who am I kidding? I don't have that kind of money to throw about.

In an unrelated incident, Marisa, who has been waitressing *a lot* recently, told me:

"Never flirt with a waitress unless she flirts with you first."

"But waitresses only flirt with you when they're trying to get a big tip."

Moral: don't flirt with a waitress unless you're prepared to pay big.

AUGUST 14, 2005
Los Angeles, California, US

It's Sunday and I'm feeling penitential because I missed church and football, and that's my usual soulful Sunday one-two. Especially church. I'm going to feel bewildered for the whole start of the week. Do you think I'm stupid to think that? Some of you will. To some of you it maybe seems like I'm upset because I forgot to pack my teddy bear or something, like I'm placing importance on charms and superstitions.

Maybe you're right. Maybe I should just embrace the brazen realities of life! Mmm. When I think of it for a second, without the promise of something else, the brazen realities seem a bit three-dimensional.

I love this little flat with the funky neighbours and palm trees

286

in the courtyard. There's always the sound of a party going on somewhere far off, and though I'm not at the party, it's nice to feel there's a party going on somewhere. I feel slightly less vacuous.

I don't want to leave. It feels like, if I wanted, I could be on the brink of making medium-term friendships if I made the effort. But I'm leaving soon enough. I never did make friends with the girl across the courtyard who always wore a hat in a distinct fashion, even when she was hanging her washing out. She was sitting on her balcony earlier, smoking and listening to *American Girl* by Tom Petty.

"Is that Tom Petty you're listening to?" I would've said to her.

"Yes, is it bothering you?"

"Oh no, carry on, carry on!" I would say.

If I came back to LA I'd want this apartment again. I got really lucky with this. There must be perhaps 120 apartments in the building, and I got one of the four I would've been completely happy with. It's at the top, on the inside corner; quiet, no traffic.

I had my friend on the phone for a couple of hours there. It was almost morning her time; she hadn't been to sleep. She'd taken an E that night at a club, so now all she wanted to do was talk and talk and talk, and that was fine. I liked listening. I opened the balcony door, stretched out on the sofa and let her spill her guts all over the phone. We both figured that it was mostly speed that she had. It always is with these things.

"Would you ever take ecstasy?"

"No. I think I'd rather make a record."

"Oh, *really*?" she says sarcastically, like she'd heard that one a thousand times.

Even if I just finished a double album and was dying to see

people, and someone put the pill on a velvet pillow, and everyone was doing it, I wouldn't be arsed. I'd go for a walk or play the piano or something. Sounds boring, doesn't it? Wonder why I wouldn't do it?

"Maybe you're so in love with yourself that you couldn't bear to be separated from your ego, even for an hour or so."

Maybe she's right.

Me and Stevie crawled out to the ballgame today. It was kind of religious. We went out there to salute a god on the mound, Pedro Martinez. He was pitching for the Mets. He pitched a no-hitter till the seventh, when unfortunately I said to Stevie:

"Oh, Pedro's got a no-hitter, and we're at the bottom of the seventh. Trouble is, now I've noticed that and drawn it to your attention, it's extremely unlikely that he'll be able to keep it going. Someone's going to get a hit, just because I said that."

Next ball, someone got a hit, got on base. The next batter stepped up and knocked it into the bleachers. Two-one to the Dodgers, and that's the game.

"Mommy, the Mets suck," some kid said to her mum as I retook my seat. The whole family laughed, and the laugh was on me as I was wearing the only Mets' T-shirt in sight. So I turned and said to the kid:

"They do, you're right. They're overpaid, they constantly underperform as a team. They lack soul."

The kid looked at me a little frightened.

AUGUST 15, 2005
Los Angeles, California, US

I'm kinda beat, and I only just made it to work. I tried to catch up on emails this morning. Then on the way to work I heard a Stones track on the radio that I really liked, and I started thinking about the time I was listening to *You Can't Always Get What You Want* while wandering in the SoMa [South of Market] district of San Francisco about six years ago.

I've never been a consistently big Stones fan, but I loved the production on this track, and the ambition, and the soul. And the groove.

It struck me that I felt some parallels with the Stones around that time. Now this may seem extremely presumptuous and all that, but a boy has to dream. They started making some of their best records around the time of *Let It Bleed*. I add them to my mental list of groups that had been kicking around for a while but had yet to make their decisive move (Stones, Bee Gees, REM). Less for the Stones, more for REM.

Ach, what does it all matter? Stevie and I talked about it on Saturday, and we realised that no matter how much we chased the prize, we would still follow our hearts before anything. And our hearts just love music, recorded music, music of the soul, smash hits, transcendent singles, trippy albums that take you by the hand and lead you to the promised land.

We talked about it while we were back in the wonderful Jukebox Café. I had some catfish and greens (for the soul) and a root beer; Stevie had the veggie burger. The atmosphere in the place was different — the light was lower and the hipster element high, a Saturday-night warming-up vibration. We just wished we were going to the same place some of these cats were going.

I went to feed the jukie, but somehow there were 20 free credits. I fed in a good few, putting in some I thought Stevie would like. While I was there a young mother came up with her child.

"I was wondering what was playing just now. Can you tell?" she asked.

"Yeah, hold on."

I flicked through the selection until I came the number that was playing.

"It's the Arcade Fire," I said. "They're the new big thing just now."

"Oh, right."

I could have dropped the 'new big thing' bit. She only wanted to know what she was listening to. Personally, I couldn't wait until it was off and I could hear *Say Hello, Wave Goodbye* by Soft Cell and *Walking on the Moon* by The Police. My selection didn't start to play until we were kicking back, ready to pay the bill.

A friend remarked to me once, in a New York bar, "If you can hear your selection coming on the jukebox, it's probably past the time when you should have left."

He was right, particularly one night when I finally heard my tunes coming through. Or I thought I heard them. My head was such a fug of hard liquor at the time. Those New York measures of Jack!

I was playing pool, perhaps swaying lightly. We acknowledged, the same friend and I, that we had heard our tunes coming on. We cordially agreed that this was a job well done, and that we should leave. Despite having some difficulty walking, we made it back to his apartment. I think his girlfriend was helping us.

I took to the couch like Puck to the bower of an ash. My friend left a precautionary saucepan next to the couch in case I should need it. I regret to report that I puked into it some time in the night. It must have been the jetlag.

Glasgow, Scotland

I'm not long back from recording a track for a charity called Warchild. The idea is that about 15 groups record a track on the same day and they're putting the album out tomorrow, in about seven hours. It's going online.

We wrote a song called *The Eighth Station of the Cross Kebab House*. I wanted to print the words out in case you download it and wonder what the hell we're on about.

It's meant to be a snapshot of a pluralist utopia, a kind of *Across the Barricades* type thing. It's a fairly true reflection of some of the impressions we took from our trip to Israel/Palestine earlier this year. I spent a happy lunch hour in said kebab house at the eighth station of the cross in Jerusalem.

By the way, Lod is pronounced 'lid'. It's a town in Israel, mostly occupied by Palestinians as it happens.

The Eighth Station of the Cross Kebab House

I'm sitting around at the checkpoint
Keeping myself to myself
My heart's going out to the girl with the gun
She is young, she is fun, she is deadly

She clocks off, goes back to the city
Goes to a club with her friends

I just took a walk through the checkpoint
Past columns of poor Arab sons
They queue through the day for a chance to make pay
For something to put in their mouths

He can't sleep at night without gunfire
The lullaby puts him to sleep

We stand there accused of the British collusion
Israel into Palestine
A victory for some an astonishing hope
But for him it has brought devastation

He lives like a prisoner in exile
He lives like a prisoner in hell

Doves black and white in the blue vault of space
Swoop around like a symbol of peace
Can they see the hawk?
They're too busy in talk of love
Why should they contemplate fear?

Everyone meets in the cramped city streets
Hipsters of Zion collide
To talk music and dross
At the sign of The Cross
We eat our falafel in peace
The girl lets her uniform slip
The boy cracks a joke, he is sweet
He listens to hip hop in Gaza
She listens to Coldplay in Lod

NOVEMBER 11, 2005
Glasgow, Scotland

I realise it's been a while since my last post. I've been involved
in all the tedious and nail-biting stuff that accompanies finishing a record. I would much rather have been having adventures
and reporting to you religiously, but there you have it. So how

do I enter again the world of electronic society? I think I'll take a few questions from the floor.

Hi. I noticed that Stuart can now "listen to repeats of Radio 4 shows in the bath". That's all well and good, but might I suggest he view The Royal Tenenbaums *for helpful hints on electro-bathtime health and safety?*

Kind regards, Stephen

It's not very clever, is it, kids? It's such a raging luxury, though. When I was a nine-year-old boy, waking up and loafing on a Saturday morning, I used to fantasise about having a screen on the wall that would play any programme or film that I wanted to see. This was way before video was around, so it was a pretty futuristic concept. Now it seems that with the wafer-thin screen of my computer and the film delivery service in which I partake, I can live the dream.

I'm so addicted to Radio 4, though. I feel a little more Middle English every day. Through times of intra-band tension, footballing wilderness and spiritual torpor, you were the only one there ...

I don't think I'm living life. How would you advise I do so? PS It's my birthday the day after the Hammersmith Apollo show, and after years of crap birthdays it looks like I'm going to have the best birthday ever now :) Thanks for the happy coincidence!

God, is anyone really living their lives? I bet you feel the same as anyone else. The odd glimpse of excitement, lots of in-between confusion, waiting for something to happen, the broad hours of humdrum. I mean, you might think it's wall-to-wall glam up in Belle and Sebastian towers, but let me assure you, I keep re-running some of the moves from football last night in my head, and that's the most fun I'm having. I wish it could be football every day!

Life is pretty great, though. Can I remind you how short it is, and then maybe you will get out and go to that pottery night class you've been putting off for months.

I'll have to think of something special we can do for Hammersmith since it's your birthday. It's too cold for a picnic. It's a Friday night, though. Perhaps we ought to have a party after the show or something. Let me think about it.

I'm wondering if you could reccomend a dance party. I'm the dancing. The dancing is where the party happens: most of the time. I think that B&S is one best for the dancing, and the shredding. Cudos! Always with the B&S bumping in the headphones.
  Your friend, Christopher M Gustafson

Well, look at Chris here. He certainly sounds like he's living life! Perhaps you could come to the party after Hammersmith and lead the way — life and soul, all that sort of thing.

As I was shifting some old boxes in the storage the other day, I came across the December 12, 1998 issue of Melody Maker. *The headline reads: "Cult heroes! Belle & Sebastian: Everything you ever wanted to know about Britain's most mysterious band." I remember when Stuart didn't give interviews and how MM made such a fuss about it ("the most publicity-shy band in the world — ever!"). Was there a conscious effort to change the band's image over the years? Do you find it harder to get the media's attention in what you do now that some of the elusiveness is gone? Did Stuart lose any sleep over that 1998 article?*
  Juyi Yoo

Ah! I did in fact lose sleep over that article. Bloody *Melody Maker*! It's karma that it folded for its lying ways! It claimed it got an interview and pictures. In fact, a man in Munich took some pictures of me and Bel when we were strolling near the river. He was a sad little guy. We were petting a dog, and he just came up. I thought that perhaps he wanted pictures of a nice young couple because he was sad and alone. Two weeks later, the pictures were on the front cover of *Melody Maker*. You may think, 'What do you expect?' and our press officer even said as much. They were more naïve days, however, and I hated the fact people were so sneaky, and they made you seem powerless.

What I hated more, though, was the fact the interview I think was taken from one I did right back when the group started, two years earlier, before I was alive to the agendas and the vacuousness of the weekly press at the time. They mixed it in, made up some stuff and claimed it was current.

Obviously, I've chilled out since then and enjoy talking to most papers and publications. The funny thing is that it was only the *NME* and *MM* that were the problem. I've seen us in *The Sun*, *The Mirror*, all over the place, and those papers, though they flirt with the facts sometimes, never do so maliciously, at least with us. (We're not exactly major bait!) I've always enjoyed reading some of the funny stuff they came up with. The *NME* and *MM* back then were so po-faced, and hated anyone who didn't jump around like a monkey and pander to their idea of what ought to fashionable at the time.

I remember Bel quite liked the picture, though. The sad wee guy managed to catch us between fights!

It's funny, though. The internet killed the need for such papers since you can get all the information you need online. You can get straight to the band (like you're doing now). But there was something glorious, for me, about *Melody Maker*,

NME and *Sounds* coming out every Wednesday, especially in the 1980s. I used to get up early to go out and buy them, scour them, cut 'em up and paste them. Back then, in Bedsitland, it felt like a necessary part of belonging to a musical fraternity. That's what I used to kid myself anyway.

JANUARY 18, 2006
Glasgow, Scotland

The world seems a particularly drab place tonight. I always moan about Saturday nights. I wish there were more shows on a Saturday so we could play our way through the pinnacle of vacuousness into Sunday and beyond. At least we would feel more at the centre of things.

Any other night of the week the moonlight on the river coming back to me through the branches of the hornbeams, from the balcony, would seem sublime. Any other night sleep would eventually take me at about 2am, as long as my closing eye had a clear view of my favourite quarter of the northern sky. Any other night the town would seem vaster, broader, more accommodating to the dreams of wide-awake visionaries and malcontents.

FEBRUARY 4, 2006
Dublin, Ireland

I'm in Dublin with little to report. This room is nice. Valentina in reception told me it was a nice room and she was not lying. It's the sort of a room where the loudest noise is the far-off hum of other buildings' air output. I think there's a lane outside, and then the back of a cinema. Rooftops. Grey sky. An amazing grey that has sat over every point of Britain we have visited in the last two weeks except Manchester, where the sun shone in the window of St Anne's Church last Sunday.

Touring with a group is an amazing thing when you're on top of your game. I like the punctuality of it all, the system and the travel. The machine and the people who drive it. The backdrop might be different every time, but every day you will find Iain, our production manager, floating about like a cigarette-rolling Jeeves, imparting exact technical knowledge without a second's hesitation.

Stevie Dreads also hovers, even more so than Iain, and we are always pleased to see him. Sometimes he's self-conscious because he has some reminder or instruction for us. Maybe we should remind him that it is only with his guidance and instruction that we have the ability to stay alive and prosper in such hostile environs! He is, after all, the perfect tour manager.

I wasn't looking forward to touring when we started. I was knackered and in need of a break. I wanted to dream and replenish myself. I wanted an ordinary life. The polar opposite of touring.

Now, a few weeks in, I'm starting to come out on the right side of the ledger. I start to become subsumed by the show. I use the show. I'm obsessed with getting the right set list for each town we visit. I try to reflect the mood the group is in. Most of all, I lean on the songs. I lean on the set list. It has, after all, to provide me with enough emotional and musical content to get me through the next 24 hours.

MARCH 9, 2006
Louisville, Kentucky, US

Ah, dear diary, how I wish there were more quality hours in the touring day, that I may furnish you with facts; a decent journal of our thoughts and adventures. But you must make do with the day-end scraps on the road to Louisville, Kentucky. Around 2am, the band eventually spilled out of a pub in the centre of Nashville, and carried on the jocularities and boozing as we spun out on to the road.

We had to kick some fellow off the bus. He seemed to be Beans' new best friend. Beans kept calling him 'old pal'. "Sorry about this, old pal, but I think we're heading off now!" The fellow didn't want to move. I'm standing there in my pyjama bottoms with my head over the sink and a face full of toothpaste. "Gwet thwe fwuck off the bwus, old pwal," I was thinking, toothbrush in mouth.

Beans apparently had been getting chatted up by a really pretty girl in the bar. He bought her a drink (just out of politeness; he was being badgered, after all) but then she vanished. It turns out she was underage and she'd been chucked out.

"She was a scientist. I asked her what E equalled. 'MC squared,' she said."

"Surely that qualifies her for a drink?" I said.

"You would have thought so," Beans said.

Sarah Wilson, the cellist (we call her Sez), came on to the bus and handed Beans a banana.

"Eat this, you'll feel better," she said.

Beans bopped her on the head with it, and a banana fight broke out. Just then, I heard Mick say to Richard:

"I think a monkey would take a glass of milk. I know they're not supposed to, though."

I seem to remember getting a pineapple on the foot at this point, and deciding to retire.

TINSELTOWN IN THE RAIN

Stockholm, Sweden

Hello friends. You find me couched in considerable luxury and isolation in the suite of a swanky hotel.

I tried to write a couple of times before; I had an entry all ready to go during the March snowstorms of Minneapolis, but my signal crashed, taking my maudlin words down with it. Perhaps just as well.

I wonder, if I continue to write, with such a leap of time behind me, whether you'll notice any difference in my outlook or personality — I've been working quite hard. I've found myself in a substantial relationship. I've been battling a sneaky and insidious winter ailment. I've been longing for art to rear its head!

I've visited many places, cushioning myself through necessity from their delights and trappings. I've become expert at instantly calling the smallest of hotel rooms my home. I forget what my home looks like.

I feel like Bilbo Baggins, called away from his house at short notice one day for an adventure. The adventure lasts a year, and on many an occasion, Bilbo wonders what might be happening at home.

I look at strange vegetation in southern cities, and obsess over the progress of spring in the Kelvin Valley in Glasgow. Are the candles lit up on the horse chestnuts yet? Are the city limes sweating drops on to car windscreens yet? Has the first swift screeched its way over the surface of the river?

All the brainwork has been done in the present campaign. The group are drifting through the summer now, entrenched in chords and song selection, in mental survival and dumb obedience. It's nice though. You just might find — in this period of comfortable continental drift — original thoughts occurring, that in passing one accidentally stumbles across a decent song or two.

Funny things, songs. Have I talked to you before about how I consider them the bastard art? Nothing's changed there. I still find them like an excuse: for a storyteller who can't sustain his story past a paragraph. For a filmmaker who gives up writing a musical after one number.

Still, there's nothing like music for capturing an immediate emotion, or for translating an abstract surge of pleasure into something tangible. And what a thing! An everlasting tangible sensation.

MAY 17, 2006
Stockholm, Sweden

I keep obsessing about natural philosophy. If only I could have been any good at it! That's what I went to university to study — physics. The funny thing is, it's the only subject at school I got a B at. I should have taken the hint.

But no, I carried on, and it stays with me still. When I was

304

failing second-year physics for the umpteenth time a friend remarked that I would have been better going into the exam and writing down a list of what I was going to play at the club that night. I would have scored slightly less, but at least the gesture would have been honest.

Yesterday I wandered around the old part of Stockholm. I passed the Nobel Museum. It was open late, so I wandered in. There was an exhibit about Einstein and general stuff about famous Nobel Prize winners in history. I stayed there for quite some time.

I was mostly concerned with the physicists, of course. Funny that in my mind there was a run from late Victorian times of men that runs as potent as a list of influential groups of the past 40 years. Maxwell, Rutherford, Thomson, Bohr, Millikan, Einstein, Planck, Feynman. The Velvet Underground, the Stooges, the Modern Lovers, Roxy Music, the Sex Pistols, Subway Sect, the Smiths.

I don't know what happened. I was young! I got distracted. I failed my first physics exam in the second year and decided I would repeat the whole year, be a part-time student, go to the lectures again, actually listen this time. In the meantime I'd get a job, earn some money and try to grow up a little. I moved into my own bedsit in Oakfield Avenue. (I loved the fact the Velvet Underground's songs were published by Oakfield Avenue Publishing!)

Instead of embracing all things physical, I drifted further away from academia. There was a girl with bobbed hair and a birth-mark who sat in the physics lectures. I think I studied her harder than anything that was written on the blackboard. It's just annoying to admit you're not very good at something, isn't it?

There's something about physics, though, that keeps engaging me. I have of course reached an age where you ought to know what you are good at, and you ought to be proud and happy to shed the aspects of your life that either don't interest you, or you obviously have no aptitude for.

I can't skate. I have no interest in the workings of a standard four-stroke motor engine, even less interest in rolling my sleeves up and trying to maintain one (though I am the only male in a far extension of my family who shows no such interest). I hate chemistry and test-tubes, can't get into botany beyond trees, am hopeless at languages, can't cook much beyond eggs.

One tends to specialise. By the age of 37 you should. See, it irks me to think of myself as a musician. I'm not. I'm not a musician in the way Maxwell was a physicist. If he was a musician he'd be Schumann or Schubert, while I'm just Shit.

When it comes to physics, I'm an admirer. I'll buy my ticket for the gig, line up and be entranced. I sometimes wonder why anybody comes to our concerts, how they can come along, look forward to and be excited by them. Sometimes the whole thing seems so humdrum, but perhaps it's the otherness they admire — the fact that by chance we found ourselves in the position of making an exhibition of ourselves through music.

I'd be a physicist if I could, but I'm not, so I'll just have to be a fan.

MAY 25, 2006
Modena, Italy

It's the last date of the European leg of the tour tonight. We get to Glasgow late on Friday (tomorrow) and leave on Monday for Japan and Australia. While the shows have been very enjoyable, and seeing different places has been terrific as usual, the in-between stuff has been starting to try us somewhat. Even Stevie is getting a little jaded with this stretch.

The days do start to merge into one. Tumble off the bus bleary-eyed, force a pastry down your gut and pray there is an internet connection. Wonder if there's time to do laundry. Dreads reminds you about that interview at 12.30pm with the *Trondheim Observer*. Scramble about for some clean underwear while trying not to wake the others. Wonder if any of the local crew notice that you're still wearing your pyjamas. Hang around.

It is of course the hanging around that drives you nuts if you let it. It's very difficult to 'plug into something' in the spare time you have allotted. It's trench warfare! You have to organise your pack precisely for making the most of any given time.

My chief joy and escape is running. No, films. I can't decide. Running or films. My energy has been pretty good of late. I've run in Paris, Brussels, Cologne, Malmo, Mainz, Berlin, Zurich. I saw a wild boar in the woods on the outskirts of Zurich at night. That was nice, running through the warm woods at night with just enough light to follow the path.

MAY 26, 2006
Milan, Italy

I fell asleep last night watching *David Holzman's Diary*. I always fall asleep on the bus with my laptop on. It's a good way to cut out any noise and commotion. The thing you crave most on the bus is fresh air. I love getting home and sleeping with the window open beside my head, breathing in unadulterated oxygen/nitrogen.

Bus air is usually part recycled, and always smells of chemical toilet. That could drive you crazy after a while. My sense of smell is highly developed. I can usually smell someone with a cigarette on a city street before they come around the corner, depending on which way the wind is blowing. On an otherwise quiet street, smell wise, I can smell them up to 150 feet away. Fascinating stuff…

Last night's show was OK, though I couldn't see the audience very well, and that's enough to kill it for me. If I can't see faces I feel I might as well be in our practice room. It becomes especially boring late on in a tour when you have the palpable sensation of the same songs coming at you night after night.

This is something we've escaped in the past, jettisoning songs the minute we get a firm handle on them simply because we can. Nowadays we plan our sets round a structure of about six songs. We vary the rest, but there's enough of a backbone to know we aren't going to stray too far and lose it completely.

What am I talking about? I just finished a four-week tour with two days off before another tour and I'm talking to you about set lists? I should be talking about puppies and kittens, or something equally pleasant or diverting!

To be honest, at this minute Oz and Japan strike me as being a drag. I know I always do this, report to you on a downer before I go on tour, then tell you about what a terrific time was had by all. It's just starting to get a bit samey.

The summer will be good because the festivals are more like guerrilla affairs, where you turn up ready for anything. You could be playing in front of 40,000 people who are really into it, or 1500 who don't know who you are. There's more time to be social, more time to dream. Gigs are terrific when you've got something, anything else happening in your day, your life. If they are absolutely everything you have, then it's going to drag you down eventually.

JUNE 2, 2006
Osaka, Japan

So we're back in Japan. We just got on the bullet train, the Shinkansen, from Osaka back to Tokyo. If you spent time here and you couldn't write a pretty good novel based on this country, then maybe you ought not to try writing a novel at all. Does that make sense? I dunno.

I've been here four or five times and I don't know what's going on. I can see peripherally; I can see the superstructure and the substructure. I can see the paddy fields rammed right up against the power plants and the houses. Every square inch of non-mountainous land is perfectly accounted for. But I still can't grasp what makes people tick, what they are really into, how they like to spend their leisure time, or anything about their true philosophy. It seems to be to want to serve, but I suppose that's the viewpoint of the average visitor simply because the average visitor is so well looked after.

JUNE 3, 2006
Tokyo, Japan

I had a terrific day in Tokyo yesterday, but I wish I could get over the jetlag. I've never had it so bad. Maybe I'm just getting old and my body doesn't like it.

It's funny the things you end up doing in a foreign city when you can't sleep. It puts you in a unique space. Even when I was actually trying to get to sleep last night I can remember at various stages:
• Trying to name all the African countries.
• Working out the set list for today's show.
• Trying to do healing on a friend (unattended, naturally).

- Going through all the goals we scored at football today. (This is a popular one among lads who are not even trying to fall asleep. In fact, it has been proven that these thoughts supersede those of a sexual nature, especially on match days.)
- Working out an arrangement of a terrific Nick Lowe song called *Surrender to the Rhythm* for the group. I pictured the moment when I walked in and said firmly: "OK, Stevie on piano, Beans on Hammond. Mick and Bob, you can fight it out for the bass or electric guitar, but one of you is going to have to sing back-up, so work that into your calculations! Sarah on percussion and singing. Richard, how about you hit the tubs?"
- Picturing some fictitious, shadowy and somewhat gratuitous ideas for record sleeves for songs which haven't been written yet, one of which is called *Love Poem by Catullus*.
- Trying to remember all the words to *This Is Just a Modern Rock Song*. I do believe this was the method which got me off to sleep.

Before trying to sleep I started making you a compilation. I was downloading stuff illegally! (I figure, what the hell, you fuckers have had your tuppence worth out of me in the past.) I was trying to see how much I could recreate of a compilation tape I left in Richard's car, and I thought I could give you a note of it if you wanted to have something to listen to. (I have all the records somewhere, but the downloading is so convenient!)

So why was yesterday so terrific? Well, when you're on top of the travelling, touring life can be pretty great, and yesterday was a day off. I hadn't looked at the tour itinerary, so it came as a pleasant surprise.

Some of us caught the bullet train pretty early. Myself, Beans and Allen were invited to a small football competition between a B&S select and members of the Japanese media/press, organised by Ichi from the record label. It was taking place in a part of Tokyo I'd never been to. It was nice to be out of Shibuya. I was determined to look around and drift.

So the football was great (as always, even when you play badly and lose), but the drifting was better! Ichi and I looked around Asakusa, the old downtown area of Tokyo. "This area was pretty hip two or three hundred years ago," said Ichi. We wandered around the temple as dusk came on fast.

I thought I'd get the subway back to the other side of the city, but I thought I could change to the overground train so I could see what the hell was going on in this town. Trouble is, when night falls in Tokyo it falls fast, at least compared to Scotland, when the dusk carries on for as long as it takes to seduce somebody, and more. In Tokyo, it would have to be a pretty swift seduction.

So it was dark by the time I had travelled two stops on the subway. It was nice to wander slowly through the Friday-night metro mayhem. I let it wash over me.

JUNE 7, 2006
Perth, Australia

I'm a bit fed up this morning. Not with life, because I know life is out there waiting to be lived, but I'm a bit fed up with myself/ the tour straitjacket.

I didn't sleep much on the journey from Tokyo and didn't get much the night before either, so I decided to dedicate the day to hanging around the hotel. But when the others are off having fun, it doesn't half make you feel worthless!

I did my laundry yesterday because I stumbled on a laundry in the hotel, and it was free — powder and everything. I thought pulling hot clothes out of the dryer and folding them myself would give me a small but much-needed sense of achievement, and I wasn't wrong. And, of course, with the hypnotic and repetitive act of organising hot linen comes the necessary delve into one's subconscious to look for songs or stories. So I was quite happy with that.

I bought a suit in Tokyo but didn't have time to get the trousers adjusted, so I took it to a tailor in Perth. The suit wasn't too expensive. Don't go to the big stores in Tokyo. They'll rip you off.

This is the first time I've bought a suit since 1986. Why was I buying a suit in 1986? Good question. I think there was still a feeling in the 1980s that every boy ought to have a suit in his wardrobe, and I gave in to the cliché.

It was such a horrible number — slightly plasticky 1980s fibre, blue with a pinstripe. The salesman said that if I bought it he would throw in a leather belt but when it came to paying for it, I had to remind him about the belt. Then he fished out this little cardboard effort and threw it in the bag. I was too young and mixed up to confront him about it.

This morning I had a couple of interviews scheduled for 8.15am and 8.45am. The first one was live on the Perth music station. You never get a chance to chat about stuff or break new ground, especially live on air. I'm not complaining though. If that was to happen maybe I'd find it too strange.

The second interview was being recorded for a Melbourne station. Now the presenter actually asked me a funny question that required me to shift a few of the pillows around (I was still in bed). He asked:

"So, if the Stuart of now was to meet the Stuart of 10 years ago, what advice would he give?"

"Advice?" I said, buying some time. "Advice?" I repeated,

trying to view the question from a couple of different angles. "I was just living from day to day back then. I don't know if I would have heeded any advice. I was so 'stuck in it'."

I can't honestly remember if that's what I answered. I probably copped out. I mean, how much advice would you have taken 10 years ago if it had been offered to you? Not much, I'll wager.

Brisbane, Australia – Glasgow, Scotland

Ah, now I feel more at liberty to talk. We've finished our concerts for the time being, the time being Saturday at 1.47am Dubai time. I'm in a plane, high over the Bay of Bengal. A short time ago, coming out of Singapore, we went through hot, moist cumulus clouds and dropped a good distance out of the air. I wouldn't have liked that much a few years ago, but I think the experience I had being a passenger in a stunt glider has made jet flight seem mundane.

I'm already fantasising about what to do when I get back to Scotland. We arrive in the middle of the day, but I know I'll be dizzy and incapable of the plans I'm hatching now, one of which involves getting straight on the bike and following the Forth and Clyde canal out to Duntocher, perhaps carrying on to Loch Lomond.

I'm trying to convince the group not to rehearse in the forthcoming week in Glasgow. We've got the show with the Strokes in Hyde Park on Wednesday and *Top of the Pops* the following Sunday, but then I think we need to not see each other for a week. Just to cleanse the soul. I also think we need to accentuate the change of season; the change from touring to festival shows.

Ha ha. I'm making it out to be such a heavy business. I guess once we've got the Hollywood Bowl over with we'll be cruising till the end of the summer, getting punchy with the rest of the touring chumps in Europe. I hope we get to meet up with some nice groups and have some good games of football and legendary frisbee sessions.

JUNE 18, 2006
Glasgow, Scotland

Life begins again at home, not on a plane. I go out looking for normal social situations. It would be funny if the people who I'm trying to run into knew I was lonely. Not that lonely, though. I don't want to stay at their house or even have a drink with them. I just want to graze by. I want to check in. I'm manipulative and shallow. God thinks so too.

I'm in a big rush to get out as soon as I come home. I throw my suitcases down in the hall. (I just wanted to see if I could get to the end of that sentence; I don't actually have a hall, my flat is very small.)

Glasgow's so wet and warm it's like a crotch. It's the crotch in the west of Scotland, so that makes it a fertile place. If anybody asks me again why so much music comes out of Glasgow this is the answer I will attempt to give them. I think it's a stupid answer, but I don't have a better one, and people do insist on asking me this.

I like jetlag sometimes. I like it today because it delivered me awake at 7am so I could get up and have time to bake some bread, soak some muesli, make a cup of tea and know I don't have to make a mad dash to get out of the house. To know I could amble up the side of the Kelvin and cross over the allotments and make it to church without breaking out into a BO-

314

inducing sweat like usual. (I don't have BO, but I ought to, the irresponsible way I carry on with layers of clothes and fluctuating levels of effort throughout the day.)

With my bread I have honey. I look at the jar and it says the name of the company and then it says: 'The Taste of Honey.' I wonder where that phrase comes from and what it means, and I'm amused that companies so readily appropriate phrases that, if they thought about it, they really shouldn't use unless they wanted everyone to think about sex every time they used their product.

The taste of honey. I don't know whether it came from the play or the film, or the song The Beatles did or the song Smokey Robinson did (*I Second That Emotion*). I'm sure, though, that on each occasion the phrase stands for sex, a little bit of sex, bait for a fish, something that will draw you in.

Sometimes I wonder what all the fuss is about and why can't people call sex sex rather than hide behind such a phrase. But then it's a nice poetic thing, and I'm glad it's around to paint a picture, act like a feint and make you think about language. If people were straight-talking copulating machines it would never have occurred to Smokey to lift up his voice and curl his tongue around the phrase in the first place, and that would have been our loss. It would have been my loss, because when it comes down to it I think I would rather have Smokey sing about it than be faced with it on a day-to-day level, to have it dished up like peas and mashed potatoes. I'd rather have Smokey sing about it and hear the crackle of the record and examine the blackness of the run-out groove. I'd rather do that, all told; rather look into the mirror of the run-out groove and be lost.

JULY 9, 2006
Maryland, US

It's the morning after the show in Baltimore, and I'm feeling a bit flat. I wish I could snap my fingers and be home in the bosom of the west end of Glasgow. We are in a hotel on the outskirts of nowhere, the sort of place that is hard to fathom for a Scots person. It seems to be a community that has grown up around commerce; it's basically a hotel on a business park.

So there's nothing doing. I don't know what would satisfy me anyway this morning. I have a nice view from my room of some grass and trees, but there's some people at the hotel pool and their voices annoy me. I think I'm a bit frazzled; I could simply do with a couple of days of being drip-fed my home town.

I wonder why that is; why I get nourishment just from being at home. I'm so pleased, those first few days; you should see me. Instead of crossing the street to avoid people, I actually make the effort to stumble into the path of those people I usually want to avoid. Local fringe characters are embraced!

I feel a bit like a knight who's been off slaying dragons, coming home to the news that the price of turnips has gone up. But I want to know about the turnips! I want to know what's been going on!

I'm at the Baltimore-Washington international airport now. I suggest to Beans that it should change its name to Washingmore. He suggests Baltington.

I'm hanging out at the gate waiting for the delayed 6.10pm to Newark, with Sarah. We're making a few practical criticisms of the show last night, starting with two technical points. It occurs to me that when we are talking, anyone who hears us might take us to be professionals in some job or other. We have our own language, enough to rank us alongside a businessman or an engineer or something in that realm of specialisation.

I'm not boasting — it's just an observation. For a minute I observe us as working adults, quite at home within the community of people we are flying with. Nothing special; but I'm digging it for just a second.

There's something about this time of year that drags me back to being a teenager. I rarely need much reason to be dragged back into reverie, but at this time, during the tennis season and with the Open Championship about to kick off, it's easy to be transported to summer jobs, to summer travelling, to summer dreaming.

Stevie Jackson comes over and relates to us a story about Iain, our just-departed production manager, and his adventure in a small jet. (We are just about to get on a small jet.) Apparently the weather was so bad, and the plane was getting blown about so much, that the landing was aborted at the last minute. The plane went in again, and again the landing was deemed too risky. Unfortunately they were running out of fuel, so they would have to land the third time. The plane was swinging from side to side. They were given a pillow and asked to adopt the brace position but landed OK the third time.

The conversation arises because Dreads is worried about the flight. He's very wary of flying, especially in small planes. Sarah thinks it's mainly because so many pop legends tend to buy it in small planes. Sarah thinks Dreads just needs his rock status clarified as 'not quite legendary', and then he ought to feel better about things.

I remember hearing Mick on a recent flight trying to reassure Stevie. Some reassuring.

"Oh yeah, put your head against the seat in front of you, like that's going to do you any good. The only reason they ask you to do that is so that your dental records are preserved for ease of recognition."

I was sitting in front of him, trying to catch his eye with a subtle 'Nooo-oooh!'

So last night's show was not terribly enjoyable. I thought it was going to be great. I actually had the time to shave, pick something to wear then walk to the amphitheatre along a lakeside, looking out for terrapins on the way. Sometimes, though, as Robert Burns pointed out, one's plans and predictions go to the dogs. I don't know what happened; maybe we had too much fun at the other shows.

Two journalists, one after the other asked me, after the show in LA: "You've played the Hollywood Bowl. Where do you go from here?"

"Down," I said, both times, like it was funny the first time.

Still, we had a lovely old time in New York and LA. I could've done without all the Phil Collins-style jumping on and off jets all the time in the last few days, but the taste of each coastal city was intoxicating. A taste of honey is sometimes better than nothing.

I liked the guy who was conducting the LA Philharmonic at the Hollywood Bowl. I was glad he was a personable type, because an orchestra is a curious entity for a pop band to behold. The powers that be had brought him in because he was young and impeccably dressed, I'm guessing. He was German, from Frankfurt. Everybody admired his trousers. In a post-rehearsal meeting, I looked at him curiously.

"Have we met before?" I asked. "Your face seems very familiar."

"Some people say I look like Kevin Bacon," he said in a resigned, German sort of way.

I was a bit sheepish. *Of course* that's why I thought I knew him. I berated myself for my tactlessness afterward. But we soon became pals. He was nice when I nicked the baton from him, and guided the orch through the last few moments of *Your Cover's Blown*. The orchestral players were just about tolerant of this idea. Never look into the soul of an orchestra, however, before you have read the manual. They will take you down.

So I'm on the plane back home now. Listening to *Tainted Love* by Gloria Jones reminds me that I met her son on Thursday night after the Hollywood Bowl show. Rolan Bolan — a very pleasant young man. I sort of wished it was Bob or Stevie who had met him. They would have got a bang out of it because he's Marc Bolan's son too. All I thought to say was: "Oh, I was dancing to T Rex last night!" Duh.

I also had a conversation with Courtney Love, though not my first. I think she was surprised when I mentioned we had met before. It was 15 years before, when her band Hole was playing at the Queen Margaret Union. I was a lowly roadie. We got talking in the lift after the show.

"What did you think?" I asked her.

"I quite liked it. You have that one song that sounds like Bauhaus."

"*Bauhaus!*"

I love the way LA smells at night, in the hills. I wanted to get on a horse straight after the show and disappear up into the trails. There would have been enough ambient light seeping from the city on to the sky then back to earth to see which way to go. Instead I ended up going to bed. I believe there was an after-show party. And an after-after-show. And an after-after-after-show party. I wanted to go somewhere and dance to *Tinseltown in the Rain* by the Blue Nile. With the horse of course, it being tutored in the way of mid-1980s student dancefloor classics.

Some fave LA movies:

Short Cuts
Pulp Fiction
The Big Sleep
Fast Times at Ridgemont High
Chinatown
Jackie Brown
Shampoo
Some Kind of Wonderful
Double Indemnity

Wow, I don't even remember writing that list. I must have been drifting off. I hit the jackpot and got three seats to myself, the first time that's happened in the modern era. (Meaning, since it's been a possibility that I might sleep on board due to absence of fear.) Also, on this flight they don't seem to be blasting the air-con, and we are landing straight into Glasgow from Newark, which is civilised beyond human conception. Yippee!

JULY 15, 2006
Barcelona, Spain

I'm in a pretty good mood this morning. No broken bones, just a bit of deafness and a touch of athlete's foot. I would *not* say no to a massage. I slept on the bathroom floor last night. Doubtless you would like me to tell you at least one tale involving sauciness or drug abuse, but, dear reader, it was the only place an old man could find the peace to drift solemnly into unconsciousness.

I'm thinking of my home town, so I'm living a double life just now. I'm feeling the quietness of the parks, the stone in the building warming up while no-one's around to see. I'm thinking about office windows left open, expanses of empty school car parks; I'm thinking about how my part of the city has stopped serving the student population and started serving itself. Women take time over their yogurts. Taxis are installed in ranks, drivers play sudoku, off-duty dogs practise looking shifty.

It was a pretty scene in the main amphitheatre of the Barca festival last night. I hope the show was OK. We tend to try to pummel audiences at festivals. We don't mean to, but that's the way it is. You have to paint in broad strokes when you're performing to 12,000 bodies. The idea is to take them and move them in a certain way; create communality, if there is such a word. It's a tricky business.

I don't really like watching bands at festivals. There you have it. How can I expect anybody to enjoy us at a festival if I admit I'm immune to the delights myself? I *have* enjoyed it in the past, but I studiously avoided going to anything resembling a festival between 1985, when I saw Queen top the bill at Knebworth, and 2001, our first appearance at Benicassim.

I'm prepared to try to enjoy myself on the stage. "Make a nice noise," I always tell the group as we're about to go on. I wonder if that even registers any more. I used to think that's all you had to do to seduce a crowd. It might not grab them like the theatrics of Sir Freddie, or the gimmicks of the Flaming Lips, but I figure they'll get home and some of them might think about the outro to *The Model* and think, "That was quite a nice noise."

I always loved taking the strings onstage when we played festivals. I felt it was the one thing in our canon that the other groups didn't have. For some numbers, we had 12 musicians working together to produce what I thought was quite a decent noise.

It's a texture I feel is missing today; at least, I miss it. I can't help it. That's just how I perceive the songs. I felt pretty satisfied when I heard certain songs at the Hollywood Bowl. The likes of *I'm Waking Up to Us* sounded right; *Caught in Love* sounded broad and dramatic. This was, after all, how the songs were conceived in the first place. It was natural to have a feeling of, 'This is what this song was *meant* to sound like.'

Right, I'm sick of talking about music. What I would like right now is a book. A book about cities. I always wonder about cities. When you fly in to so many of them, you get to thinking, 'How did this one grow up? What inspired this agglomeration?' I could do with a book of about 1200 pages, with 60 chapters, each covering a city. Twenty pages each, covering origins, a bit of geography and history. Does such a book exist? Probably. I know I could get books about individual cities, but I'd like it all to come from one source, so that I can get a feel for the different stories, while the editorial feel is consistent.

JULY 28, 2006
Reykjavik, Iceland

I'm in a hotel room listening to a Felt track called *Mexican Bandits*. I was watching a film called *The Son's Room* by Nanni Moretti but I've turned it off momentarily because it got to a sad part; I'll go back to it later. I like the way he paces films. It reminds me of Ang Lee, who is also very good.

When I woke up this morning the first thing I did was get my computer, point it toward the door (where the best wi-fi signal seems to come from) and tune into BBC 6 Music. I listened to the second part of a Morrissey interview from 1984 that I found in the archive section. I lay back and listened to the interview, which was called *My Top 10*. I remember listening to this series in the 1980s. I think it was on a Saturday afternoon. I can't remember hearing the Morrissey one before though. If I'd stumbled upon it in 1984 I would have perhaps listened, uncommitted.

I remember hearing the programme with Simon Le Bon of Duran Duran; it must have been a few years later. I was amazed that he chose a Cocteau Twins song, a track called *Little Spacey* from the *Victorialand* album. I remember being infinitely annoyed when the interviewer called the track *Victorialand* as if he couldn't be bothered to lean over and read the label on the record to see what the song was called. (I'm listening to the song right now. If I veer off into the impenetrable for a second or so it's because of the aural tickle that I feel.)

Well, I liked listening to Morrissey. He was so talkative; passionate about his small world; affable, even. His choice of music was good. I particularly liked the Sandy Posey track he picked. So there I am listening to Morrissey talking about how the Smiths will never play another festival, I'm listening to the Cocteau Twins, I'm thinking that when I get back to Scotland I might try to get a job in the holiday camp I used to work in.

I was looking round the breakfast table this morning, wondering if I'll ever feel the same way about this time, this trip, as I feel now about, say, the summer of 1986 when I worked at Butlins. Twenty years. That's enough to make any small adventure seem legendary. Many of you reading this probably can't think back 20 years because that would represent the vast majority of your life. I say to you: listen kids, enjoy yourself. Drink in every moment, because as you get older life starts to pass you by at an exponential rate. Enjoy yourself, so that when you look back 20 years and your life looks like a film, then it's a good film, with nice cinematography and a plot straight out of the nouvelle vague. Oh yeah!

I'm not being a 'down' old man here. I've never liked life so much. There was a moment a couple of days ago that was unsurpassed for pleasure and completeness. It involved my bicycle.

My bicycle is 20 years old, so too is the star of the nouvelle vague film I was talking about earlier. She was the star, but is also still around. That makes her a legend now. My bike is a legend. She's called Laura for some reason. Calling your bike Laura is a bit of a mistake really, but it was a long time ago that I christened her thus, so I can forgive myself. My facilities of taste were still green.

I needed to take a pile of laundry to the laundrette. It's quite a distance because I have to negotiate the River Kelvin. It was hot, so I would have been a sticky hot person if I'd simply shouldered the burden, and I wanted to remain relatively clean in case I ran into my girl later. So I thought I'd put the washing on the handlebars and push.

This was fraught, however. I kept running into the kerb. So I wondered if I could get up on the bike while the washing sat on the handlebars. It really worked! I launched myself into the road and marvelled at the invention called the bicycle. It made the whole carrying business effortless.

I parked it up against the glass front of the laundry. I've been parking that bike up against shop fronts for years. That's why there's nothing better. That's why I started having such a great time. I was home, I had some errands to run, it was a boiling-hot day and I was drifting about staying cool, sitting back on the saddle of my bicycle. I was early for Ciara because I made it to the laundry so fast, so I went for a celebratory circumnavigation of the west end, through the park to the office, along

324

past the newly reopened Kelvingrove Art Gallery and Museum, and up Byres Road.

I'm up in a plane now, listening to *Wild Horses*, Mick Jagger moaning plaintively over the Nashville tunings and the rhythms of the veteran Stones. We're off to the far east of Iceland in a prop plane, reminiscent of the kind you might find in *Indiana Jones and the Temple of Doom*.

I'm feeling pretty good. OK, you know, earlier when I was going on about Morrissey and the 1980s and Simon Le Bon and Butlin's, and my bicycle — I dunno. It's just my way of wanting to disappear into something. Seeing the past as a film. I enjoy curling up in hotel rooms and disappearing into another world. Perhaps I should grow up, perhaps I should have got outside and seen a bit of Reykjavik, but I didn't feel like it. I'd have rather stayed in and read about Reykjavik on the internet — how it sprang up, what its major industries and culture are, etc. I'm in that kind of mood. Endless games of Scrabble and jigsaws, like a sick kid from a Barry Hines novel.

(I'm listening to *From the Hip* by Lloyd Cole and the Commotions, which was one of their best tracks. It was the second or third single from their third album. It's great, but just by releasing a song like that, it's as if you're giving up. In a commercial sense, I mean. Nobody played it; it was forlorn. What were they thinking? I would probably have done the same thing.)

JULY 29, 2006
Borgarfjordur, Iceland

There are voices downstairs. I can hear Sarah talking to the mayor of Borgarfjordur. I'm upstairs in a little house. My room is cosy, being not much bigger than the size of a single bed. The sloping roof dominates the headspace. I've got a lump on my napper from banging it, twice, while coming through the miniature door.

We're in a beautiful part of the world, or at least it's been beautiful since we got here. It's way out on the east of Iceland. When we got in, we played football with the local kids in what is easily the most beautiful place I've ever played, surrounded by green mountains still patched with snow.

We had our dinner in the village hall, then we were taken out on one of the fishing boats. They managed to load a pile of beer and schnapps on board before we went out at 10pm with the sun still up. The whole business was ridiculously picturesque. I have been craving my own country for a while now, but this will suffice for the minute. This will do fine.

We zipped along at a fair rate, eventually stopping under some high cliffs, a cathedral of green vaulted heights inhabited by thousands of puffins and gulls. It was peaceful though when we stopped the engines and hung out for a while. I felt like we were invading the birds' night-time routine.

When you find yourself somewhere like that, especially if someone takes you there, you should try to fill up on it. Everyday life is full of strain, but when I'm somewhere like that, I feel like a car at a filling station, like I'm being pumped full of something. It isn't food or drink, but I'm definitely refreshed. The bonus is that you can shut your eyes for days to come and be transported back.

We headed out into deeper water, stuck some lines in the water and soon started pulling in fine big cod. The gulls got very interested as the guts flew over the side. Up till that point they had been poking disinterestedly at some jellyfish just under the surface.

When we returned to the village we went back to the hall where some live music was happening. Some fellow was ploughing through a selection of pub favourites on his acoustic guitar. He was raucous and pretty amusing. Stevie shouted for the Stones, and he came back with *Paint It Black* like he had written it himself.

There was a piano at the back, so I sat down and started accompanying the singer, just for my own amusement. No-one could hear it over the sound of the PA. Still, pretty sharpish, the bar lady came over, said, "No," and practically brought the lid down on my fingers!

The singer exalted and damned himself in equal measure as he played selections from the Kinks, the Lovin' Spoonful and the Pixies, but also that awful song with that woman screeching: "And I think to myself, WHAT'S GOIN' ON?"

JULY 30, 2006
Borgarfjordur, Iceland

So the gig happened yesterday. This town was invaded by an inordinate number of people (where did they come from?). Plays about elves were acted out. Bonfires were burned. Folk songs were sung. A big derby football match was played (in which I played for some of the second half!).

A man, drunk, delirious and soon to be married, took over in goal for a short time while the regular keeper went to the toilet. He was dressed like a student doctor, but he also had a black afro on his bald head. He let in a goal in somewhat comedic fashion. The goalkeeper came back from the toilet and seemed genuinely dismayed at the loss, haranguing the drunken man in the white overalls. 'What did you expect?' I thought to myself, as I took off my jeans and readied myself for the fray.

I know I've mentioned the Stones a couple of times already in this bulletin (Stevie would be proud of me), but I heard a story this morning that I must relate. The biggest Stones fan in Iceland (apparently) lives one fjord to the north of here. (I think I saw his car yesterday. It had a massive transfer of the Stones' logo and the 'The Rolling Stones' written on the bonnet.)

A couple of years ago, Mick Jagger sailed his yacht into one of the fjords. He took his bicycle ashore and was riding around. Who did he run into, but the chap I already mentioned. (I must stress that we're at the centre of all things happening here, and there are about 50 houses. Wherever our Stones fan lives must be even more deserted. Partially surfaced, the roads are the kind that if you stop and step off into the heather for a second, you will know the meaning of real quiet. You could hear a worm preparing to dine.) So the Stones fan thought he was hallucinating. I think they had a chat. Then Jagger got back on his bike and cycled off.

Talking about quiet roads, we're now on the road back to the airfield. We stopped the van for a minute because, worryingly, Grimur spotted some tracks that seemed to leave the road and veer off the side of a cliff. Being a trainee mayor, it's doubtless part of his civic duty to make sure his constituents are safe. He makes a call, and it turns out that whoever went off the road at that point has been dealt with already. Whatever that means ...

"It's not the right place to exit," says Grimur, master of understatement.

AUGUST 3, 2006
Glasgow, Scotland

What a boring old day! I've done nothing. I walked down the street and picked up the *NME* because we were in it. (Are you disappointed in me?) They had this thing called The Recommender which I spoke to them about a while back. Thing is, I wrote it out for them in April but I don't think they liked the answers or something, so they did it down the phone. Here's what I wrote to them, back then.

What I'm listening to

Tracey Ullman – *They Don't Know*

I haven't heard this for a while, but the last time I heard it I welled up slightly on account of the richness and beauty of the production.

Cyndi Lauper – *Girls Just Want to Have Fun*

I've been listening to this song quite a lot recently. There is one naff synth sound on this record, but apart from that I give it my highest award.

Madonna – *Borderline*

I always listen to this song. It's her best one, pretty gay, but not outrageously so. It's sincere, and that's probably why I like it. Plus, it's musical genius. And her voice sounds like spacedust going off in your ear.

Hall and Oates – *She's Gone*

From *The Old Grey Whistle Test* DVD. I've had a thing about them for a while. Should I be worried?

The Blue Aeroplanes – *Ceiling Roses*

I like bespectacled men spouting their 'poetry' over pretty meshes of guitar and violins. Kill me if you like.

Delays – *Valentine*

I'm so happy I can include a new one! Apologies, I just don't listen to new music like I used to.

Furniture – *Brilliant Mind*

I wiped my iPod recently by mistake, but somehow this survived, so I listened to it every day for two months when we were making our last LP.

The Flirtations – *Nothing But a Heartache*

A stalwart of soul dancefloors around these parts for so long. I've never owned a copy, but I'm listening to it in my head just now.

Freda Payne – *Band of Gold*

I crapped out of singing this at karaoke recently — cowardice personified. Another great soul anthem.

Blondie – *Denis*

From *Top of the Pops* in 1978. I always thought she was singing about another girl. I thought 'crush' meant she wanted to hang out with this other girl and maybe share make-up or books or something. That's the first time I heard the word 'crush'. Damn, it's so good when the second electric guitar comes in halfway through the verse.

A guilty pleasure

Vintage Scottish passenger ferries. I've got a thing for them. My dad worked for Caledonian MacBrayne, and my brother works for them.

Any chance I get, when home for a few days, I'll organise a photo session for a record sleeve, or I'll go scouting for video locations. More often than not it will involve a trip on one of Caledonian MacBrayne's antiquated 1960s steamers, somewhere on the west coast of Scotland. From the classic black, yellow and red livery to the whisky and fried egg rolls served in the tiny wood-lined galleys, it's way more than just a mode of transport!

I've considered trying to capture the smell (a mixture of ship's diesel and fresh paint) in spray form so I can enjoy it around the house whenever I like.

330

My biggest influence

God. An irritating answer in some regards, but I find it hard to see past the omniscient one. I'm firmly of the opinion that everything good comes from Him, from a chord change in a Beatles song to the sound of the drums on a Joy Division record. Of course, The Beatles and Joy Division are perfectly entitled to disagree with me.

My favourite new bands

Regina Spektor

I don't know how 'new' she is, but she's new to me. I was in the bath a while ago, listening to Janice Long on Radio 2, and Regina Spektor was in session. I only heard one song; I think this was called *Fidelity*. Well, I knew straight away that I was within earshot of some kind of greatness! I haven't bought her record yet, so lazy am I, but I'm pretty excited about seeing her play live.

The Royal We

I missed their debut show in Glasgow recently, at a party on West Princes Street. My girlfriend assures me they were very good, even though she was off her face at the time. I'd probably recommend them anyway. The name's so good, how could they possibly fail?

Camera Obscura

They're not that new, but they've got a new album coming out. I heard a track at a club the other day and it sounded amazing. They're from Govan in Glasgow, where ships used to come from. The sort of group the *NME* traditionally ignores then sucks up to when they realise how popular they've become!

Other stuff

DVDs

I've become addicted to *Seinfeld*. I'm such a retard. I always get into stuff way after everyone else. I think I'm just addicted to season five, though. I'm scared to watch any more in case they fall below the level of comedy perfection practised by season five.

Books

I'm really into postcards. My girl just bought me a book called *Boring Postcards*. To me, they are things of great beauty, though. They look like the postcards I always scavenge for in secondhand stores. There's also a book called *The Postcard Century*, which is a large volume of cards and messages.

The web

When you're on tour the best thing is BBC Radio 4 online. Not only can you tune in live and get a bit of Blighty whenever you want, you can listen to Melvyn Bragg or *Gardeners' Question Time* or whatever you're into by going to the archive section.

AUGUST 20, 2006

Belgium – Holland

I bust my iTunes so I can only listen to single tracks. I may never listen to another LP. Perhaps that is a good thing; my searching for individual tracks on my computer filing cabinet is this century's version of lifting a 7-inch single and dropping it lovingly on to the spindle. The only thing I miss is the smell of the warm motor and the female companion that often accompanies a 7-inch single session in an attic room.

I'm listening to *Half a Person* by the Smiths. I've spent longer than six years on your trail, Steven Patrick Morrissey. I saw you racing from the scene of your Salzburg gig the other night. I blew you a kiss as you got into your big, black car and headed for the Alps. I wonder if you made it back to Rome.

He was good that night. Everyone from the group who travelled up to the site enjoyed Morrissey. I wish he'd hung around the next day. I do feel quite isolated at festivals. I feel I have far more in common with Moz than the garlands of young rockers that turn up at these Eurocamps.

Let me tell you about default festival rockers these days. Skinny, painted-on black jeans, pointed patent shoes with laces in the wrong place. Spiked hair, tight vintage Japanese T-shirt, or shirt and thin tie. Converse shoes. They're a bit of a bore, but not all the groups are like that. I saw and heard Arctic Monkeys, and they seem more interesting, yet look more normal. How does that work? Perhaps they have more substance at their core.

I had a great day at Pukkelpop yesterday. Our merchandising girl Fiona told me as I got up that Midlake were on somewhere in a tent. I had a lot of energy today so I ran out of the bus and right round the site, making a game of running up to people and dodging round them at the last minute. I watched Midlake and they were great. I didn't see all the songs, but what I saw I loved unreservedly. They are my new favourite group. They gave me their record a few weeks ago in Spain and it is the best record anyone has ever given me, in the look-what-I've-done category. They are to Fleetwood Mac what Stillwater are to Led Zeppelin. I don't mean that in a bad way, I just wanted to write it because it seemed clever. They are very, very good.

I'm really enjoying this run of festivals. I think we're getting the hang of it. Leicester was great, Frequency, Pukkelpop, St Malo; so much fun, long drives and long waits aside. At least I'm getting good sleeps on the bus.

I often think of a line from The Beatles' song *I Should Have Known Better*: 'This could only happen to me.' I don't know what the intention was, but whoever wrote it felt uniquely blessed at that particular moment with the circumstance of his love.

I had nipped off the camp to find a hotel with a bath. I was in the middle of one of the longest baths in pastoral-rock history, watching *The Maggie* on my semi-aquatic laptop, when it occurred to me that *this could only happen to me*. This is the payoff. This is the hiatus before new work and anguish begin. Surely, moments that good can't go on for ever. Or maybe I'm just easily pleased. Or oddly pleased.

Allen and I were throwing the Photo Jenny frisbee around near the buses. I always badger people into playing. Allen is a good thrower so I usually badger him first. I often badger Sez, our cellist, but she insists on only throwing before showering because she always has to run after the thing. How that hunk of (perfectly weighted) plastic raises the spirits! Even aforementioned Default Festival Rocker will have a go. (Limply, with no aim or acumen, but we encourage the effort nonetheless.)

We turn up at these festivals with such swank. We only throw our own (competition-weight) frisbees, we carry Belle and Sebastian canteens to drink out of and, when the weather is inclement, we shelter in the uniform chic of Belle and Sebastian silver rain macs. We must seem like not so much a band as a council of community workers.

Indeed, it is as so that I feel. Rooted to headlining the second stage in western European campaigns, rock ambition seems almost ignoble. With our combined ages, any thinking collective ought to have more to offer fans and co-workers alike than just *rocking the house*. We should be running the union, or something.

POMONA BOOKS

Pomona is a wholly independent publisher dedicated to bringing before the public the work of prodigiously talented writers. Our books can be purchased on-line at:

www.pomonauk.com

Pomona backlist